HEDGING FINANCIAL INSTRUMENTS

A Guide to Basis Trading for Traders, Investors and Portfolio Managers

JEFF L. McKINZIE

&

KEITH SCHAP

Probus Publishing
Chicago, Illinois

332.645
M15%

© 1988 by Jeff L. Mckinzie and Keith I. Schap.

ALL RIGHTS RESERVED. No part of this publication may be
reproduced, stored in a retrieval system, or transmitted, in any form
or by any means, electronic, mechanical, photocopying, recording,
or otherwise, without the prior written permission of the publisher
and the copyright holder.

This publication is designed to provide accurate and authoritative
information in regard to the subject matter covered. It is sold with
the understanding that the publisher is not engaged in rendering legal,
accounting or other professional service. If legal advice or other expert
assistance is required, the services of a competent professional person
should be sought.

FROM A DECLARATION OF PRINCIPLES JOINTLY ADOPTED
BY A COMMITTEE OF THE AMERICAN BAR ASSOCIATION
AND A COMMITTEE OF PUBLISHERS.

Library of Congress Cataloging in Publication Data
McKinzie, Jeff L.
    Hedging financial instruments.

    Includes index.
    1. Hedging (Finance)   I. Schap, Keith.   II.   Title.
HG6041.M385 1987   332.64'5   87-29176
ISBN 0-917253-87-6

Printed in the United States of America
1   2   3   4   5   6   7   8   9   0

MB

Dedication

To our fathers:
Tony McKinzie
Ed Schap

University Libraries
Carnegie Mellon University
Pittsburgh, Pennsylvania 15213

Contents

Preface

Basis trading—the basis is the mathematical relationship between the current price of an underlying commodity or asset and its futures price—has been used successfully for decades by grain and commodity traders to reduce the impact of price fluctuations and market volatility. As if by "magic," grain brokers, traders and other buyers of commodites have protected themselves from market extremes.

Experienced traders know, of course, that their success has nothing at all to do with luck or magic, but with skillful applications of basis trading principles.

It is to these principles of basis trading that this book is dedicated; but rather than just the grain and commodities markets, we will show how basis trading can be applied to the financial instruments so prominent in today's investment arenas. Like the grain traders of the past and present, bankers, financial managers, traders, corporate treasurers and portfolio managers can employ basis trading to protect and enhance a broad range of financial instruments—bonds, mortgages, currencies and interest rate futures and options.

Most importantly, we designed this book to be a practical guide in a financial world that is experiencing ever-increasing volatility. The recent and rapid declines in the financial markets make basis trading all the more useful to manage price risk, to protect mortgage portfolios from rate volatility, to prevent erosion in the value of cash reserves, to derive better than long-term returns from short-term investments, to lock in a future lending rate, to enhance the yield of an investment portfolio, and to design an effective foreign currency swap program.

In addition to helping readers understand the mechanics of basis trading, we offer a system for charting the basis and establishing a basis trading program. In our opinion, the best learning will come from careful analysis and application of the more than twenty different basis trading strategies that have been culled from real-world examples.

Finally, we recognize that the art and science of basis trading expands and changes as market conditions evolve; nevertheless, we believe that if readers understand and apply the fundamentals of basis trading correctly, they will be in an even better position to enhance profits and to reduce losses whatever the condition of the market may be.

Acknowledgements

Many people contributed to this book—some information and insight others, equally important, moral support. All helped to make this a better book. Special thanks are due:

Don Brouillette, who created the environment where these ideas could develop and be put to practical use, and who encouraged subsequent basis trading efforts;

Ray Hennady, a master basis trader who is also a patient and resourceful teacher;

Tony Freeland, whose wealth of basis lore and willingness to discuss new ideas, theoretical and practical, sped the development of these ideas;

Kevin Commins, whose reading of crucial parts of the manuscript and helpful discussion of how to present complex ideas in writing improved the presentation;

Marguerite Regas, who read much of the text and whose comments did much to clarify the writing;

Howard Marubio, Kurt Green and Jeanine Freeland, whose good-natured help made the task easier;

Probus Publishing, a sympathetic and encouraging publisher, whose suggestions improved the book from conception to execution;

Richard Victor, Curtis Calvert, and the other Moonrakers for their infusions of spirit.

I
Beginnings

1

Why Risk Management

Consider the case of an institutional borrower with a $300 million line of credit. What happens if the prime rate goes from 7.5% to 8%?

Or of a mortgage banker who packages mortgages worth $100 million to Freddie Mac every 30 days or so. What happens if, during one of these holding periods, interest rates suddenly dive?

Or of a financial manager with a cash reserve of $100 million who puts his money in short-term T-notes for liquidity. What if the next auction is down three-fourths of a percent?

To some those are descriptions of disaster. Wiser money managers just smile in a relaxed way, for they have discovered a way

- to assure a borrowing rate 2% less than normal prime no matter what the prime does
- to protect, with certainty, their mortgage portfolios
- to invest short-term money that yields significantly more than the short-term rate.

The ability to manage risk, even to profit from it, is highly sought after. Indeed, "risk" has probably become the biggest four letter word circulating in business circles these days. The reasons are not hard to find.

The risk managers who accomplish these feats have learned some facts about the current financial world which seem contradictory at first.

They take it as a "sure thing" that a hedger selling long-term debt futures will lose money. They know that shrewd investment managers at major institutions regularly position themselves to have balanced hedges using long-term Treasury bond futures. As a result, outsiders often think good risk managers are practicing sleight of hand, or worse. Those risk managers have figured out what Georges Andre, a giant of the grain trade, meant when he said that "the secret of success in this business is to buy high, sell low, and still make money."

Unpredictable weather, fickle markets, whimsical foreign policies make the grain trade a cyclical business in the calmest of times and a tempestuous one much of the time. To cope, the grain traders invented hedging, the essential risk management strategy. Financial executives who follow their lead can, as Cargill's Whitney McMillan says, "thrive on cyclicality."

Sadly, people new to risk management have tended to follow the lead of the textbook writers and exchange personnel who hold that, since cash and futures are highly correlated, hedgers need only establish a futures position "equal and opposite to their cash position."

These writers ignore the underlying market features which govern hedging success. Any risk manager who does likewise will find what he intends as risk management tactics to be extremely expensive. To speak plainly, the notion that cash and futures correlate closely is a pernicious fiction.

Others seem to believe that, since they are dealing with the so-called "interest rate futures," what they do is separate from what the grain traders do. It is true that the strategies financials hedgers use often appear to depart from classical hedging, to be mathematically more sophisticated. However, that turns out to be more a matter of appearance than fact.

Crucial to all risk management is an understanding of "the basis." The basis provides a way of describing the economic energy inherent in the markets—*all* markets. Technically, and traditionally, the basis represents the difference between cash and futures prices. It allows one to relate cash and futures and to understand what drives commodities into and out of storage. A mathematical relationship, the basis provides a coherent point of reference in spite of price chaos. Given that, the reason for focusing on the basis may be obvious.

Critics of American business have suggested that, while companies like Cargill may thrive on cyclicality, Wall Street in general does not. Some think an urge to obliterate the cycles, a tendency to see them as evil, goes far to explain the willingness of corporate America to "pay premiums" to diversify into unrelated businesses. Afraid, they are trying to smooth out the cycles—to establish consistency by main strength. But, as Cargill's MacMillan says, "Foolish consistency is the hobgoblin of public managers."

People who understand the basis, on the other hand, can escape that trap. In a sense, the basis resembles a natural force—like a fast flowing river—or a socio-economic force like the ones John Naisbitt calls megatrends.

People can stand in the middle of a river, oppose it, but it will sweep them away before it. Or they can use its flow to their benefit—to drive an electric generator, say. As Naisbitt says, these forces "are easier to ride in the direction they are already going." When risk managers make a decision that is compatible with the real market forces, like the basis, the market helps them along.

A study of the basis can lead to a genuine understanding of the markets. "Within a simple framework," Naisbitt writes, "we can begin to make sense of the world. And we can change that framework as the world itself changes." In risk management, that framework starts with the basis.

All risk management strategy derives from the generations-old practice of the grain traders which, referred to in general terms, might well be called basis trading. All risk management strategy involves balancing positions in related cash and futures markets in such a way that the basis trader can *take advantage of an expected basis change.*

Risk managers who make the effort to understand the basis learn that cyclicality is only an apparent problem. Once their understanding penetrates the presumptive fog, they can find in cyclicality wonderful opportunities to protect their assets from risk, fix borrowing rates, and enhance profits.

2

Backgrounds

Financial executives currently face unprecedented challenges to the profitable operation of their companies. Foreign competition, spiraling costs, insurance problems, and questions of litigation are among the problems that erode profits. What all this says is that financial executives are operating in a marketplace that puts a premium on shrewd financial management. Those who will do well in this situation are those with highly developed coping skills.

Chief among these coping skills are the techniques and strategies collectively known as hedging, or basis trading. All of these coping skills derive their effectiveness from the cash-futures relationship known as the basis. Commodity prices are often chaotic. In contrast, the basis provides a solid point of reference. Since it reflects real market needs—especially concerning the storage or circulation of commodities—the basis represents an economic force whose energy risk managers can harness.

Sweet are the Uses of Adversity

Financial managers can "thrive on cyclicality" because volatile economic situations give rise to futures markets. Originally, and until quite recently, the strongest futures markets were agricultural, primarily in the grains. Since the mid-1970s, the financials, especially U.S. Treasury bonds, have emerged as the dominant futures markets. Along the way, exchanges have introduced contracts of various kinds. Some have failed. Some have succeeded. There are reasons for failures and successes alike.

Many aspects of business defy certain prediction. No one can know what corn, heating oil, or U.S. Treasury bonds will cost six months or a year from now. That uncertainty creates risk. Risk creates a climate in which futures markets can flourish. This simple notion lies behind recent commodities developments which make financial risk management possible.

For decades prior to the late 1970s, interest rates were closely controlled in the U.S. They held between 3% and 6%. Figure 2-1 illustrates the U.S. interest rate history since 1930.

Then, in 1979 the Federal Reserve Board changed the rules, deciding to replace interest rate control with control of the money supply. At roughly the same time, an escalating Federal deficit motivated the issuing of a huge volume of bonds. With interest rates following market pressure, this became an area of great volatility in our economy. For years banks and others had managed risk through the use of back-to-back cash contracts. By the end of the 70s, though, this tool had become inadequate to the task. As a result, a number of very successful financial futures contracts developed. Now they dominate the trading scene.

In contrast, the grain trading activity, once the primary futures area, has shrunk remarkably. Few contracts trade, compared with a decade or so ago, as Table 2-1 amply demonstrates.

Table 2-1   Annual Volume (in futures contracts traded)

	Corn	Wheat	Soybeans	U.S. Treasury Bonds
1976	23,046,296	14,869,140	27,370,894	——
1986	6,160,298	2,090,316	6,133,668	52,598,811

In 1976, the T-bond contract did not yet exist. Ten years later, it at least doubled the 1976 volumes of the major grain contracts. The reason for that remarkable change in grain volume (to somewhat oversimplify) is that government programs have taken over. Farmers sell grain only

**Figure 2-1 Ater Adjusting for Inflation, Interest Rates Remain New
Record Highs**

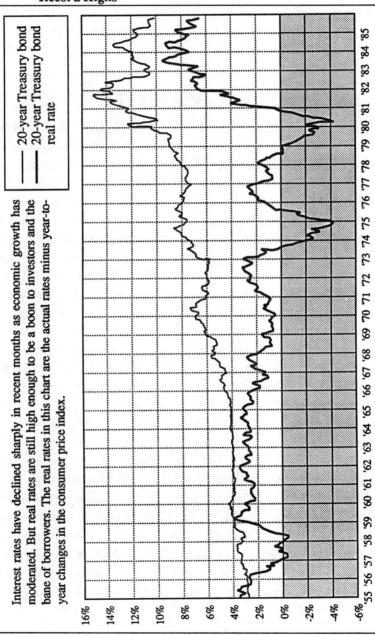

Interest rates have declined sharply in recent months as economic growth has moderated. But real rates are still high enough to be a boon to investors and the bane of borrowers. The real rates in this chart are the actual rates minus year-to-year changes in the consumer price index.

— 20-year Treasury bond
— 20-year Treasury bond real rate

when the cash price beats the support level. Otherwise the farmers default to the government, and the grain goes into storage instead of going to market. Where so little grain goes for sale, a stable situation replaces a volatile one and futures trading loses relevance.

Given that overview, it should be clear why the markets have developed as they have.

A Stage Where Every One Must Play a Part

Risk management requires the market presence of a variety of people, some of whom might seem to be working at cross-purposes. In fact, they are not. An important idea, one often overlooked, is that risk never just evaporates. There is a kind of homeostasis in the markets. The risk inherent in a situation shifts from one player to another.

Some people and businesses are more vulnerable to risk than others. For example, the officers of a manufacturing company who are planning a plant expansion may decide that if borrowing rates increase beyond a certain point, their project will lose feasibility. Yet they may also believe that unless they increase production capacity they will be hard pressed to fight effectively for market share. Mortgage lenders, portfolio managers, bond dealers and corporate money managers may all seek protection from similar risks. To all of those people, risk is anathema. If at all possible, they want to shift their risk to someone else.

Curiously, others welcome risk. The possibility of sizeable profits makes it worthwhile, in their view, to take a chance.

Accordingly, the first group become classical hedgers—the second, speculators.

In the most general terms, the hedger—or risk manager or basis trader—trades the unknown for the known. Theoretically, the cost of the money he needs for the plant addition, to stick with that example, could go up or it could go down. If it goes up, he suffers—down, he benefits. Yet by hedging he willingly sacrifices the chance to benefit from the decrease in exchange for a known, acceptable cost that protects him from the adverse possibility. Classical hedging provides just that kind of defensive strategy, whatever the details.

The risk takers, or speculators, believe that with careful analysis of markets they can time their moves to take advantage of whatever situation crops up. They balance the hedgers in the market by sacrificing slow and steady for more risky but larger profits.

Speculator is an undeservedly suspect term in many quarters. Hedgers cannot hedge unless there are people willing to take the other side. In fact, positions must balance. There must be as many buyers as sellers in the market. When everyone wants to do the same thing—buy or sell—the markets shut down. They "lock limit up" or "lock limit down." Clearly, what is needed is a commodity of good names. It takes both sides to have a market.

Notice that the risk has not gone away. The hedger has shifted it to the speculator. In effect, he says: If I can have a well-defined situation I can achieve my business goals, so I will let you make whatever money can be made from this situation if you will take over this risk. The speculator takes on the risk, saying, in effect: For the chance to make a profit, I will take the chance that I might take a loss.

Actually, that obscures the complexity of the situation. The hedger may not entirely give up the chance to enhance the yield of his investment. The speculator may not always be all that exposed. Nevertheless, that is the essence of the risk management drama, and those the principle players.

From Risk Management to Profit Potential

Traditional hedging is primarily a defensive strategy. The very term "risk management" shows that, whatever the particular strategy, the defensive element remains very much a central concern.

Defense alone hardly justifies the effort that goes into designing an effective basis trading strategy, though. Going to a bank and negotiating a line of credit at a favorable rate is probably far less work than designing bond hedges or foreign currency swaps. And the bank bears the risk exposure. Cash reserves are perfectly safe when financial managers invest them in U.S. Treasury bills or simply put them in a bank at short-term rates.

Why not just do that? Why bother with basis trading? Simply because the short-term rates are so low. The money, though safe, produces noncompetitive returns. On the other side, deftly crafted foreign currency swaps can help risk managers reduce borrowing rates or improve investment yields. A good bond hedge or reverse repurchase strategy can earn significantly more than short-term yields. Sometimes those strategies can even surpass the standard long-term rates.

Along with the defensive value of risk management, the possibility of enhancing yields or otherwise benefitting from the effort makes hedging worth the extra trouble.

It is important to recognize that the profit potential side of risk management need not conflict with the risk protection side. The factors that propel effective risk management are eminently predictable—more so in the case of the financials than in the case of the traditional physicals. The bond market behaves in a certain way, consistently . Bond prices can do anything, and often do. Bond futures prices also can do anything. To a price watcher these markets can be perplexing indeed. Yet year in and year out the fundamental feature of the bond market— the relationship of cash to futures—to which knowledgeable risk managers pay attention describes consistent patterns. To risk managers, who focus on neither cash price nor futures price but on the *relationship* between cash and futures, the extra profits or borrowing advantages are there for the taking. The strategy that produces them will be essentially as safe as the options that do not earn those profits—like short-term bank accounts.

For all the theoretical neatness of this system, it remains puzzling to many observers of the commodities scene that so many participants have spotty records. They do less well, by far, than it appears they should. The news media carry such items with alarming frequency— today the stories feature a major mortgage lender which thought it was hedging, yet suffered astronomical losses; tomorrow they feature someone else. Not surprisingly, those results are predictable, too—to anyone who has developed a genuine understanding of risk management.

Hedging is not the problem in those cases. The news stories reporting the disasters invariably quote a participant to the effect that there are no perfect hedges, or the market failed to behave as expected.

However, the unfortunate people who make the news have an incomplete grasp of how the markets work. They pay attention to obvious information, such as prices, when they should be paying attention to more fundamental market characteristics. They overlook the meticulous record keeping that disciplined risk management requires. As a result, these people fail in their hedging attempts because, typically, they

- are not fully hedged
- fail to match their cash exposure
- make no effort to manage the basis
- select the wrong hedge structures
- design an ill-advised cross hedge
- fix a bad price.

In short, they fall prey to a common curse of mankind, folly and ignorance. They tend to confuse the roles of hedger and speculator. They take dangerous chances when they should be creating more positive risk protection. Yet such people never say to a reporter that they apparently didn't understand hedging as well as they should have.

To Know What Were Good to Do

As the basis trading story unfolds, a variety of mathematical relationships emerge—between cash and futures, yield rates and portfolio values, or bond maturities and prices, to name a few. It is important to distinguish between those relationships and the so-called technical analyses that some people promote. The technical analysts observe futures prices, chart them, and conduct statistical studies, in an effort to locate patterns which might guide their trading. For all the appearance of rigor those people promote, they are essentially speculators. Because that is so, technical analysis has no place in the thinking of serious risk managers.

Maintaining perspective is important. Many find current events as chaotic and impossible to make sense of as prices. If what the market does follows entirely from some OPEC action, from a Soviet or Argentine crop failure, or from how the Japanese respond to a Treasury bond auction, then the task is hopeless to many of the would-be hedgers. No one can forecast any of those things in a useful way.

In the actual case, what OPEC, the USDA, or the Federal Reserve does is important. It is well worth the effort to be able to determine how those events affect the markets. Risk managers who understand the forces which drive cash-futures relationships have powerful interpretive tools at hand. Since the markets respond to certain fundamental phenomena which can be described in terms of the basis (the difference between cash and futures prices), they become far more predictable. Given an understanding of those phenomena, risk managers can frame useful responses.

There is no magic. Risk managers really can know what to do; and when profits might be only 1% or 2% of sales in a good year, that is important. The kind of uncertainty the U.S. economy has been experiencing not only creates risk. It threatens the entire business structure.

Typical financial managers strive to eliminate or control any factor that threatens those narrow margins, to say nothing of their peace of mind. Many of the factors are beyond control. The higher medical costs go and the more people sue, the higher the insurance rates. Regulatory agencies add their bit of misery. There seems to be no help for it. On the financial side, though, risk managers can take effective action—if they master the discipline make the effort to understand cash-futures relationships.

II

The Strategic Essentials of Basis Trading

Financial managers face situations which create risk. Identifying that risk defines a motive for a certain kind of risk management strategy. After developing a general sense of how the relevant strategy works, risk managers need to develop an understanding of why it works, a rationale. The rationale is important because risk management by rote or by habit tends to be ineffective and to cause major losses. Understanding of the underlying market forces allows managers to overcome misguided habits and misconceptions. Moreover, managers who grasp the rationale for this or that strategy will be able to see additional opportunities and create strategic refinements that can enhance yields. The essential risk management theme unfolds in four stages:

- motive
- strategy
- rationale
- refinements

15

The first stage is to look at a rather generic situation, review common risk management approaches, compare results, and then work towards a rationale for those results.

The rationale focuses on the ideas which are the keys to all successful risk management—the cash-futures relationship known as the basis and the so-called storage problem. No matter how subtle and sophisticated the approach, these notions are the foundation. Every modification and refinement involves an adaptation to some aspect of the basis phenomenon. The storage problem supplies a conceptual framework which makes sense of the basis developments and guides strategic decision making.

As a result, these discussions, as they present increasingly varied and sophisticated strategies, reiterate and develop these central notions. The strategies are most often the focus of attention, but risk managers need to keep in mind that without the conceptual underpinnings they signify nothing.

Notes on Method

For expository simplicity, most of the examples throughout the book hold the yield to maturity constant—an arguable assumption. Because cash and futures will move in equal and opposite magnitude changes, with the exception of the basis change, only the basis change is important. Changing yield to maturity, therefore, only complicates the math without having an impact on the hedge result.

Further, interest rates can be, and often are, volatile. At the same time, it is often true that over a period of several months, the yield may go up a percentage point and then drop almost as much. In effect, there is little or no change.

The stable yield assumption creates an additional effect which is especially interesting. A stable yield defines a flat market. Speculators often sit out the flat times because the common wisdom holds that it takes change to find profits in the markets. It is supposed to be difficult to do well in the absence of volatility. Investors flock to a bull market, thinking (incorrectly, as it turns out) that a bull market is the friendliest situation for making money. Yet, in time the savage bull doth bear the yoke.

Curiously, the fundamental nature of bond basis is such that it creates opportunity even in a supposedly flat market. In a normal yield curve market, the basis has to change a great deal just to hold the yield constant. Since basis change constitutes opportunity for a hedger, even a flat market produces basis trading opportunity. In short, an apparently weak assumption turns out to lead to a strong claim for the usefulness of basis trading strategies. They produce excellent results at any time.

3

How Basis Trading Works

Financial people have been quick to sense the potential of the new financial futures contracts. Using futures opened up new possibilities for coping with such problems as volatile interest rates or short-term money management needs. Financial managers flocked to the exchanges to try their hands at "futures-based" risk management. Some have done well. Others have become disillusioned. That is sad because the problems are unnecessary. The basic ideas of risk management are simple, although they do require careful thought.

Essentially, financial managers have two choices when using futures-based risk management: to follow the lead of the so-called "common sense" hedgers, or to learn how hedging really works. Curiously, the common sense group dominates the exchange research staffs and the business school faculties.

Chief among the misleading "common sense" ideas now in circulation is the claim that cash and futures prices correlate so closely that hedgers can safely ignore the basis—the difference between cash and futures prices. Nothing could be less true, or more costly to a hedger. Circulated most often by exchange economists, this mistaken belief leads to the equally mistaken notion that hedging only requires taking a futures position equal and opposite to a cash position. In the trade vernacular, hedging to those people requires little more than balancing the longs and the shorts. Looked at that way, "common sense" hedging seems attractively simple. Attractive until it is time to add up the results.

In contrast, a substantial group of people, mostly in the grain trade, mastered the "basis trading" techniques and the related hedging strategies generations ago. By following their lead, people in other businesses can easily find out what has made hedging work so well for those grain trade veterans. Early in their study, they will have to get used to ideas that appear to contradict long-cherished thought patterns which most people have come to regard as common sense. Among the bothersome ideas that confront people new to risk management:

- risk managers must be astute enough not to pay too much attention to price,
- T-bonds are the appropriate futures instrument for many kinds of short-term risk control,
- often when it seems logical to sell futures, risk managers have to buy futures (there's more to it than just balancing shorts and longs),
- most "textbook" hedging examples often lose in an actual market situation.

Admittedly, the idea that the price of the bond, or bond futures, is of little or no importance calls for a hard swallow. So does the claim that the instrument of choice for short-term protection is a long-term U.S. Treasury bond. Further, no one lightly questions the expertise of the university and exchange people. Once would-be risk managers put "common sense" behind them, though, they can focus on what really does make for successful hedging and risk management in actual practice.

In fact, hedgers who master the market fundamentals discover that they can routinely design successful risk management strategies. Good risk management is not problematic at all. That is why it is good risk management. These strategies not only allow managers to achieve their risk protection goals, they are safe and often lead to enhanced profits.

The best way to begin understanding the implications of the two primary risk management options is to start thinking about examples of hedging strategies—some of which characteristically disappoint, some of which routinely succeed.

Hedging a Treasury Bond Portfolio

Financial managers in many kinds of business can improve their companies' cash positions significantly by contructing hedges with Treasury bonds and T-bond futures. This can be a useful way to deal with cash reserves. In general, it provides an interesting short-term investment.

Traditionally, hedging involves shifting price risk by establishing balanced cash and futures positions. Thus it seems wise management, when buying bonds, to protect the cash position by selling futures. To complete that kind of hedge (or, in the vernacular of the trade, to "unwind" the strategy), the hedger would sell the cash bonds and buy back his futures contracts. Figure 3-1 graphically summarizes such a classical hedge.

Figure 3-1

CASH	FUTURES
buy T-bond	sell T-bond futures
sell T-bond	buy T-bond futures

One aspect of that strategy that attracts many newcomers to the market is the attractively high coupons of many of the bonds. At a time when short-term yields hover below 7%, the idea of a 13.25% coupon return, or even an 8% bond yield, has a certain allure. Moreover, word in some circles has it that a hedger can get the higher return on a short investment. Maybe so. But it is not always easy to see how to do that.

Consider what might happen in an actual case. Assume that a would-be hedger, thinking along those lines, bought on June 24, 1987, $100 million par worth of the 13.25% May 2009-14 T-bond issue which was then selling at 153.70931 and yielding 8%. To protect that position, he sold 1532 contracts of December futures at 96-00.

Bond price quotes do not give a dollar value. Rather, they indicate a percentage of the par (or face) value. For cash bonds, the minimum unit has a $1,000 par value. Thus $100 million par implies 100,000 bonds. The "practical" minimum in cash bond trade is $1,000,000 par, or 1,000 bonds (each with a $1,000 par value). In this case, one bond of the 13.25% May 2009-14 issue has a cash value of $1,537.09 as of June 24, 1987. The standard Chicago Board of Trade T-bond futures contract has a par value of $100,000. Accordingly, on June 24, 1987, $100,000 par worth of the 13.25% May 2009-14 bond (100 bonds) had a cash value of $153,709 while a December futures contract had a cash value of $96,000.

Those two prices are not comparable, yet one hedging requirement is balanced positions. To remedy that, the Chicago Board of Trade has developed Conversion factors (Cf), multipliers which align the price of a given bond with the generic, 8% yield futures contract. The Cf also supplies a hedge ratio (HR), the number of futures contracts required to balance a cash position of $100,000 par. In this case, the Cf and the HR is 1.5320.

The number of contracts actually needed depends on the size of the cash position. To determine that, hedgers can use the formula:

$$\frac{\text{Cash Value}}{1000 \text{ x Cash Price}} \quad \text{x} \quad \text{Cf} = \text{No. of Contracts}$$

$$\frac{153,709,310}{1000 \text{ x } 153,709} \quad \text{x } 1.5320 = 1532$$

That formula allows a hedger to determine that this strategy requires 1532 futures contracts to balance the cash position.

This hedger, assuming no change in yield, planned to sell the cash bonds and buy back his futures on December 1 of that year. Figure 3-2 presents his trade sequence in detail.

Because this strategy assumes an absence of yield change, the difference in the cash bond price between June 24 and December 1 is due to the time difference. The Cash Result is a $476,620 loss.

But that is exactly why people hedge. The idea, after all, is to let the futures side protect the cash in just such a case.

On the futures side, the first signs are not encouraging. Obviously, a hedger who sold low (96-00) and bought high (100-00) is looking at a

Figure 3-2

CASH	FUTURES
June 24, 1987	sell
buy T-bond	Dec 87 T-bond @96-00
13.25% coupon May 2009-14,	Cf: 1.5320
@ 153,709, yield 8%	HR: 1.5320
Par Value: $100,000,000	No. of Contracts: 1532
Cash Value: $153,709,310	
December 1, 1987	buy
sell	Dec 87 T-bond @100-00
13.25% coupon May 2009-14,	
@ 153.23269, yield 8%	
Par Value: $100,000,000	
Cash Value: $153,232,690	
June 24 to December 1: 160 days	

$$\text{Cash Sale} \quad - \quad \text{Cash Purchase} \quad = \quad \text{Cash Result}$$
$$153,232,690 \quad - \quad 153,709,310 \quad = \quad -476,620$$

loss. *How much?* is the question. Bond traders deal in minimum units of one 32nd of a percentage point. That is, a futures price of 96-08 means 96 and 8/32nds, or 96.25%. One 32nd has a cash value of $31.25 for each $100,000 par. To determine the futures result, traders use this formula:

$$\begin{matrix} \text{Futures Change} \\ \text{(in 32nds)} \end{matrix} \quad x \quad 31.25 \quad x \quad \text{Contracts} = \text{Futures Result}$$
$$128 \quad x \quad 31.25 \quad x \quad 1532 \quad = \quad -6,128,000$$

The sum of the cash and futures results reveals a capital loss of $6,604,620.

Because the hedger holds the cash bond for 160 days, he earns $5,808,219 in coupon interest. Bond coupon pays the stated rate on the par value. To figure the interest income, hedgers determine the coupon earnings for a year, divide by 365 to establish daily yield, and multiply by the number of days of bond ownership.

$$\text{Par Value} \quad x \quad \text{Coupon} \quad \div \quad 365 \quad x \quad \text{Days} \quad = \quad \text{Interest Income}$$
$$100,000,000 \quad x \quad .1325 \quad \div \quad 365 \quad x \quad 160 \quad = \quad 5,808,219$$

The net result of the strategy is the sum of the hedging loss (the capital loss) and the interest income.

-6,604,620	Capital Loss
+5,808,219	Interest Income
- 796,401	Net Hedging Result

The net loss, taking everything together, is $796,401 which amounts to a -1.2% annualized return.

It is important to realize that the interest income is really separate from the hedge. An unhedged bond holder would earn the coupon return also. He would have to deal with cash market changes, too, but he would not have made a futures trade.

This hedger would have done better to put his money in a safety deposit box. At least that would keep the principal intact. Though it hardly makes a case for hedging, this example is typical of the kind of results that follow from the shallow approach that regards hedging as merely balancing the longs and the shorts and thinks no more deeply.

A Basis Trading Approach

That kind of disappointing result is far from inevitable. Consider another approach to the same problem. Assume that on June 24, 1987 another hedger, one who might be properly called a "basis trader," initiated a slightly different strategy. On the cash side, instead of just buying the bond, he forward purchased it for September 1 delivery. In a forward purchase, buyer and seller contract "now" to complete a transaction at some future time. The September 1 invoice price will be 153.47334 rather than 153.70931. The September 1 price is not fixed but is floating with the market. This price difference is predictable given an assumption of unchanging yield. His other initial move, to buy 1534.7 September T-bond futures at 98-00 is in anticipation of taking delivery of his bond purchase.

It is important to notice that, besides the forward purchase, this basis trader *buys* futures. He does not sell them. Also, it is the September contract at 98-00 which he buys, not the December at 96-00.

Then on September 1, the basis trader prices and takes delivery of his cash bond, and eliminates his futures position. All one action, really. The way he handles the futures is a bit complex. In effect, he sells them to himself. (The important thing here is not to worry about the nature of this paper trade but to focus on its effect.)

Finally, on December 1 he sells his bonds at 153.23269. Figure 3-3 illustrates this trade sequence.

Figure 3-3

CASH	FUTURES
June 24, 1987	
forward purchase 13.25% May 2009-14, (153.70931) 8% yield, for September 1 delivery	buy Sep T-bond @98-00 Cf: 1.5347 HR: 1.5347 No. of Contracts: 1534.7
September 1, 1987	
buy (take delivery on forward purchase) 13.25% May 2009-14 @ 153.47334, 8% yield Par Value: $100,000,000 Cash Value: $153.,473,340	sell Sep T-bond @100-00 (through delivery)
December 1, 1987	
sell 13.25% May 2009-14, @153.23269, 8% yield Par Value: $100,000,000 Cash Value: $153,232,690	

June 24 to December 1: 69 days
September 1 to December 1: 91 days
June 24 to December 1: 160 days

At first glance, this strategy seems complicated. That is really an illusion. More importantly, it delivers very satisfying results. To start with there is a $240,650 cash loss, though such a minor amount is of no real concern (it amounts to -0.15% of the cash price).

$$\text{Cash Sale} - \text{Cash Purchase} = \text{Cash Result}$$
$$153,232,690 - 153,473,340 = -240,650$$

Also, having held the cash bond between September 1 and December 1, the basis trader earns $3,303,425 in coupon income for those 91 days.

The futures side is especially interesting. Although the figure says *through delivery*, the hedger really does not want to get involved in the complexities of that process. *Delivery* here is a shorthand for the idea that the hedger will, in effect, sell the futures to himself. He will "price them out" at zero basis and his account will be debited the invoice amount. If he were selling futures in the usual sense, he would realize a $3,069,400 futures gain.

$$\begin{array}{cccccc}
\text{Futures Change} \\ \text{(in 32nds)} & \text{x} & 31.25 & \text{x} & \text{Contracts} & = & \text{Futures Result} \\
\\
64 & \text{x} & 31.25 & \text{x} & 1534.7 & = & 3{,}069{,}400
\end{array}$$

That offsets the cash loss and leaves a capital gain of $2,828,750. The way this hedger has designed the strategy, that reduces the purchase price of the bond for all purposes.

The net result of the strategy is the sum of the hedging result (the capital gain) and the interest income.

+ 2,828,750	Capital Gain
+ 3,303,425	Interest Income
+ 6,132,175	Net Hedging Result

That $6,132,175 amounts to a 9.11% annualized return. That is a 14% better yield than the stated 8% yield of the bond itself.

On the face of it, the first strategy is a failure, the second a success. In general that is true, yet some hedgers might have business goals which make the loss of the first strategy seem a reasonable premium for price insurance. Finally, winning and losing depends on what the hedger wants to accomplish, on his business goals.

People new to hedging often think in terms of "fixing a rate" or "locking in a price." Some think also about "price neutrality." The two general kinds of hedging strategies differ markedly with regard to those notions.

A hedger using the first strategy has no price exposure. Because he always has balancing cash and futures positions, he is indifferent to price change. Basis traders would say he is "price neutral."

A hedger using the second strategy has all kinds of price exposure, but he has fixed his cash price. The price exposure results from the fact that the futures position and the cash position are in place at separate times. Yet the futures purchase effectively locks in the purchase price of the cash bond. That is a somewhat remarkable turn of events, since both the September 1 cash and futures prices are floating with the market. Though both prices are predictable given certain assumptions, the hedger cannot know in advance exactly what they will be. The fact that the futures position will move essentially with the cash market locks in the price. When it comes time to cash out the futures, the futures gain will at least make up for the change in the cash price from June to September.

The numbers are indeed unequivocal. Neither outcome is accidental. That brings up the questions—why are the results of these two strategies what they are, and how they are so predictable to basis traders? Or, what did the second hedger know that the first did not?

4

Why Basis Trading Works

U nlike the physical markets, people tend to think of the financial markets as abstract entities. They also apparently assume that a different set of rules apply. Neither of those assumptions is true. Worse, they make the financials seem more difficult to understand than they really are and obscure from view the forces that drive risk management strategies in *all* markets.

The Storage Problem

The easiest way to grasp what market forces make financial risk management work the way it does is to refer back to the grain trade. Those people invented the risk management business, after all. And their central problem is relatively easy to see.

People in the grain business face a more or less fixed demand but a seasonal supply. A corn processor, for example, needs the same amount of corn each month. A hardgoods manufacturer who has to deal with such a customer can regulate production to match customer needs. This is not so for a grain dealer. There is only one harvest a year. Since processors have no desire to buy a year's supply, an obvious supply problem results. Part of the year, there is too much corn, other times not enough. Compounding the problem, some years farmers harvest

29

bumper crops. Other years weather or disease cause crop failures. Then the users either have to tap previously stored supplies or face the problem of shortages. In any event, there is a storage problem.

Moreover, corn users have an aversion to paying a premium at the end of the crop year when the supply has dwindled. Grain traders have an aversion to accepting too low a price just after harvest, when there is an oversupply.

Both sides need a way to regulate the flow of the commodity into the market. They need a way to "even out" the market and limit the risk that the cyclical nature of their business imposes on them. The system these people developed over the years involves the use of futures in a variety of hedging strategies. Crucial to all of those strategies is the ability of the risk managers to know when the market wants to store corn, or any other commodity, and when it does not.

Risk managers need a reliable "gauge" of what the markets want. In addition, risk managers need a way to "anticipate" the market. If they just react to it after the fact, that is damage control, not risk management.

The grain traders discovered just such an indicator in *the basis*. The basis expresses a relationship between cash and futures prices. Prices may differ widely from year to year. Yet the basis, since it expresses the relationship rather than the price level, provides a stable point of reference. Make no mistake, the basis often fluctuates hundreds of points in a few weeks or months. Yet it creates a reliable, even predictable, point of reference. That is why the basis is valuable to risk managers.

In fact, basis traders pay less attention to absolute basis levels than to how the basis changes as a general rule. The exception is the extremes. There is definite value in the extremes. When the basis moves in a negative direction, it is said to be widening. When it moves in a positive direction, it is narrowing. Figure 4-1 illustrates the distinctions.

At points W1 and W2, the basis is wide. At point N, it is narrow. But moving from W1 to N, it is narrowing. From N to W2, it is widening.

Generally speaking, a wide basis or the anticipation of a narrowing basis prompts storage. Such a restriction of the flow of bonds might occur after a bond auction or a flood of mortgages. In that situation, risk

Figure 4-1 Narrowing and Widening Basis

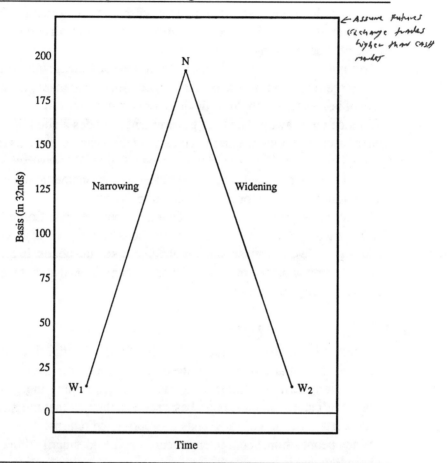

managers want to be *long the basis*. They want to buy cash and sell fu-tures. A narrow basis or the anticipation of a widening basis dis-courages storage. Such an opening up of the flow of bonds might occur between bond auctions, when the government has debt ceiling problems, or when rates are falling fast. Then risk managers want to be *short the basis*. They want to sell cash and buy futures.

That is the essence of risk management strategy. The storage impera-tive drives the basis. The basis prompts the basis trader's moves. All hedging strategies involve either short basis positions or long basis positions. A hedger is short the basis when he sells cash and buys futures. He is long the basis when he buys cash and sells futures. Many are the variations. Yet however sophisticated they seem, all come down to one of those two kinds of position.

To some people, the worlds of the grain trade and the financial community seem far removed from each other. But if risk managers conceive of bonds, for example, as devices for storing money, the apparent difference melts away. The U.S. government provides a good illustration of just how similar the grain markets and the financial markets really are. The Federal Reserve issues money. The U.S. Treasury issues bonds. The crucial issue for the Federal Reserve is whether to put more money into circulation, or to pull some into storage.

To circulate more money, the Federal Open Market Committee (FOMC), a branch of the Federal Reserve, buys bonds. When the policy makers think less money should circulate, they sell the bonds. In effect, that pulls money off the market and into storage. Looked at that way, a bond is a storage bin for money.

Understanding Bond Basis

Traditionally, the basis represents the cash-futures relationship. In the case of the financial commodities, the basis also represents the interplay between long-term and short-term rates. Besides issuing the general "store-don't store" signals, bond basis reflects the fact that the market exacts certain costs. It always tends to erode stated returns.

When people think about interest accruing, they ordinarily think of a pattern like that in Figure 4-2.

The case of a bond is more complex. A 13.25% coupon bond, to refer to the instrument of the earlier examples, may never quite pay that return. The stated coupon rate indicates the return to par. That is, if par is $100,000, and someone holds the 13.25% bond for one year, it will pay him $13,250. However, if he had to pay $160,000 for that bond, rather than $100,000, then the $13,250 represents an 8.3% return, not a 13.25% return.

Figure 4-2   Normal Interest Accural Concept

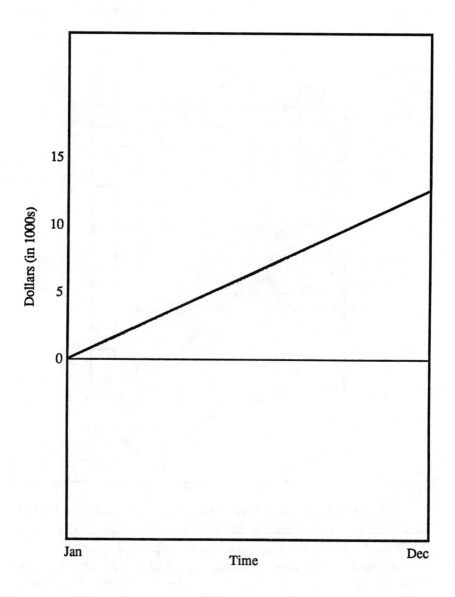

A good way to illustrate these forces is to use a graph like the one in Figure 4-3. Though an idealization, this figure nevertheless illustrates several important notions.

Figure 4-3   Coupon, Carry and Basis

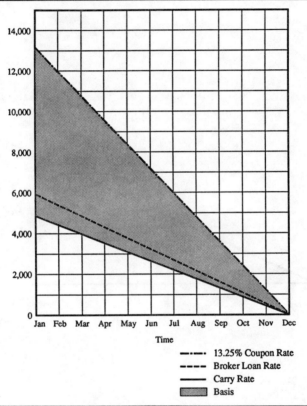

The broken upper line indicates the coupon return. At the far left point, the graph indicates that the coupon return is $13,250, the full 13.25%. At six months it shows a $6,625 return, and so on.

The next line illustrates the short-term lending rate—the so-called "broker loan rate" which is, in effect, a broker's prime rate. The lowest line represents the net yield of a trader's activity when he buys bonds and sells futures. The shaded area between the coupon line at the top and the net yield line at the bottom is the basis.

In reality, the yield and the basis do not move in such a neat, straight line. Figure 4-4 displays an actual basis chart showing the 12.5% August 2009-14 bond.

Figure 4-4   Seven-Month Bond Basis

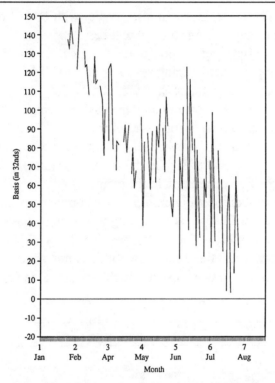

For all the complexity of the actual basis chart, it should be clear that Figure 4-3 illustrates the general tendency of bond basis.

In a normal yield curve market, certain basis phenomena may be taken as axiomatic:

1. The basis widens as the delivery date of the futures contract approaches.
2. The basis of all bonds converge *toward* zero.

These are the "knowns" that basis traders can count on.

How much and at what rate the basis will widen depends on a variety of factors—coupon size, yield, maturity, market conditions. One bond, the cheapest to deliver, always attains zero basis at delivery. But so regular are the basis tendencies that those factors only contribute to degree. Risk managers can predict with assurance what the general basis trend will be. Therefore, they can also predict with equal confidence what the result of any trading strategy will be.

A widening basis gives a "don't store" signal. In that case, it is generally the appropriate hedging response to establish a short basis position (sell cash, buy futures). Exceptions exist, but generally a hedger who establishes a position long the basis (buying cash and selling futures) will be "on the wrong side of the basis." That is the right strategy when the market wants hedgers to store the commodity. But in the face of this "don't store" signal, the short basis strategy is the one that creates a position of strength in the market.

For illustration, consider Figure 4-5 which summarizes the strategy of the first hedge in Chapter 3, expanding it to include basis information. In these examples, notice the assumption that yield rates do not change. That simplifies the discussion but does not affect the results. Both hedging strategies will work in essentially the same way.

Figure 4-5

CASH	FUTURES	BASIS
June 24, 1987		
buy 13.25% coupon May 2009-14, @153.70931, 8% yield 　Par Value: $100,000,000 　Cash Value: $153,709,310	sell Dec T-bond @96-00 　Cf: 1.5320 　HR: 1.5320 　No. of Contracts: 1532	212
December 1, 1987		
sell 13.25% coupon May 2009-14, @153.23269, 8% yield 　Par Value: $100,000,000 　Cash Value, $153,232,690	buy Dec T-bond @100-00	
June 24 to December 1: 160 days		

STRATEGIC SUMMARIES

Introductory Note

Readers can use this book as a repository of "hot tips." For those readers, these strategic summaries may be especially useful. They're also a good review or refresher mechanism.

If the problem and goals of the summary match those of a risk manager, this might very possibly be the strategy he wants. On the whole, however, it is much better to regard these as suggestions which can guide the risk manager in designing the particular strategy that will be right for the particular situation.

"Might" because risk managers must always guard against slavish imitation. Knee-jerk reaction tends to cost money.

Every strategy implies a certain kind of market situation — for example, a normal yield curve and a widening basis. Usually, in that situation, a long basis strategy is going to be unsuccessful. Yet there are times when long the basis is the way to be. That is the strategy that will get the job done.

So every strategy has to follow from careful thought. At the very least, a risk manager must:

1. identify a risk
2. define business goals
3. analyze the basis (or spreads)
4. design a strategy

Step three implies the presence of a basis book and an awareness of the storage problem.

Each strategic summary conforms to a standard format for ease of reference and comparison. In outline:

A. The Problem — a note on the problem, the goal, the strategic response

B. Preliminaries
1. Basis calculations
2. Futures Position Size
   (Par Units)

C. The Strategy — the T-chart

D. Results and Evaluation
1. Cash Result
2. Futures Result
3. Capital Gain or Loss

4. Interest Expense
5. Interest Income
6. Net Hedging Result
7. Annualized Yield
8. Basis Value
9. Hedge Check

Steps 3, 4, and 5 do not apply in every case. When there is no interest income or expense, then the Capital Gain or Loss and the Net Hedging Result will be identical, and Net Hedging Result will be the term used. The Capital Gain or Loss is important to focus on the result of the hedging strategy in cases where interest results might obscure it. After all, in situations where a hedger has interest expense and income, so does an unhedged operator. Clearly, that expense or income is independent of the hedge, an important point to keep in mind.

For ease of reference, these are the formulas for deriving the information necessary to think about hedging strategy.

B. Preliminaries

1. *The Basis*

   Cash Price − (Futures × Cf) = Basis

2. *Futures Position Size*

   $$\frac{\text{Cash Value}}{1000 \times \text{Cash Price}} \times \text{Cf} = \text{No. of Contracts}$$

   $$\frac{\text{Cash Value}}{1000 \times \text{Cash Price}} = \text{No. of 100,000 Par Units}$$

C. Results and Evaluation

1. *Cash Result*

   Cash Sale − Cash Purchase = Cash Result

2. *Futures Result*

   Futures Change × 31.25 × Contracts = Futures Result

3. *Capital Gain or Loss* (where needed)

   $$\begin{array}{r} \text{Cash Result} \\ + \ \text{Futures Result} \\ \hline \text{Capital Gain or Loss} \end{array}$$

4. *Interest Expense* (where applicable)

   $$\begin{array}{r} \text{Amount Financed} \\ \times \ \text{Rate} \\ \hline \text{Annual Expense} \\ \div \ 365 \text{ days} \\ \hline \text{Daily Expense} \\ \times \ \text{Days in Hedge} \\ \hline \text{Interest Expense} \end{array}$$

5. *Interest Income* (where applicable)

Par Value
× Coupon Rate
Annual Income
÷ 365 Days
Daily Income
× Days in Hedge
Interest Income

6. *Net Hedging Result*

Sum of 3, 4, 5 (if there is no interest expense or income, Net Hedging Result replaces Capital Gain or Loss and sums 1 and 2)

7. *Annualized Yield*

Net Hedging Result
÷ Cash Value
Return
÷ Days in Hedge
Daily Yield
× 365 Days
Annualized Yield

8. *Basis Value*

Basis Change × 31.25 × Par Units = Basis Value

9. Basis Value should equal sum of Cash Result, Futures Result

WHY BASIS TRADING WORKS

Strategy 1

A. The Problem

To protect an investment from value erosion while earning a long-term yield on a short-term investment, a risk manager might think selling futures a useful hedge. This trader has achieved "price neutrality," a major hedging goal in the minds of many. Yet, in a normal yield environment, the storage fundamentals work against this long basis position (buy cash, sell futures).

B. Preliminaries

1. *The Basis*
    a. $153.70931 - (96 \times 1.532) = 6.63731 \ (\times 32) = 212.39392$
    b. $153.23269 - (100 \times 1.532) = 0.03269 \ (\times 32) = 1.04608$

2. *Futures Position Size*

$$\frac{153,709,310}{1000 \times 153.70931} \times 1.5320 = 1,532$$

C. The Strategy

CASH	FUTURES	BASIS
June 24, 1987		
buy	sell	
13.25% coupon May 2009-14,	Dec T-bond @96-00	212
@153.70931, 8% yield	Cf: 1.5320	
Par Value: $100,000,000	HR: 1.5320	
Cash Value: $153,709,310	No. of Contracts: 1532	
December 1, 1987		
sell	buy	
13.25% coupon May 2009-14,	Dec T-bond @100-00	1
@153.23269, 8% yield		
Par Value: $100,000,000		
Cash Value: $153,232,690		
June 24 to December 1: 160 days		

D. Results and Evaluation

1. *Cash Result* (loss)

    Cash Sale   − Cash Purchase = Cash Result
    153,232,690 - 153,709,310   = −476,620

2. *Futures Result* (loss)

    Futures Change $\times$ 31.25 $\times$ Contracts = Futures Result
      (in 32nds)
           128       $\times$ 31.25 $\times$ 1532   = −6,128,000

3. *Capital Loss*

− 476,620	Cash Loss
− 6,128,000	Futures Loss
− 6,604,620	Capital Loss

4. *Interest Expense* (not applicable)

5. *Interest Income*

100,000,000	Par Value
× .1325	Coupon Rate
13,250,000	Annual Income
÷ 365	Days
36,301.37	Daily Income
× 160	Days in Hedge
5,808,219	Interest Income

6. *Net Hedging Result* (loss)

− 6,604,620	Capital Loss
+ 5,808,219	Interest Income
− 796,401	Net Hedging Result

7. *Annualized Yield*

− 796,401	Net Hedging Result
÷ 153,709,310	Cash Value
− 0.0051812	Return
÷ 160	Days in Hedge
− 0.0000324	Daily Yield
× 365	Days
− 0.0118196	= − 1.18% Annualized Yield

8. *Basis Value*

Basis Change × 31.25 × Par Units = Basis Value
−211.34784 × 31.25 × 1000   = 6,604,620

9. Basis Value = Capital Loss
6,604,620   = 6,604,620

This hedger apparently followed his intuitive sense, unaware of the basis or the direction of the basis change. His "common sense" response was that of a buyer of bonds, but he wanted to be a seller of futures— the classical storage hedge in which the hedger constructs a long basis position. The storage hedge is appropriate any time the market signals "store," any time the hedger can anticipate a narrowing basis. Notice that the basis on June 24 is 320 over. By December 1 it widened (become less positive) to 114 over. To be long the basis in that situation is what veteran basis traders refer to as being on the wrong side of the basis.

The basis trader, on the other hand, used the basis change to good advantage. Figure 4-6 summarizes the strategy of the basis trader from Chapter 3, expanding it to include basis information.

Figure 4-6

CASH	FUTURES	BASIS
June 24, 1987		
forward purchase 13.25% May 2009-14, (154.70931) 8% yield, for September 1 delivery	buy Sep T-bond @98-00 Cf: 1.5347 HR: 1.5347 No. of Contracts: 1534.7	106
September 1, 1987		
buy (take delivery on forward purchase) 13.25% May 2009-14 @153.47334, 8% yield Par Value: $100,000,000 Cash Value: $153,473,340	sell Sep T-bond @100-00	0
December 1, 1987		
sell 13.25% May 2009-14 @153./23269, 8% yield Par Value: $100,000,000 Cash Value: $153,232,690		

June 24 to September 1: 69 days
September 1 to December 1: 91 days
June 24 to December 1: 160 days

The structure of this trade sequence turns the predictable basis change to advantage. Specifically, the basis went from 106 over to zero (basis traders keep track of whether the basis is positive or negative by referring to a number like +106 as 106 over and a number like -236 as 236 under, where over and under refer to the relationship to zero just as + and - do). Correctly anticipating the widening basis in this case, the basis trader designed a strategy which, in effect, allowed him to short the basis. At first glance the strategy seems to entail a complicated process. In reality it does not.

Like master craftsmen, basis traders have control of all the tools of their trade. They know what each can do and when to use it. The first hedger knew about buying and selling. Apparently that is as far as his expertise reached. Along with those rudimentary moves, basis traders understand such details as forward purchase (or "cash forwards" as they are often called) and how to assess the market potential of basis change, variations in conversion factors, and cash and futures price changes.

Most importantly, basis traders understand the storage problem and what it means in terms of strategic response. That is, basis traders know that

- bond basis widens in a normal yield curve market
- a widening basis issues a "don't store" signal
- the short basis position is the correct response to the "don't store" signal.

Risk management newcomers stall out on the notion that a short basis position (sell cash, buy futures) is even possible. To invest, their thinking seems to run, people *buy* bonds; talk of selling them makes no sense.

In a way they are right. Study of Figure 4-6 indicates that the basis trader agreed. Yet his forward purchase tactic creates the *effect* of a cash sale at the outset of his trading sequence. He is, for all intents and purposes, short cash. He is not holding inventory—as, indeed, his basis analysis shows him he must not.

In sum, the basis trader's mastery of all the possibilities the markets afford has allowed him to respond creatively and effectively. It has allowed him to escape the bonds of superficial thought and to see the genuine logic of the situation. Because of that, he can accomplish what he set out to do.

Strategy 2

A. The Problem

To profit from favorable market conditions when they must delay entering the market, hedgers often find forward purchase strategies useful. In effect a short basis position (sell cash, buy futures), this does not eliminate price exposure, but locks in the cash bond purchase price and takes advantage of the predictable basis change to enhance returns. Normally, the futures gain will at least make up for the change in cash prices.

B. Preliminaries

1. *The Basis*

    Cash   − (Futures x Cf)   = Basis
    a. $153.70931 - (98 \times 1.5347) = 3.30871 \ (\times 32) = 105.87872$
    b. $153.47334 - (100 \times 1.5347) = 0.00334 \ (\times 32) = 0.10688$

2. *Futures Position Size*

$$\frac{153,709,310}{1000 \times 153.70931} \times 1.5347 = 1534.7$$

C. The Strategy

CASH	FUTURES	BASIS
June 24, 1987		

forward purchase 13.25% May 2009-14, (153.70931) 8% yield, for Sept, 1 delivery	buy
	Sep T-bond @98-00
	  Cf: 1.5347
	  HR: 1.5347
	  No. of Contracts: 1534.7
		106

September 1, 1987		

buy
(take delivery on forward purchase) 13.25% May 2009-14 @153.47334, 8% yield
    Par Value: $100,000,000
    Cash Value: $153,473,340
	sell
	Sep T-bond @100-00
	  (through delivery)
		0

December 1, 1987		

sell
13.25% May 2009-14
@153.23269, 8% yield
    Par Value: $100,000,000
    Cash Value: $153,232,690		

June 24 to September 1: 69 days		
September 1 to December 1: 91 days		
June 24 to December 1: 160 days		

D. Results and Evaluation

1. *Cash Result* (loss)

   Cash Sale   − Cash Purchase = Cash Result
   153,232,690 − 153,473,340   = −240,650

2. *Futures Result* (gain)

   Futures Change × 31.25 × Contracts = Futures Result
   (in 32nds)
       64   × 31.25 × 1534.7   = 3,069,400

3. *Capital Gain*

− 240,650	Cash Loss
+ 3,069,400	Futures Gain
−21,828,750	Capital Gain

4. *Interest Expense* (not applicable)

5. *Interest Income*

100,000,000	Par Value
x .1325	Coupon Rate
13,250,000	Annual Income
÷ 365	Days
36,301.37	Daily Income
× 91	Days in Hedge
3,303,425	Interest Income

6. *Net Hedging Result*

2,828,750	Capital Gain
+ 3,303,425	Interest Income
6,132,175	Net Hedging Result

7. *Annualized Yield*

6,132,175	Net Hedging Result
÷ 153,473,340	Cash Value
0.039956	Return
÷ 160	Days in Hedge
0.0002497	Daily Yield
× 365	Days
0.0911495	= 9.11% Annualized Yield

8. *Basis Value*

   Basis Change × 31.25 × Par Units = Basis Value
   105.77184   × 31.25 × 1000   = 3,305,370

9. Basis Value = Futures Result (+ Cash Result)*
   3,305,370   = 3,305,370

   * (Cash Result) refers to the 235,970 cash value change
   between June 24 and September 1.

5

Basis Trading Refinements

R isk managers who overcome "common sense" concern with price and master the ways of the basis can refine their strategies to achieve extra benefits.

Basis traders know flat prices are inscrutable. A record of prices for a period of several years defines chaos. No amount of study or analysis can make them reveal anything of value. For some reason, people find that surprising.

Price watchers apparently assume that patterns will emerge to guide their decision making, if only they look at enough data. The developer of one computer trading program, speaking of his own misconception concerning the usefulness of price history, said that no patterns emerged over the ten-year period he studied. Price watching breeds only a sense of futility.

Basis information is far more useful for bond basis responds in a uniform way time after time. Graphs of bond basis show tendencies which almost copy each other—invaluable information which provides risk managers with something they can count on to quide their strategic thinking.

Basis Variations that Make a Difference

A fundamental of bond basis is that it converges toward zero in a normal yield curve market. Figure 5-1 shows an idealization of that truth.

Figure 5-1   Idealized Basis Graph

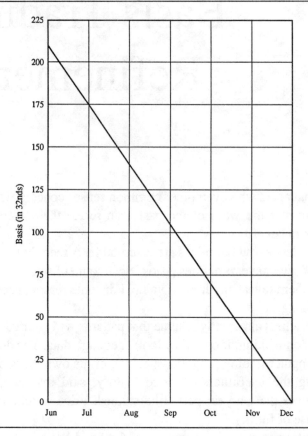

The simple fact that bond basis characteristically widens, or becomes more negative, establishes the foundation for risk management strategy. A widening basis rewards a short basis strategy, one in which the basis trader sells cash and buys futures. A long basis strategy, in which the trader buys cash and sells futures, will also perform predictably. The basis will work against that position in forseeable ways.

The variations that occur within the general tendency create useful trading opportunities. Figure 5-2, though still an idealization, comes closer to the reality.

Figure 5-2 Bond Basis Abstraction

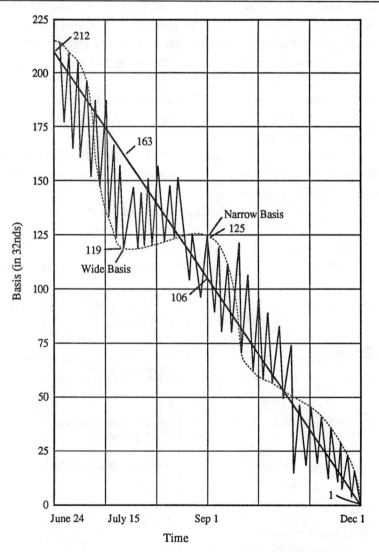

The solid straight line shows the basis converging to zero. The wavy dashed line shows the basis narrowing and widening away from the central tendency. These variations result from events like Treasury refinancings, interest rate changes, developments in foreign trade or fluctuating foreign exchange rates.

A shrewd basis trader, keeping track of such variations, might trade in and out of some portion of his positions as the basis widens (becomes more negative than the norm) and narrows (becomes more positive than the norm). Good basis traders always stay at least a little short (sell cash, buy futures). That is why, in a case like this, they will only trade part of their positions in response to the basis variations. Keeping their eyes on developments, and refining their strategy accordingly, they can derive extra profit opportunities.

Imagine that Figure 5-2 describes the basis situation for the 13.25% May 2009-14 bond relative to December 87 T-bond futures between June 24, 1987 and December 1.

To see what kind of opportunities might ermerge, risk managers should be aware, first, of what the outcome of a relatively conservative approach would be. A hedger who established a short basis position (sell cash, buy futures) on June 24 could just hold his position until December 1 and then unwind. To create that kind of strategy, given a $10 million par position in the 13.25% May 2009-14 bond, the hedger would structure his trade like those in Figure 5-3.

Figure 5-3

CASH	FUTURES	BASIS
June 24, 1987		
sell	buy	
13.25% May 2009-14	Dec 87 T-bond @96-00	212
@153.70931, 8% yield	Cf: 1,5320	
Par Value: $10,000,000	HR: 1.5320	
Cash Value: $15,370,931	No. of Contracts: 153.2	
December 1, 1987		
buy	sell	
13.25% May 2009-14,	Dec 87 T-bond @100-00	
@153.23269, 8% yield		
Par Value: $10,000,000		
Cash Value: $15,323,269		
June 24 to December 1: 160 days		

Cash Result

Cash Sale	–	Cash Purchase	=	Cash Result
15,370,931	–	15,323,269	=	47,662

Futures Result

Futures Change (in 32nds)	x	31.25	x	Contracts	=	Futures Result
128	x	31.25	x	153.2	=	612,800

Net Hedging Result

47,662	Cash Gain
612,800	Futures Gain
660,462	Net Hedging Result

Annualized Yield

9.8%

BASIS TRADING REFINEMENTS

Strategy 3

A. The Problem

To enhance short-term returns to cash reserves or other "cash" holdings, a short basis position (sell cash, buy futures) is an excellent ploy. In a normal yield environment, it assures the hedger of being on the right side of the basis. Keep in mind that the yield of the hedging strategy enhances a standard short-term investment (say, 6% T-bills) for the term of the hedge.

B. Preliminaries

1. *The Basis*

   Cash $-$ (Futures $\times$ Cf)   = Basis
   a. $153.70931 - (96 \times 1.5320) = 6.63731 (\times 32) = 212.39392$
   b. $153.23269 - (100 \times 1.5320) = 1.04608 (\times 32) = 1.04608$

2. *Futures Position Size*

   $$\frac{15,370,931}{1000 \times 153.70931} \times 1.5320 = 153.2$$

C. The Strategy

CASH	FUTURES	BASIS
June 24, 1987		
sell	buy	
13.25% May 2009-14	Dec 87 T-bond @96-00	212
@153.70931, 8% yield	Cf: 1.5320	
Par Value: $10,000,000	HR: 1.5320	
Cash Value: $15,370,931	No. of Contracts: 153.2	
December 1, 1987		
buy	sell	
13.25% May 2009-14,	Dec 87 T-bond @100-00	1
@153.23269, 8% yield,		
Par Value: $10,000,000		
Cash Value: $15,323,269		
June 24 to December 1: 160 days		

D. Results and Evaluation

1. *Cash Result* (gain)

   Cash Sale $-$ Cash Purchase $=$ Cash Result
   $15,370,931 - 15,323,269$ $= 47,662$

2. *Futures Result*

   Futures Change $\times$ 31.25 $\times$ Contracts $=$ Futures Result
      (in 32nds)
         128 $\times$ 31.25 $\times$ 153.2 $= 612,800$

3. *Capital Gain* (not applicable)
4. *Interest Expense* (not applicable)
5. *Interest Income* (not applicable)
6. *Net Hedging Result*

$$
\begin{array}{rl}
47,662 & \text{Cash Gain} \\
+\ 612,800 & \text{Futures Gain} \\
\hline
660,462 & \text{Net Hedging Result}
\end{array}
$$

7. *Annualized Yield*

$$
\begin{array}{rl}
660,462 & \text{Net Hedging Result} \\
\div\ 15,370,931 & \text{Cash Value} \\
\hline
0.0429682 & \text{Return} \\
\div\ 160 & \text{Days in Hedge} \\
\hline
0.0002702 & \text{Daily Yield} \\
\times\ 365 & \text{Days} \\
\hline
0.0986377 & = 9.86\%\ \text{Annualized Yield}
\end{array}
$$

8. *Basis Value*

Basis Change $\times$ 31.25 $\times$ Par Units = Basis Value
211.34784 $\times$ 31.25 $\times$ 100   = 660,462

9. Basis Value = Net Hedging Result
   660,462   = 660,462

This strategy produces an excellent result. The $660,462 net hedging result amounts to a 9.8% annualized yield. That is 22.5% better than the stated yield of the cash bond.

A basis trader who recognizes the opportunities depicted in Figure 5-2 might do even better. The segment labelled Wide Basis bottoms about July 15. The segment labelled Narrow Basis peaks about September 1.

Given the unchanging yield assumption, the cash and futures prices might be something like these:

Date	Cash	Futures
June 24	153.70931	96-00
July 15	153.70931	97-30
Sept. 1	153.47334	97-20
Dec. 1	153.23269	100-00

The basis along the "normal" line might be 212, 163, 106, and 1 for those four dates. The actual basis values, instead, are 212, 119, 125, and 1.

To capitalize on those variations from the basis norm, a basis trader could begin, just as in the conservative strategy, by selling cash and buying futures to establish a short basis position on June 24, 1987. Specifically, he will sell $10 million par of the 13.25% May 2009-14 bond at 153.70931 and 8% yield, and buy 153.2 December 87 T-bond futures contracts at 96-00.

On July 15, he will take advantage of the wide basis by buying cash and selling futures. Given that good traders always stay somewhat short, assume that this trader traded out of half of his positions—cash and futures. To do that, he will buy $5 million par of the 13.25% May 2009-14 bond at 153.70931 and sell 76.6 futures contracts at 97-30.

Seeing the narrow basis on September 1, he will unwind the partial position by selling the $5 million par cash bond now at 153.47334 and buying 76.6 December futures at 97-20. At that point, his positions on both sides are right where they were at the start—short $10 million par cash and long 153.2 December futures contracts.

Figure 5-4 summarizes that complex of trades.

Figure 5-4

CASH	FUTURES	BASIS
June 24, 1987		

sell
13.25% May 2009-14
@153.70931, 8% yield
   Par Value: $10,000,000
   Cash Value: $15,370,931
	buy
	Dec 87 T-bond @96-00
	   Cf: 1.5320
	   HR: 1.5320
	   No. of Contracts: 153.2
		212

July 15, 1987		

buy
13.25% May 2009-14
@153.70931, 8% yield
   Par Value: $5,000,000
   Cash Value: $7,685,465.5
	sell
	Dec 87 T-bond @97-30
	   Cf: 1.5320
	   HR: 1.5320
	   No. of Contracts: 76.6
		119

September 1, 1987		

sell
13.25% May 2009-14
@153.47334, 8% yield
   Par Value: $5,000,000
   Cash Value: $7,673,667
	buy
	Dec 87 T-bond @97-20
	   Cf: 1.5320
	   HR: 1.5320
	   No. of Contracts: 76.6
		125

December 1, 1987		

buy
13.25% May 2009-14
@153.23269, 8% yield
   Par Value: $10,000,000
   Cash Value: $15,323,269
June 24 to December 1: 160 days
	sell
	Dec 87 T-bond @100-00
		1

Strategy 4

A. The Problem

To take advantage of events which create variations in storage demands, like refundings and yield changes, basis traders might alter their hedge positions as the basis narrows (becomes more positive) or widens (becomes more negative) away from the norm. Good traders always stay somewhat short. Their market sense determines what portion of their positions they trade in response to these opportunities.

B. Preliminaries

NOTE: The trader maintains a constant short position equal to half his cash position (the proportion varying with the individual case). He trades in and out of the other half. To calculate results, he figures the "short segment" and the "enhancement segment" separately.

1. *The Basis*

   Cash   − (Futures × Cf)   = Basis

   "short segment"

   a. $153.70931 - (96 \times 1.5320)$ $= 6.63731\ (\times\ 32) = 212.39392$
   b. $153.23269 - (100 \times 1.5320)$ $= 1.04608\ (\times\ 32) = 1.04608$

   "enhancement segment"

   a. $153.70931 - (96 \times 1.5320)$ $= 6.63731\ (\times\ 32) = 212.39392$
   b. $153.70931 - (97.9375 \times 1.5320)$ $= 3.66906$ $= 117.40992$
   c. $153.47334 - (97.625 \times 1.5320)$ $= 3.91184$ $= 125.17888$
   d. $153.23269 - (100 \times 1.5320)$ $= 1.04608\ (\times\ 32) = 1.04608$

2. *Futures Position Size*

   $$\frac{7,685,465.5}{1000 \times 153.70931} \times 1.5320 = 76.6$$

   $$\frac{7,685,465.5}{1000 \times 153.70931} \times 1.5320 = 76.6$$

C. The Strategy

CASH	FUTURES	BASIS
June 24, 1987		
sell	buy	
13.25% May 2009-14	Dec 87 T-bond @96-00	212
@153.70931, 8% yield	Cf: 1.5320	
Par Value: $10,000,000	HR: 1.5320	
Cash Value: $15,370,931	No. of Contracts: 153.2	
July 15, 1987		
buy	sell	
13.25% May 2009-14	Dec 87 T-bond @97-30	117
@153.70931, 8% yield	Cf: 1.5320	
Par Value: $5,000,000	HR: 1.5320	
Cash Value: $7,685,465.5	No. of Contracts: 76.6	

CASH	FUTURES	BASIS
September 1, 1987		
sell	buy	
13.25% May 2009-14	Dec 87 T-bond @97-20	125
@153.47334, 8% yield	Cf: 1.5320	
Par Value: $5,000,000	HR: 1.5320	
Cash Value: $7,673,667	No. of Contracts: 76.6	
December 1, 1987		
buy	sell	
13.25% May 2009-14	Dec 87 T-bond @100-00	1
@153.23269, 8% yield,		
Par Value: $10,000,000		
Cash Value: $15,323,269		

D. Results and Evaluation

"short segment"

1. *Cash Result* (gain)

   Cash Sale   − Cash Purchase = Cash Result
   7,685,465.5 − 7,661,634.5   = 23,831

2. *Futures Result* (gain)

   Futures Change × 31.25 × Contracts = Futures Result
   (in 32nds)
        128   × 31.25 × 76.6   = 306,400

3. *Capital Gain* (not applicable)

4. *Interest Expense* (not applicable)

5. *Interest Income* (not applicable)

6. *Net Hedging Result*

         23,831 Cash Gain
   + 306,400 Futures Gain
   _____
      330,231 Net Hedging Result

7. *Annualized Yield* — see below

8. *Basis Value*

   Basis Change × 31.25 × Par Units = Basis Value
   211.34784   × 31.25 × 50   = 330,231

9. Basis Value = Net Hedging Result
   330,231   = 330,231

"enhancement segment"

Time Segments
(1) June 21 to July 15: 21 days
(2) July 15 to September 1: 47 days
(3) September 1 to December 1: 91 days

1. *Cash Result* (gain)

Cash Sale   − Cash Purchase = Cash Result
(1) 7,685,465.5 − 7,685,465.5 = 0
(2) 7,673,667   − 7,685,465.5 = − 11,798.5
(3) 7,673,667   − 7,661,634.5 = + 12,032.5
                     Total   + 234

2. *Futures Result* (gain)

Futures Change × 31.25 × Contracts = Futures Result
   (in 32nds)
     (1) 62   × 31.25 × 76.6   = 148,413
     (2) 10   × 31.25 × 76.6   = 23,938
     (3) 76   × 31.25 × 76.6   = 181,925
                      Total   354,276

3. *Capital Gain* (not applicable)

4. *Interest Expense* (not applicable)

5. *Interest Income* (not applicable)

6. *Net Hedging Result* (totals)

       234   Cash Gain
+ 354,276   Futures Gain
   354,510   Net Hedging Result

7. *Annualized Yield* — see below

8. *Basis Value*

Basis Change × 31.25 × Par Units = Basis Value
(1) 94.984   × 31.25 × 50   = 148,413
(2) 7.7696   × 31.25 × 50   = 12,140
(3) 124.1328 × 31.25 × 50   = 193,958

9. Basis Value = Cash Result + Futures Result
(1) 148,413 = 148,413
(2) 12,140   = 12,140
(3) 193,958 = 193,958

Total Hedging Result

     330,231   Net Hedging Result "short segment"
+ 354,510   Net Hedging Result "enhancement segment"
     684,741   Total Hedging Result

Annualized Yield

       684,741   Total Hedging Result
÷ 15,370,931   Cash Value
   0.0445478   Return
       ÷ 159   Days in Hedge
   0.0002802   Daily Yield
      × 365   Days
   0.1022638   = 10.23% Annualized Yield

Notice that, although this hedger buys cash on July 15, he is still short $5 million par of the cash bond. Similarly, at that time, he is still long 76.6 futures contracts. When the hedger trades out of the "refinement" on September 1 (selling $5 million par of cash and buying back 76.6 futures contracts), he is right back where he started on June 24—in terms of position size.

In effect, to total the results of the strategic refinement, the hedger works with two separate segments. On the one hand, half the position behaves just like the positions in the more conservative strategy.

Cash Result

	Cash Sale	–	Cash Purchase	=	Cash Result
	7,685,465.5	–	7,661,634.5	=	23,831

Futures Result

Futures Change (in 32nds)	x	31.25	x	Contracts	=	Futures Result
128	x	31.25	x	76.6	=	306,400

Net Hedging Result

23,831	Cash Gain
306,400	Futures Gain
330,231	Net Hedging Result

It takes a three-stage calculation to figure the results on the "refinement" half. The hedger has to calculate both cash and futures results (1) for the June 24 to July 15 segment, (2) for the July 15 to September 1 segment, and (3) for the September 1 to December 1 segment. Then he has to sum the results.

Cash Result

Cash Sale	–	Cash Purchase	=	Cash Result
7,685,465.5	–	7,685,465.5	=	0
7,673,667	–	7,685,465.5	=	-11,798.5
7,673,667	–	7,661,634.5	=	+12,032.5
			Sum	+234

Futures Result

Futures Change (in 32nds)	x	31.25	x	Contracts	=	Futures Result
(1) 62	x	31.25	x	76.6	=	148,413
(2) 10	x	31.25	x	76.6	=	23,938
(3) 76	x	31.25	x	76.6	=	181,925
				Sum		354,276

Net Hedging Result

234	Cash Gain
354,276	Futures Gain
354,510	Net Hedging Result

Total Hedging Result

330,231	"Conservative" Result
+ 354,510	Refinement Result
684,741	Total Hedging Result

Annualized Yield

10.23%

The total result of this hedging strategy is the sum of the "conservative" portion and the refinement. Notice that the cash gain from the more active trading is much less than the result of the conservative strategy. Yet the futures side improvement more than overcomes that. A victory is twice itself when the achiever brings home full numbers.

The refinement produces an annualized return of 10.2%, which is 27.5% better than the stated bond yield.

Basis traders might trade in and out this way several times. The number of trades and the size of the partial positions would depend on what the hedger thinks of the market, how strong he thinks the opportunities are. Specific earnings are not the point to focus on. Because of varying market conditions, the same opportunities are not always available. But "opportunity" is the key word.

Risk managers who study bond basis and understand how the market responds to current events, in basis terms, will notice opportunities that others miss.

Besides knowing which moves to make, basis traders have to worry about timing their moves. Perhaps rising interest rates caused a narrowing of the basis. Then the trader needs to think about what will drive the basis back to the normal level. That kind of anticipation helps them time their moves into and out of their positions.

Market veterans often remark that less experienced traders typically hold onto losing positions too long, and abandon profitable positions too soon. While that remark applies especially to speculators, it also applies to basis traders trying to enhance the performance of their strategies. Waiting for the right moment to trade out of a position can be agonizing. Staying in another day may produce additional earnings, but the market may reverse and destroy some of the gains.

Finally, the decision to pursue a relatively conservative or a more aggressive trading policy depends on what overall business goals motivate the risk management program. If protecting against risk is the overriding goal, then playing it safe is best. On the other hand, some business people can tolerate a certain degree of risk. They may decide it worthwhile to pursue the extra profit.

What The Markets Tell Us

Futures Quotes and Spreads

Commodities analysts persist in trying to use futures to predict commodities prices. Futures do not predict future prices. Once again, price

obsession blinds people and obscures the market's real message—
which turns out to be extremely important.

Though they vary in form, futures quotations in newspapers and elsewhere all list a series of prices for subsequent contract months which
are called spreads. Figure 5-5 displays a typical series.

Figure 5-5   U.S. Treasury Bond Futures—March 16, 1987

Mar	Jun	Sep	Dec	Mar88	Jun	Sep	Dec
101-21	100-17	99-17	98-19	97-22	96-27	96-01	95-08

Basis traders use the spreads for a quick check on the storage situation of the market. Spreads are related to, but not exactly the same as,
the basis. Where the basis relates cash and futures prices, spreads relate
pairs of futures prices. In Figure 5-5, the spread between June 87 and
September 87 is 32/32nds (or one percentage point, also called a handle). Bond prices, recall, indicate a percentage of the par value, and the
fractions are 32nds of one percent. Thus, 101-21 means one hundred
one and twenty-one thirty-seconds percent of par. Par for a T-bond futures contract is $100,000, so on March 16, 1987 one March 87 con-
tract cost $101,656.25—1.0165625 of 100,000.

Spreads have useful predictive power, though not with regard to
price. Essentially, the spreads tell risk managers the same story as the
basis charts do concerning questions of storage.

A wide basis signals a carry market. It tells risk managers to store the
commodity in question, to buy cash. A narrow basis gives the opposite
signal—that this is a noncarry market so risk managers should not store,
they should sell cash. So it is with spreads.

Yet the spreads offer one further advantage, at least in some cases.
The basis is, in a sense, a microeconomic indicator. It is unique to the
individual bond, even to the individual bond trader's situation. Spreads
are macroeconomic indicators. They are as generic as the futures contracts themselves and refer to the possibilities of the entire market.

However, spreads for financials differ superficially from the physicals. In the case of physicals, two basic kinds of spread patterns occur. For example, on March 12, 1987, these corn spreads described a carry market:

Corn (a carry market)

Mar	May	Jul	Sep	Dec	Mar88	May
155.75	157.25	160.75	165.00	173.25	180.75	182.00

On that same day, the No. 2 heating oil spreads signalled a noncarry, or inverse, market:

No. 2 Heating Oil (an inverse market)

Apr	May	Jun	Jul	Aug
0.5040	0.4923	0.4821	0.4798	0.4728

When physical spreads go steadily higher, as with these corn spreads, they signal a carry market, just as a wide basis does. So, naturally enough, basis traders call spreads like these for corn "wide spreads." Wide spreads, like a wide basis, tell a basis trader to store the commodity, to buy cash.

Spreads like those for No. 2 oil signal a noncarry market just as a narrow basis does. Narrow spreads, where the prices go steadily lower, tell basis traders not to store, to sell cash.

Bonds appear different because they virtually never exhibit spreads like the corn example, given the assumption of a normal yield curve market. Since financial basis characteristically widens, the spreads, like the oil example, always exhibit a declining series of prices as in Figure 5-6.

Figure 5-6

T-bond

Jun	Sep	Dec	Mar88	Jun
100-13	99-14	98-17	97-21	96-27

Succeeding futures months always show lower prices. Yet risk managers who pay attention to the degree of price change can derive the same information from the T-bond spreads as they can from the physicals. The spreads for financial commodities vary in terms of how great the price intervals are between futures months.

They might exhibit a small absolute difference, as in Figure 5-7, where the prices drop only 16/32nds from one month to the next.

Figure 5-7

Jun	Sep	Dec	Mar88
88-00	87-16	86-00	86-16

"Wide" spreads like these imply a carry market. Like the corn spreads, they tell basis traders that the market is rewarding storage. It is time to buy cash.

The spreads might exhibit a greater absolute difference, as in Figure 5-8, where the prices are a whole point apart.

Figure 5-8

Jun	Sep	Dec	Mar88
88-00	87-00	86-00	85-00

Or the intervals might be quite large, as in Figure 5-9 where the prices vary a point and a half.

Figure 5-9

Jun	Sep	Dec	Mar88
88-00	86-16	85-00	83-16

These "narrow" spreads signal a noncarry market. It is time to sell cash rather than store.

A useful way to focus on the parallelism of the basis and the spreads is to compare the kind of relationship each defines. The basis is the cash-futures difference, as in these examples.

Cash Price	–	(Futures Price x Cf)	=	Basis
153.70931	–	(97.9375 x 1.5320)	=	212
153.70931	–	(99.904086 x 1.5320)	=	21

A very positive, narrow basis like 212 issues a "don't store" signal. In contrast, a relatively more negative wide basis like 21 urges storage.

Spreads define the difference between nearby and deferred futures months, as in these examples.

Nearby	–	Deferred	=	Spread
88-00	–	87-16	=	0-16(+0.5)
88-00	–	86-16	=	1-16(+1.5)

The 0-16 (or 0.5) spread is less positive than one like 1-16 (or 1.5). The former, therefore, is a wide spread which implies a carry market. It urges storage. The latter, more positive, spread is a narrow spread which discourages storage.

Figure 5-10 summarizes the relationship of spreads and the basis with regard to the storage signals.

Figure 5-10   Storage Signals

	Store	*Don't Store*
Basis cash-futures	wide (more negative)	narrow (more positive)
Spreads nearby-deferred	wide (more negative)	narrow (more positive)

Risk managers who concentrate on the storage problem as they read the markets find this a useful way to look at spread phenomena. After all, the focus of concern is not prices but what message there is concerning storage.

III

Basis Records
and Bond Data

A risk management operation in a sense resembles theater. The strategies and trading are what everyone notices. Behind those who spend a few minutes in the public eye are others who spend hours laboring behind the scenes to make it all happen. In risk management, the moments of trading achieve success only if countless behind-the-scenes tasks are attended to carefully.

Anticipation is the name of the risk management game. The adept practitioners think ahead. They calculate possible outcomes and think about each possible turn of events. They design strategic responses for each possibility. And they predict, within narrow limits, what the result will be in each case.

To be able to anticipate, basis traders do several kinds of background work. They have to understand why cash prices behave as they do—how coupon, yield, and maturity relate. They have to understand how to calculate and chart the basis. In fact, the better risk managers will chart in several different ways, each approach providing different kinds of insights.

No glamor is attached to these tasks. Yet when they are omitted or overlooked, the glamor of the other areas tarnishes, or vanishes altogether. To prevent that, basis traders discipline themselves to meticulous record keeping.

6

Understanding Cash Bond Pricing

Newcomers to financial risk management face what appears to be a wilderness of data. Once they grasp the function of each bit of information, though, chaos gives way to order and utility. An important task for a trader in financials, is to understand the information the market develops and how to derive it.

The financial papers, for example, provide daily reports on more than 150 cash Treasury issues. The bonds are those with maturities greater than ten years. Treasury notes have maturities between one and ten years. And Treasury bills have maturities of one year or less. Of all of the bonds, only about three dozen are deliverable against the futures contracts. These examples refer to just the five listed in Table 6-1— which illustrates a typical quotation format.

Seasoned bond traders can learn a great deal from all of this information. To start with, though, focus on just four facts:

- coupon rate
- maturity
- bid-ask prices
- yield.

Table 6-1   Selected Treasury Bonds (June 25, 1986)

Rate	Mat.	Date	Bid	Ask	Bid Chg.	Yld.
15.750%	2001	Nov	166-08	166-16	+.5	8.11
11.625%	2002	Nov	132-10	132-18	+.22	8.02
7.625%	2002-07	Feb	97-20	98-04	+.4	7.81
10.375%	2007-12	Nov	123-22	123-30	+.9	8.02
12.500%	2009-14	Aug	145-27	146-03	+.17	8.07

The rate column shows the coupon rate, not to be confused with overall bond yield. Recall that in the earlier hedging examples, the coupon earnings softened the disaster for the hedger with the unsatisfactory strategy and improved the basis trader's already good result. For the first bond listed, the coupon is 15.75%. Held for a year, a $100,000 investment in this bond would earn $15,750. The third bond listed would earn $7,612.50 under similar circumstances.

The second bit of information, 2001 Nov, indicates the date of maturity. Nov means November 15 of the relevant year because, by convention, the government normally pays coupons on the fifteenth. So the first bond here reaches maturity on November 15, 2001. The fifth bond achieves maturity on August 15, 2014 (2009, the first date in the hyphenated pair, indicates a call date which simply suggests that the government has the right to prepay the note annually after this year).

The bid-ask prices indicate at what prices a trader can sell or buy this bond. The trader selling the second bond can get 132-10. Buying it, he will pay 132-18. The fractions in U.S. bond listings are 32nds, not decimals (corporates are quoted in eighths). A listing of 166-08 (or 166.08) means 166 and 8/32nds, while 97-20 means 97 and 20/32nds. Decimal equivalents would be 166.25 and 97.625. Also, the price expresses a percentage of par. For example, the buyer of the second bond listed will pay $1,325.60 for every $1000 worth of face value (it is possible to buy in increments of $1,000 par though the practical minimum is really $1 million par). For a $100,000 bond, he will pay $132,562, plus accrued interest. In the case of the third bond, the 98-04 means that he will pay $9,813.00 for every $1000, or $98,130 for a bond with

$100,000 par (par refers to the amount to be repaid at maturity, in effect the face value of the bond). Traders call bonds selling at less than par "discount" and those selling over par "premium" bonds.

The bid change figure is the price change from the previous day.

The yield figure is the final useful fact. The first bond will yield 7.81% if held to maturity, the fourth bond 8.02%. Yield and coupon are separate matters. Coupon rates represent periodic payments to the bond holder. Yield represents the economic return for holding the bond. In bond trade language appreciation is the difference between a discounted purchase price and par. Depreciation is the difference between a premium purchase price and par. Appreciation and depreciation, at least gains and losses, can also occur as short-term price fluctuations in either case.

Pricing

People commonly refer to interest rate hedging, and there are books with titles like *The Interest Rate Futures*. Actually, risk managers cannot hedge interest rates. They can only hedge prices. As with the trading of physical commodities, the basis, the difference between cash and futures prices, is the most important single fact to know. But of course the basis figure reflects a relationship between prices. So once again basis traders have a need to know the price of the bond they are trading.

Basis traders can follow bond and futures prices in the newspaper lists or in the listings of the various electronic reporting services. However, careful traders often need more than that information. Seldom will any trader hold a bond to maturity. Moreover, in placing a hedge they often need to know what the price will be at some future time. So being able to calculate price is important.

Basis traders know one essential fact about a bond at the outset. At maturity its price will be par, and it will produce its stated yield—given the constant reinvestment assumption concerning coupon earnings. Actually, if the coupon is reinvested at a higher rate the yield will be understated. If the coupon is reinvested at a lower rate the yield will be overstated.

Using these standard bits of information, risk managers can quite easily determine the bond price at any moment, present or future.

Bond price depends on two things—the present value of a future sum, as people in finance say, and the present value of an annuity. The future sum is fixed at par. It is the repayment of principal. The annuity is the constant stream of coupon or interest payments.

The formula for all that looks nasty, but it is tamable. To find the present value of the future sum, bond traders use this formula:

$$\text{PVFS} = \frac{1}{(1+i)^n}$$

Here, i indicates the yield rate (per period), and n indicates the number of periods till maturity. Since n is an exponent, it must be accurate or the results will be useless. Also, since bonds usually pay on coupons semi-annually, traders use half the stated rate and calculate maturity in terms of the number of six-month periods between the target time and the maturity date (and remember that, unless the bond says otherwise, 2009 Nov means November 15, 2009).

For practice, let's derive the stated price of the 15.75% 2001 Nov bond listed in Table 6-1. The yield for that bond is 8.11% so half of that is 0.0406 (after all, 8.11% = 0.0811). As of June 25, 1986, there were 30.79 six month periods till maturity. Again, the 0.79 in that number is very important. To derive it, find the number of six month periods and the remainder in days. Convert the days left into a decimal fraction. In this case, 144 days is 0.79 of 365/2. Inserting those numbers into the formula, bond traders can solve for the Present Value of a Future Sum (PVFS), the principal value, as follows:

$$\text{PVFS} = \frac{1}{(1+.0406)^{30.79}} = \frac{1}{3.4054057} = .2936508$$

That is the principal repayment value to which the coupon value, or present value of an annuity, is added.

To derive the Present Value of an Annuity (PVA), the coupon value, traders use a similar formula:

$$PVA = C \left| \frac{1 - (PVFS)}{i} \right|$$

The only new term here is C, the coupon rate. For this bond the coupon is 15.75%, half of which is 0.0788. Substituting into the formula, traders solve for PVA as follows:

$$PVA = .0788 \left[\frac{1 - \dfrac{1}{(1 + .0406)^{30.79}}}{.0406} \right] = .0788 \left[\frac{1 - .2936508}{.0406} \right]$$

$$.0788 \left[\frac{.7063492}{.0406} \right] = .0788 \ [17.397764] = 1.3709438$$

The sum of the annuity figure, 1.3709438, and the future sum, 0.2936508, is 1.6645946. Multiplying that times 100 produces 166.45946 or, in 32nds, 166-15—a number close to the stated ask.

Using the same arithmetic, basis traders can determine price of that bond at any point along the way. The only two figures that can vary are i and n. So they simply substitute new values for those and calculate the result.

Traders can domesticate this math by breaking the process down into four segments and moving through each step by step:

1. Solve for PVFS
2. Solve for PVA
   Notice that the portion in parentheses in this formula is identical to the PVFS formula. As a practical matter, just insert the value derived for PVFS.
3. Add the PVFS to the PVA
4. Multiply the sum in 3) times 100 to derive the BOND PRICE, as a percent of par.

Using the same bond, and assuming no yield change, traders can calculate what the price will be on, say, November 15, 1996. At that time, there will be 10 time periods till maturity. The four step process produces these calculations.

1) $PVFS = \dfrac{1}{(1 + .0406)^{10}} = \dfrac{1}{(1.4888)} = .671679$

2) $PVA = .0788 \left[\dfrac{1 - (.671679)}{.0406} \right] = .0788 \left[\dfrac{.328321}{.0406} \right] =$

$.0788\ [8.0867241] = .6372338$

3) $.671679 + .6372338 = 1.3089128$

4) $1.3089128 \times 100 = 130.89$ (BOND PRICE)

The price of the 15.75% Nov 2001 bond on November 15, 1996 is 130-28 (where 28 refers to 32nds).

Again assuming no yield change, traders can calculate the price of this bond just one year before maturity. Here the exponent is 2—two six-month periods. Accordingly, the four step process now produces these calculations.

1) $PVFS = \dfrac{1}{(1 + .0406)} = \dfrac{1}{(1.0828484)} = .02349$

2) $PVA = .0788 \left[\dfrac{(1 - .92349)}{.0406} \right] = .0788 \left[\dfrac{.0765096}{.0406} \right] =$

$.0788\ [1.8844729] = .1484964$

3) $.92349 + .1484964 = 1.0719865$

4) $1.0719865 \times 100 = 107.20$ (BOND PRICE)

An important price to calculate might be the one for the 15.75% Nov 2001 bond three months after the June 25 purchase date (in the hedging example illustrated in Figure 4-6, the basis trader held a bond for three months). This requires changing the exponent from 30.79 to 30.29, because maturity is three months or half a time period closer. Every other detail remains constant.

1) $\text{PVFS} = \dfrac{1}{(1 + .0406)^{30.29}} = \dfrac{1}{3.3383122} = .2995525$

2) $\text{PVA} = .0788 \left[\dfrac{(1 - .2995525)}{.0406} \right] = .0788 \left[\dfrac{.7004475}{.0406} \right] =$

$.0788 \ [17.252401] = 1.3594892$

3) $.2995525 + 1.3594892 = 1.6590417$

4) $1.6590417 \times 100 = 165.90 \ (\text{BOND PRICE})$

That involves a change of 16/32nds, which is the same as the spreads listed at that point. Inasmuch as the bond value is expected to decline by 16/32nds, basis traders can see from this that it was something other than random forces which caused the spreads to vary about 16/32nds each month.

Yield fluctuation can affect bond price just as much as time. Staying with the 15.75% Nov 2001 bond, assume the Nov 1996 maturity point and also assume that yield drops from 8.11% to 7.9% (remember, half of that will be 0.0395).

1) $\text{PVFS} = \dfrac{1}{1 + .0395)^{10}} = \dfrac{1}{1.4731431} = .6788206$

2) $\text{PVA} = .0788 \left[\dfrac{(1 - .6788206)}{.0395} \right] = .0788 \left[\dfrac{.3211794}{.0395} \right] =$

$.0788 \ [8.1311241] = .6407325$

3) $.6788206 + .6407325 = 1.3195532$

4) $1.3195532 \times 100 = 131.96$ (BOND PRICE) [131.31, in 32nds]

At 8.11% yield, the November 15, 1996 price was 130-28. At 7.9% the price on that date would be 131-31, 3/32nds higher. This price should be higher because the yield is lower, and it is a law of the bond market that bond price and yield vary inversely.

Of course, traders need not always calculate bond prices by hand. Besides referring to quotations in newspapers, they can program computers to process the information. Certain standard tables can be useful in this way also. The point is, risk managers need a first-hand appreciation of how yield and maturity affect bond prices.

These examples reveal several other interesting tendencies. As bonds move toward maturity, their prices tend towards 100—which means 100% of par. For example, with the 12.5% Aug 2014 bond, the prices change as Table 6-2 shows.

Table 6-2

Purchase Date	Maturity Date	Price
6-24-1986	8-15-2014	146.03
9-24-1986	8-15-2014	145.29
8-15-2009	8-15-2014	115.05
8-10-2014	8-15-2014	100.02

Similar results derive from a similar exercise with any other bond. The discount bond would increase in price where the others decrease, but all prices would move closer to 100, or par, as maturity drew closer.

Four Price Rules

So regular are bond price phenomena that risk managers can see several general rules at work. *First, price and yield vary inversely.* Mortgage lenders are painfully aware of that. As rates climb, portfolio value drops. The same thing can happen to other investors—thus the need for risk management.

The *second* rule states that *for bonds alike in all respects save coupon size, a given change in yields will cause the price of a lower coupon bond to change more in percentage terms.* Table 6-3 illustrates that.

Table 6-3 Price Change for 15-Year Maturity, Coupon Varies

Yield	Coupon (price)			Coupon (price change)		
	8%	10%	12%	8%	10%	12%
14%	62	75	87			
12%	72	86	100	10	11	13
10%	84	100	116	12	14	16
8%	100	118	136	16	18	20

On this table, observe the change from 10% yield to 8%. The 8% coupon changes 16 points (from 100 to 84), the 10% coupon changes 20 points (from 118 to 100), and the 12% coupon changes 20 points (from 136 to 116). The larger the coupon, the larger the numerical increment. However, 16 is 19% of 84, 18 is 18% of 100, and 20 is 17% of 116; so, as the rule says, the smaller the coupon, the greater the percentage price change.

The *third* rule states that *for bonds alike in all respects save maturity, a given change in yields will cause the price of a longer maturity bond to change more in percentage terms than a shorter maturity bond.* Table 6-4 illustrates that point.

Table 6-4 Price for 8% Coupon, Maturity Varied

Yield	Maturity (years)			Maturity (price change)		
	10yr	15yr	30yr	10yr	15yr	30yr
14%	68	62	58			
12%	77	72	68	9	10	10
10%	88	84	81	11	12	13
8%	100	100	100	12	16	19

Here the 2% yield change from 10% to 8% causes the 10 year bond to change 14%, the 15 year bond to change 19% and the 30 year bond to change 23%. Interestingly, the rule holds also for the first yield increment, from 14 to 12, where the numerical changes for the two longer bonds are both 10. The percentages here are 13%, 16%, and 17% for the 10, 15, and 30 year bonds, respectively.

The *fourth* rule says that *for any bond, a given increase in yields will cause a smaller percentage price change than a decrease in yields of the same size.* Table 6-5 demonstrates that notion.

Table 6-5

Yield	Price	Yield Change	Price Change	% Price Change	Yield Change
12%	125.9200				
		+2%	-18.5728	12.85%	
10%	144.4928				3%
		-2%	23.0992	15.99%	
8%	167.5920				

For a reference point consider the 15.75% Nov 2001 bond. At 10% yield, the price for an August 8, 1986 purchase should be 144.4928 or 144-15. If the yield rises to 12%, all else staying the same, the price goes down to 125.92 or 125-29. If the yield drops to 8%, all else stable, the price goes up to 167.592 or 167-19, as it should, given the first rule. The yield changes are of the same magnitude—both 2%. But the increase causes a 13% change while the decrease causes a 16% change.

A casual reading of a day's bond price listings does not suggest the presence of any especially systematic phenomena. Yet these examples aptly demonstrate that bond pricing responds to market stimuli in regular ways. What is behind all of this is that the market has to adjust the prices of many issues with widely varying coupons and maturities so they will have more consistent yields.

To accomplish that, the market demands a premium for high coupon bonds, bonds whose coupons are higher than the yield. It allows a discount for low coupon bonds, those whose coupons are lower than the yield. That makes the interest received less or more in relationship to the expected future principal payment. Premiums decrease the expected yield. Discounts raise the yield.

Since risk managers can state rules for these changes, they can actually predict how bond prices will respond to various kinds of changes. More importantly, given a sense of bond price structure, risk managers can use that knowledge to derive the basis—which is even more stable, and more predictable, than prices.

7

Charting the Basis

A task of first-order importance in any risk management operation is basis record keeping. Mere calculation is not enough because all of the strategies—simple or complex—depend on how the basis changes, on the basis trader's being able to predict what the basis will do during a given period of time. Success in risk management requires, at the very least,

- an informed prediction of how the basis will change
- a strategy that puts the trader on the right side of the basis, given that change
- a selection of instrument that will maximize the advantage of that situation.

Meticulous charting of the basis pays off every step of the way.

Calculating the Basis

The basis, for any commodity, describes the relationship between cash and futures prices. For the physical commodities, the basis is the cash price less the futures price:

$$\text{Cash} - \text{Futures} = \text{Basis}.$$

On a given day, the financial news services might publish futures quotations like the ones for foreign currencies in Figure 7-1.

81

Figure 7-1   Foreign Currency Futures Quotations

Thursday, April 30, 1987

Currency	June	Sept	Dec
British Pound $ per pound	1.6350	1.6265	1.6215
Japanese Yen $ per yen (.00)	0.7132	0.7189	0.7251
Swiss Franc $ per franc	0.6816	0.6867	0.6921
W. German Mark $ per mark	0.5558	0.5601	0.5644

Similarly, the reports quote cash currency information like that in Figure 7-2.

Figure 7-2   Exchange Rate Quotations

Country	US $ equivalent
Britain	1.6435
Japan	0.007100
Switzerland	0.6793
W. Germany	0.5537

British pound futures on that day are $1.6350 (basis traders normally use the "nearby month" in these calculations, which in this case is June). The cash market is selling pounds at $1.6435. According to the formula, therefore, the British pound basis is 0.0080 over.

$$\text{Cash} - \text{Futures} = \text{Basis}$$
$$1.6435 - 1.6350 = +0.0080$$

(Basis traders refer to *over* and *under* rather than *plus* and *minus*, in the sense that the pound basis here is "80 over the June.")

That same day Deutsch mark futures were $0.5558, and cash was $0.5537. Therefore, the Deutsch mark basis is 0.0021 under.

$$Cash \ - \ Futures \ = \ Basis$$

$$0.5537 \ - \ 0.5558 \ = \ -0.0021$$

The pound and the Canadian dollar normally have a positive basis, as in the case of the pound here, because interest rates in those countries are typically higher than in the U.S. The West German mark, Swiss franc, and Japanese yen normally exhibit negative basis because interest rates in those countries are lower than in the U.S.

Calculating the basis is that simple.

U.S. Treasury bonds present a special case. Because of their different coupons, yields, and maturities, bonds are not as neatly equivalent to each other as two shipments of oil or soybeans. To overcome these variations among bonds, the Chicago Board of Trade has developed a system of conversion factors (conventionally abbreviated Cf) which have the effect of aligning a given bond with the generic futures price. So the basis for bonds is the cash price less the product of the futures price and the conversion factor:

$$Cash \ - \ (Futures \ x \ Cf) \ = \ Basis.$$

Since every bond has its own price, each has its own basis. As a result, where a grain trader might only need to plot one basis figure, financial risk managers must typically plot several. To calculate bond basis, then, basis traders must

- develop price information
- locate appropriate conversion factors
- calculate the basis according to the formula.

Consider the 13.25% May 2009-14 bond whose cash price, on June 24, 1986 is 157.965 (this is the bond used in the hedges of Chapters 3 and 4). On June 24, the September '86 futures price was 98-05, and the Cf for that bond for the September '86 futures is 1.5439. Substituting those values in the formula, risk managers can derive the basis for that bond on that day.

$$
\begin{array}{llll}
\text{Cash} & - & (\text{Futures x Cf}\quad) & = & \text{Basis} \\
157.965 & - & (96\text{-}00 \ \text{x} \ 1.5414) & = & \\
57.965 & - & (96.00 \ \text{x} \ 1.5414) & = & \\
157.965 & - & 147.9744 & = & 9.9906 \\
(9.9906 & \text{x} & 32 \ = \ 319.6992 & = & 320)
\end{array}
$$

Basis traders normally quote bond basis in 32nds. The basis in this case, then, is 320.

Basis traders need to calculate the basis daily. Staying with the 13.25% May 2009-14 bond, for example, a basis trader would develop a set of information like that in Table 7-1, which shows the basis for that bond during the month of April, 1987.

Table 7-1

		Cash price	Futures Price June 1987	Cf	Basis in 32nds
April	1	151-31	97-23	1.5368	57
	2	152-02	97-08	1.5368	84
	3	151-23	97-24	1.5368	48
	6	151-23	98-04	1.5368	30
	7	151-16	97-08	1.5368	66
	8	151-18	97-13	1.5368	60
	9	149-08	95-23	1.5368	69
	10	147-18	94-22	1.5368	66
	13	146-05	93-30	1.5368	57
	14	143-22	92-20	1.5368	43
	15	145-15	93-08	1.5368	69
	16	146-18	94-07	1.5368	57
	17		No Markets	1.5368	
	20	144-16	92-18	1.5368	72
	21	144-08	92-19	1.5368	63
	22	143-24	92-06	1.5368	66

	23	141-23	91-14	1.5368	38
	24	140-01	89-18	1.5368	77
	27	144-08	91-06	1.5368	58
	28	143-24	92-07	1.5368	62
	29	142-27	91-26	1.5368	56
	30	144-24	93-02	1.5368	55
May	1	143-16	91-26	1.5368	77

Similarly, the 7.625% February 2002-07 bond yields April '87 price and basis data like that in Table 7-2.

Table 7-2

		Cash price	Futures Price June 1987	Cf	Basis in 32nds
April	1	97-20	97-23	0.9709	88
	2	97-14	97-08	0.9709	97
	3	97-16	97-24	0.9709	83
	6	98-00	98-04	0.9709	87
	7	97-09	97-08	0.9709	92
	8	97-13	97-13	0.9709	91
	9	95-30	95-23	0.9709	96
	10	94-24	94-22	0.9709	90
	13	93-28	93-30	0.9709	85
	14	92-02	92-20	0.9709	68
	15	93-14	93-08	0.9709	93
	16	94-04	94-07	0.9709	85
	17		No Markets	0.9709	
	20	93-18	92-18	0.9709	118
	21	92-12	92-19	0.9709	79
	22	92-00	92-06	0.9709	80
	23	91-02	91-14	0.9709	73
	24	89-03	89-18	0.9709	68
	27	90-31	91-06	0.9709	78
	28	91-22	92-07	0.9709	69
	29	91-11	91-26	0.9709	70
	30	92-16	93-02	0.9709	69
May	1	91-20	91-26	0.9709	79

Conversion Factors

Conversion factors bring the price of a more valuable bond in line with the price of a less valuable bond, or with the price of the generic instrument of the futures contract. More specifically, the Cf adjusts the relative value of a particular bond coupon and maturity so it is in proportion to a standard 8% bond.

To calculate a Cf, basis traders can use the standard bond price formula with the yield (i) being the given 8%. The 10.375% November 2007-12 bond has a Cf of 1.2350 relative to the September 87 futures contract. To derive that, a trader could solve as follows:

$$\frac{1}{(1 + .04)^{40}} + .051875 \; \frac{1 - (PVFS)}{.04} = 1.2350$$

Again, PVFS is the result of the first segment of the problem—the portion to the left of the plus sign.

Each bond has its own Cf Moreover, the Cf for any bond varies with time to maturity. That is because prices for all bonds come to par at maturity. But at a point distant from maturity, the price will be farther from par than it will half way to maturity. Accordingly, the Cf for the earlier point will have to be larger than the one for the later point, because it will have to accommodate a bigger price difference than the later one.

Each futures month requires a separate Cf Table 7-3 displays the Cf values for two bonds over a two year period.

Table 7-3

	12.5% Aug 2009-14	13.25% May 2009-14
Dec 86	1.4662	1.5414
Mar 87	1.4640	1.5394
Jun 87	1.4623	1.5368
Sep 87	1.4601	1.5347
Dec 87	1.4583	1.5320
Mar 88	1.4560	1.5299
Jun 88	1.4542	1.5270
Sep 88	1.4517	1.5248

The usual source for Cf values is the Chicago Board of Trade, where the T-bond futures contract trades. The CBOT publishes a booklet which lists Cfs for all coupon rates and maturities.

Figure 7-3 Conversion Factor to Yield 8.00%

				COUPON RATE				
YRS-MOS	12%	12⅛%	12¼%	12⅜%	12½%	12⅝%	12¾%	12⅞%
15-0	1.3458	1.3566	1.3675	1.3783	1.3891	1.3999	1.4107	1.4215
15-3	1.3485	1.3594	1.3703	1.3812	1.3921	1.4030	1.4139	1.4248
15-6	1.3518	1.3628	1.3738	1.3847	1.3957	1.4067	1.4177	1.4287
15-9	1.3544	1.3654	1.3765	1.3876	1.3987	1.4098	1.4208	1.4319
16-0	1.3575	1.3686	1.3798	1.3910	1.4022	1.4133	1.4245	1.4357
16-3	1.3599	1.3712	1.3825	1.3937	1.4050	1.4162	1.4275	1.4387
16-6	1.3630	1.3743	1.3856	1.3970	1.4083	1.4197	1.4310	1.4423
16-9	1.3653	1.3767	1.3882	1.3996	1.4110	1.4224	1.4339	1.4453
17-0	1.3682	1.3797	1.3912	1.4027	1.4143	1.4258	1.4373	1.4488
17-3	1.3705	1.3821	1.3937	1.4052	1.4168	1.4284	1.4400	1.4516
17-6	1.3733	1.3850	1.3966	1.4083	1.4200	1.4316	1.4433	1.4549
17-9	1.3755	1.3872	1.3989	1.4107	1.4224	1.4342	1.4459	1.4576
18-0	1.3782	1.3900	1.4018	1.4136	1.4254	1.4373	1.4491	1.4609
18-3	1.3802	1.3921	1.4040	1.4159	1.4278	1.4397	1.4516	1.4635
18-6	1.3829	1.3948	1.4068	1.4187	1.4307	1.4427	1.4546	1.4666
18-9	1.3848	1.3969	1.4089	1.4209	1.4330	1.4450	1.4570	1.4691
19-0	1.3874	1.3995	1.4116	1.4237	1.4358	1.4479	1.4600	1.4721
19-3	1.3893	1.4014	1.4136	1.4258	1.4379	1.4501	1.4623	1.4744
19-6	1.3917	1.4039	1.4162	1.4284	1.4407	1.4529	1.4651	1.4774
19-9	1.3935	1.4058	1.4181	1.4304	1.4427	1.4550	1.4673	1.4796
20-0	1.3959	1.4082	1.4206	1.4330	1.4453	1.4577	1.4701	1.4824
20-3	1.3976	1.4100	1.4224	1.4349	1.4473	1.4597	1.4722	1.4846
20-6	1.3999	1.4124	1.4249	1.4373	1.4498	1.4623	1.4748	1.4873
20-9	1.4015	1.4141	1.4266	1.4392	1.4517	1.4643	1.4768	1.4894
21-0	1.4037	1.4163	1.4289	1.4416	1.4542	1.4668	1.4794	1.4920
21-3	1.4053	1.4180	1.4306	1.4433	1.4560	1.4686	1.4813	1.4940
21-6	1.4074	1.4201	1.4329	1.4456	1.4583	1.4711	1.4838	1.4965
21-9	1.4089	1.4217	1.4345	1.4473	1.4601	1.4728	1.4856	1.4984
22-0	1.4110	1.4238	1.4367	1.4495	1.4623	1.4752	1.4880	1.5009
22-3	1.4124	1.4253	1.4382	1.4511	1.4640	1.4769	1.4898	1.5027
22-6	1.4144	1.4274	1.4403	1.4533	1.4662	1.4792	1.4921	1.5051
22-9	1.4158	1.4288	1.4418	1.4548	1.4678	1.4808	1.4938	1.5068
23-0	1.4177	1.4307	1.4438	1.4569	1.4699	1.4830	1.4960	1.5091
23-3	1.4190	1.4321	1.4452	1.4583	1.4714	1.4845	1.4976	1.5107
23-6	1.4209	1.4340	1.4472	1.4603	1.4735	1.4866	1.4998	1.5129
23-9	1.4221	1.4353	1.4485	1.4617	1.4749	1.4881	1.5013	1.5145
24-0	1.4239	1.4371	1.4504	1.4636	1.4769	1.4901	1.5034	1.5166
24-3	1.4251	1.4384	1.4517	1.4650	1.4782	1.4915	1.5048	1.5181
24-6	1.4268	1.4402	1.4535	1.4668	1.4802	1.4935	1.5069	1.5202
24-9	1.4280	1.4413	1.4547	1.4681	1.4815	1.4949	1.5082	1.5216
25-0	1.4296	1.4431	1.4565	1.4699	1.4833	1.4968	1.5102	1.5236
25-3	1.4307	1.4442	1.4576	1.4711	1.4846	1.4980	1.5115	1.5250
25-6	1.4323	1.4459	1.4594	1.4729	1.4864	1.4999	1.5134	1.5269
25-9	1.4334	1.4469	1.4605	1.4740	1.4876	1.5011	1.5147	1.5282
26-0	1.4350	1.4485	1.4621	1.4757	1.4893	1.5029	1.5165	1.5301
26-3	1.4359	1.4495	1.4632	1.4768	1.4904	1.5041	1.5177	1.5313
26-6	1.4375	1.4511	1.4648	1.4785	1.4921	1.5058	1.5195	1.5331
26-9	1.4384	1.4521	1.4658	1.4795	1.4932	1.5069	1.5206	1.5343
27-0	1.4399	1.4536	1.4674	1.4811	1.4948	1.5086	1.5223	1.5361
27-3	1.4407	1.4545	1.4683	1.4821	1.4958	1.5096	1.5234	1.5372
27-6	1.4422	1.4560	1.4698	1.4836	1.4974	1.5113	1.5251	1.5389
27-9	1.4430	1.4569	1.4707	1.4846	1.4984	1.5123	1.5261	1.5400

Even more convenient are the periodically issued supplements to *The Financial Futures Professional,* a CBOT publication, which list Cfs for all U.S. Treasury bonds eligible for delivery into the CBOT's T-bond futures contract.

Figure 7-4 Deliverable T-Bond Conversion Factors

Listed below are all Treasury Bonds eligible for delivery into the CBT T-Bond futures contract along with their conversion factors as of May 7, 1987.

Coupon	Maturity	Amount ($ Billions)	Jun 87	Sep 87	Dec 87	Mar 88	Jun 88	Sep 88	Dec 88	Mar 89
7-¼	May 15, 2016	18.82	.9159	.9163	.9163	.9167	.9167	.9171	.9171	.9175
7-½	Nov 15, 2016	18.51	.9436	.9439	.9439	.9442	.9441	.9445	.9444	.9447
7-⅞	Nov 15, 2002-07	1.50	.9889	.9892	–	–	–	–	–	–
8-⅜	Aug 15, 2003-08	2.10	1.0335	1.0330	1.0330	1.0325	1.0324	–	–	–
8-¾	Nov 15, 2003-08	5.23	1.0673	1.0670	1.0663	1.0660	1.0652	1.0648	–	–
*8-¾	May 15, 2017	9.25	1.0844	1.0845	1.0841	1.0841	1.0837	1.0837	1.0833	1.0833
9-⅛	May 15, 2004-09	4.61	1.1026	1.1021	1.1011	1.1005	1.0995	1.0989	1.0979	1.0973
9-¼	Feb 15, 2016	7.27	1.1395	1.1390	1.1389	1.1383	1.1382	1.1376	1.1375	1.1369
9-⅜	Feb 15, 2006	4.76	1.1316	1.1306	1.1300	1.1289	1.1283	1.1272	1.1266	1.1255
9-⅞	Nov 15, 2015	6.90	1.2086	1.2083	1.2076	1.2073	1.2065	1.2062	1.2054	1.2051
10	May 15, 2005-10	2.99	1.1876	1.1866	1.1851	1.1841	1.1826	1.1815	1.1799	1.1787
10-⅜	Nov 15, 2004-09	4.20	1.2199	1.2186	1.2168	1.2155	1.2136	1.2122	1.2103	1.2089
10-⅜	Nov 15, 2007-12	11.03	1.2360	1.2350	1.2336	1.2326	1.2310	1.2300	1.2284	1.2273
10-⅝	Aug 15, 2015	7.15	1.2916	1.2907	1.2902	1.2892	1.2887	1.2876	1.2871	1.2860
10-¾	Feb 15, 2003	3.01	1.2418	1.2396	1.2378	–	–	–	–	–

10-3/4	May 15, 2003	3.25	1.2436	1.2418	1.2396	1.2378	-	-	-	-
10-3/4	Aug 15, 2005	9.27	1.2600	1.2581	1.2566	1.2546	1.2532	1.2511	1.2495	1.2474
11-1/8	Aug 15, 2003	3.50	1.2793	1.2768	1.2748	1.2723	1.2702	-	-	-
11-1/4	Feb 15, 2015	12.67	1.3593	1.3581	1.3574	1.3561	1.3554	1.3541	1.3534	1.3521
11-5/8	Nov 15, 2002	2.75	1.3158	1.3134	-	-	-	-	-	-
11-5/8	Nov 15, 2004	8.30	1.3357	1.3337	1.3311	1.3289	1.3262	1.3240	1.3211	1.3188
11-3/4	Feb 15, 2005-10	2.65	1.3500	1.3473	1.3452	1.3425	1.3403	1.3374	1.3351	1.3322
11-3/4	Nov 15, 2009-14	6.01	1.3866	1.3853	1.3833	1.3820	1.3799	1.3785	1.3764	1.3749
11-7/8	Nov 15, 2003	7.26	1.3487	1.3463	1.3433	1.3408	1.3376	1.3350	-	-
12	May 15, 2005	4.26	1.3755	1.3733	1.3705	1.3682	1.3653	1.3630	1.3599	1.3575
12	Aug 15, 2008-13	14.76	1.4037	1.4015	1.3999	1.3976	1.3959	1.3935	1.3917	1.3893
12-3/8	May 15, 2004	3.76	1.3996	1.3970	1.3937	1.3910	1.3876	1.3847	1.3812	1.3783
12-1/2	Aug 15, 2009-14	5.13	1.4623	1.4601	1.4583	1.4560	1.4542	1.4517	1.4498	1.4473
12-3/4	Nov 15, 2005-10	4.74	1.4516	1.4491	1.4459	1.4433	1.4400	1.4373	1.4339	1.4310
13-1/4	May 15, 2009-14	5.01	1.5368	1.5347	1.5320	1.5299	1.5270	1.5248	1.5219	1.5196
13-3/4	Aug 15, 2004	4.00	1.5293	1.5252	1.5217	1.5175	1.5139	1.5095	1.5057	1.5011
13-7/8	May 15, 2006-11	4.61	1.5653	1.5623	1.5586	1.5554	1.5515	1.5483	1.5442	1.5408
14	Nov 15, 2006-11	4.90	1.5840	1.5810	1.5773	1.5743	1.5705	1.5672	1.5633	1.5599

*Most recently auctioned 30-yr. bond eligible for delivery.

Although the CBOT provides the standard Cfs, risk managers need to keep in mind that the CBOT economists have embodied some arguable assumptions in their Cfs which cause them to exhibit some quirks. In their calculations, they

1. round maturities back to the nearest quarter
2. assume that callable bonds will be called.

For the 13.25% bond, that may be a valid assumption, but low coupon bonds like the 7.625% Feb 2002-07 do not get called. Rounding maturities has the effect of making premium bond Cfs slightly higher than actually should be the case, and it makes the Cfs of discounts slightly lower.

Hedge Ratios

In the discussion of the bond hedges in Chapters 3 and 4, recall that it took over 1500 futures contracts to balance the cash-side position. Effective hedging requires balanced positions. In physical hedging, that is simple. To hedge 5 million bushels of wheat, a risk manager buys that number of futures.

Because of the lack of comparablility among the various bonds and the futures contract, financials hedgers must use a hedge ratio (HR) to achieve position balance. Basically, HRs tell basis traders how many futures contracts they will need to balance cash positions. One way risk managers calculate hedge ratios is with this formula:

$$\frac{\text{Bond Position Cash Value}}{1000 \ \times \ \text{Bond Price}} \ \times \ \text{Cf} \ = \ \text{HR}$$

Referring still to the 13.25% May 2009-14 T-bond, assume that on April 7, 1987 a risk manager wanted to hedge a $100 million par cash position using June 1987 T-bond futures. The bond price was 151-16 (or 151.5), the June 87 futures price is 97-08 (or 97.25), the June 87 Cf for the 13.25% bond is 1.5368, and the basis for that bond is 66 (32nds). Using the HR formula, the risk manager discovers that he needs 1,536.8 futures contracts.

$$\frac{151,500,000}{1000 \times 151.5} \times 1.5368 = 1000 \times 1.5368 = 1536.8$$

At the 97-08 futures price, the April 7 futures position has a dollar value of $149,450,000. Notice that the cash and futures do not quite match.

$151,500,000	Bond Position Cash Value
- $149,450,000	Futures Position Cash Value
$ 2,050,000	Difference in Cash Value

However, the $2 million difference does not mean the HR is in error.

The difference between the dollar values of the cash and futures positions should relate to the dollar value of the basis. The formula

$$\frac{\text{Bond Position Cash Value}}{1000 \times \text{Bond Price}} \times \text{Basis} \times 31.25 = \text{Basis Value}$$

determines the cash value of the basis on a given day for a given hedge. Using the April 7 figures, a risk manager will discover the dollar value of the basis to be $2,050,000 (the basis value of 66 results from rounding up from 65.6).

$$\frac{151,500,000}{1000 \times 151.5} \times 65.6 \times 31.25 =$$
$$1000 \quad \times 65.6 \times 31.25 = \$2,050,000$$

The 1536.6 HR is demonstrably the right one for this situation.

Charting the Basis

Important as determining the basis is, tracking or charting is an even more crucial part of basis trading. Basis charting is more complicated with financials than with physicals. Besides the need for conversion factors, there is the need to calculate the basis for each bond. So, too, with charting. Seldom does a basis trader track just one bond. More often he charts three or more. The essence of financial risk management is to be aware of how the basis is likely to change and to have a strategy ready which can turn that change to advantage.

Once basis traders have assured themselves that they are "on the right side of the basis," they must choose the cash instrument appropriate to their needs. Bonds with higher coupons converge toward zero at a greater rate than bonds with lower coupons, though at a given moment any of the deliverable bonds might be cheapest to deliver. If the predictable basis change is working in the basis trader's favor, he wants to use the cash bond which produces the most basis change. That may or may not be the cheapest to deliver bond. In some cases, he will prefer a bond that produces minimal basis change. Oversimplification can create problems. Only careful charting of an assortment of bonds allows risk managers to make the right choice with assurance.

Complexities notwithstanding, the essentials of charting are the same for all commodities. Using the data of Table 7-1, a basis trader might chart the basis of the 13.25% May 2009-14 bond for April 1987 as in Figure 7-5.

A central paradox of basis trading is that the basis simultaneously fluctuates markedly, is eminently predictable over time, and provides a stable point of reference.

In the actual case, there is no contradiction in that. To understand how that can be so, consider a few of the details of this simple chart. The zero line, across the bottom, indicates the relevent futures price. The zero provides a stable point of reference. The futures price fluctuates, as does the cash. Notice that the basis was 66 over on three different days—April 7, 10, and 22. The futures price was 97-08, 94-22, and 92-06, respectively. The basis, though, refers to a relationship, not the price; and the zero is a base to plot from. The basis on those three days is 66 over. Sometimes veteran basis traders describe such a basis with a remark like "The April 7 basis is 66 over the June." That is to say, the basis is 66/32nds over whatever the June futures price is on that day. In that way, the futures price provides a stable though shifting point of reference which the chart captures through the device of the zero line.

Figure 7-5 Bond Basis Chart Plotting 13.25% May 2009-14 Against June '87 T-Bond Futures

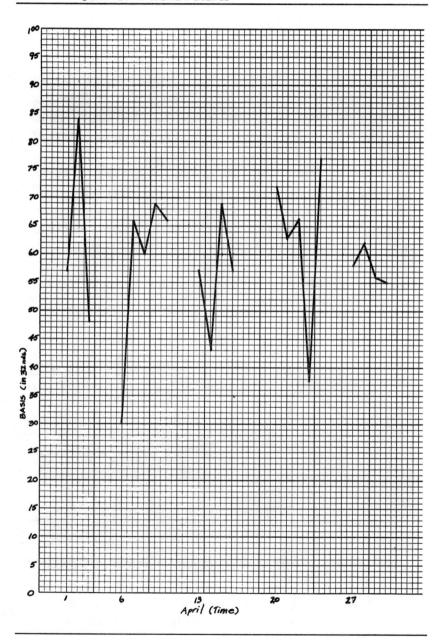

The prices on those three days vary, yet there is a sense in which the situation is stable. That is more important information to a risk manager than the news about prices.

Charting Foreign Currency Basis

For basis charts to be really useful, they should extend over fairly long periods of time. In many cases, the ideal period is a year. Nevertheless, charts extending over even a few months often provide interesting information. A few typical foreign currency basis charts demonstrate that.

Figures 7-6 to 7-10 show that, without exception, these currency basis plots tend toward zero, as is typical of financials. The British pound and the Canadian dollar widen—become less positive. The West German mark, Japanese yen, and Swiss franc narrow—become less negative. Those are completely normal basis patterns for these markets.

Figure 7-6　British Pound Basis—Cash Against March '87 Futures, Weekly Average

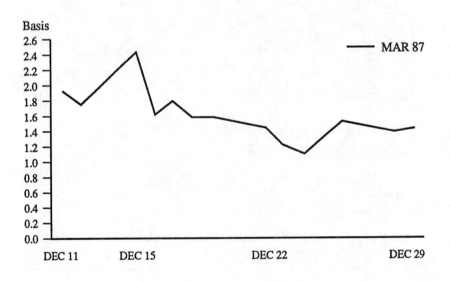

Figure 7-7 Canadian Dollar Basis—Cash Against March '87 Futures, Weekly Average

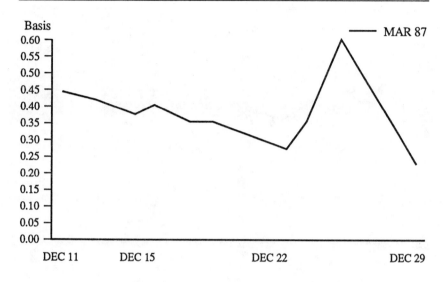

Figure 7-8 Deutsch Mark Basis—Cash Against March '87 Futures, Weekly Average

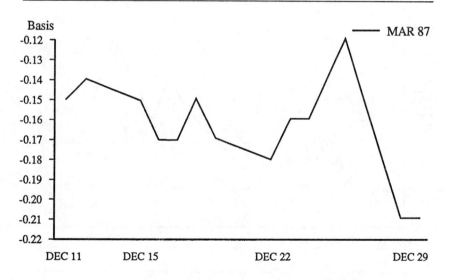

Figure 7-9   Japanese Yen Basis—Cash Against March '87 Futures, Weekly Average

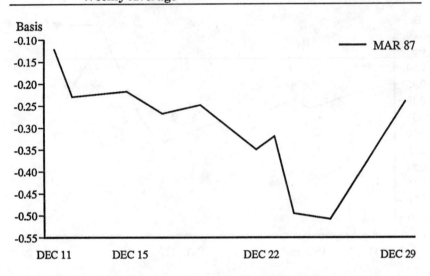

Figure 7-10   Swiss Franc Basis—Cash Against March '87 Futures, Weekly Average

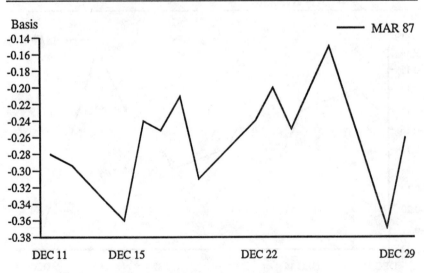

They result from the way the markets adjust to the fact that British pound and Canadian dollar yields are higher than that of the U.S. dollar, and West German mark, Japanese yen, and Swiss franc yields are lower than that of the U.S. dollar. The market adjusts the basis in these ways to hold a constant return to storage.

Charting Bond Basis

Bond basis differs from that for any of the physical commodities, and even some other financials, in that it deteriorates by definition—but never, in a normal yield curve market, to a point much less than zero. In that market, zero is the floor. In an inverted yield curve market, zero is the ceiling. The reason zero is an effective floor, in a normal market, is that a negative basis results in a short-term yield which is greater than the long-term yield. A bond trader can then use a long basis strategy (buy cash, sell futures) to earn a greater than long-term return on a short-term investment. Opportunities like that are fleeting, evanescent, because arbitragers pounce on them and that drives the basis back to at least zero. While there are variations within the trend, that describes the essential case.

Figure 7-11 represents an idealization of that pattern for one bond.

Figure 7-12 describes the actual case of the 12.5% August 2009-14 bond during a seven month period.

Some basis traders use graphs that show a continuous line throughout the given time period. Others prefer this convention, thinking that leaving spaces for the weekends, when no trading takes place, clarifies the picture.

To get a real picture of the basis pattern, it is best to chart six months or more of information. Often, when people figure the basis, they just use the nearby futures quote—a perfectly natural approach. That means that the data will range over the three months of one contract, then three months of the next, and so on. Charting that data will produce something like Figure 7-13.

Figure 7-11   Idealized Basis Graph

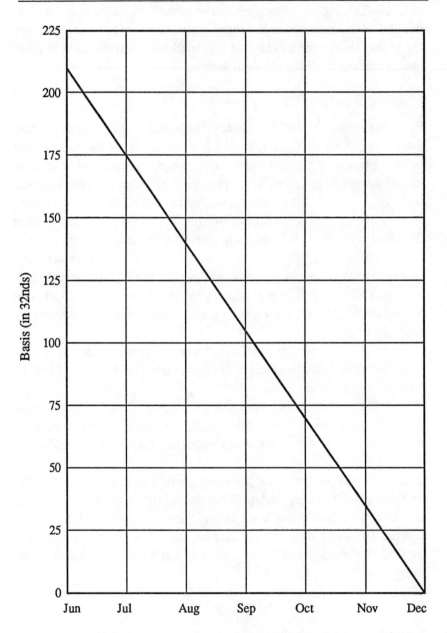

Figure 7-12   Seven-Month Bond Basis

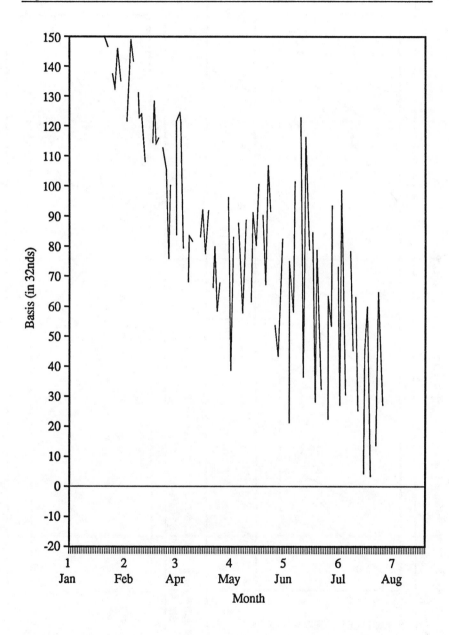

Figure 7-13 Typical Basis Charted Against Three Nearby Futures Months

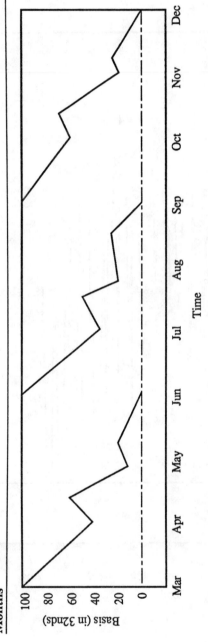

Figure 7-14 The Basis More Volatile with Approaching Delivery, Seem Almost Flat in Effect

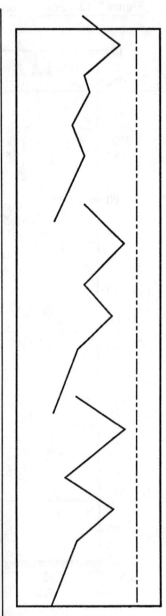

Each line signifies a successive futures month—for example, June, September, December. Among the weaknesses of that approach—the bond basis often seems "choppy" because the basis may be especially volatile closer to delivery, and just after delivery it may even narrow a bit. As a result, a chart limited to nearbys may seem to contradict the general claim of basis deterioration. Figure 7-14 shows a fairly likely, and somewhat misleading, circumstance in which the basis seems relatively flat.

In contrast, if a basis trader, in early April, begins charting the September or December basis (that is, uses the September or December futures quotes and Cfs in deriving the basis), his chart will show a picture which more nearly reveals the actual situation.

Seldom will risk managers watch only one bond, though. They could chart each one that interests them separately in a sequence of charts like Figure 7-12. But that makes it hard to sense the relationship between the bonds—which can be very important. So a more usual basis chart would be like the one in Figure 7-15 which plots the basis for three bonds—the 12.5% Aug 2009-14, the 7.265% Feb 2002, and the 10.375% Nov 2007-12. Plotting these is no different from plotting a single bond. It just requires more arithmetic. The results, in terms of useful information, are well worth the effort.

This chart shows the 12.5% August 2009-14 bond to be cheapest to deliver, since it arrives at zero while the others only approach zero. Also, that bond undergoes the greatest basis change of the three. A trader whose strategy puts him on the right side of the basis will definitely prefer to use that bond in his hedges.

The basis of the cheapest to deliver converges near zero slightly before, or on, the First Notice Day (the official "delivery" day for a contract). As a delivery month approaches, the basis for the various bonds becomes more divergent. Often, at a time remote from delivery, several bonds will move more or less parallel to each other. Closer to delivery, their paths separate. Lower coupon issues appear to tail off or flatten out. The higher coupon bonds become more volatile, and a definite cheapest to deliver emerges. Then, after the delivery month, there may well be a narrowing for a short time.

Figure 7-15   Static Basis Convergence

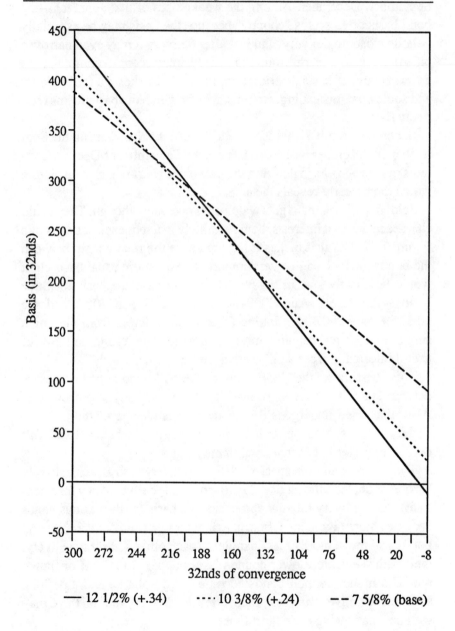

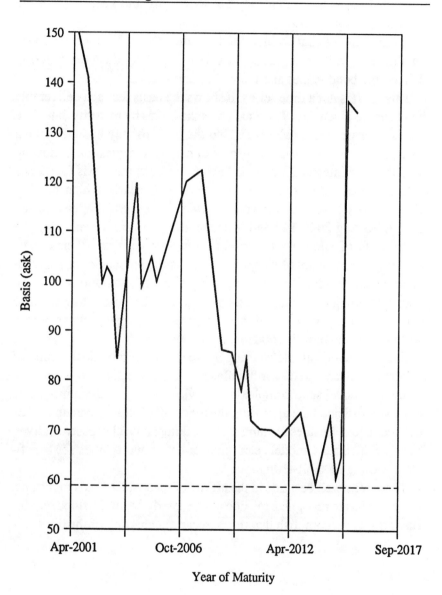

Figure 7-16 All Deliverable Basis for Thursday, April 24, 1986
Plotted Against June 1986 Futures

Year of Maturity

Each of these situations creates opportunity for basis traders, and good charting is the means they use to identify and keep track of the emerging possibilities.

A third kind of chart, which can be extremely useful, plots all bonds on a given day, as in Figure 7-16. Charts like this reflect the differing deliverable bond values and the yield curve effects.

This chart is not a time series. It shows the basis for each deliverable bond for the given day. The x axis lists the bonds by maturity date. The y axis indicates basis values. To find the basis for any bond on such a chart, simply locate the maturity date of the bond in question, follow up until that line intersects the basis line, and refer to the y axis for a basis value. Among other things, this chart shows clearly which bond is cheapest to deliver. The horizontal dashed lines show that on this day the 12.5% Aug 2009-14 bond is cheapest to deliver. Understating the importance of good basis charting is impossible. From their charts, basis traders can learn to recognize the essential tendencies of the commodities they trade. They can use them to identify variations from the norm that suggest strategic refinements. Good charts allow them to determine at a glance which instrument is cheapest to deliver, which will provide the most favorable basis change.

Even relatively simple charting approaches can provide that kind of information. It is well worthwhile, however, to incorporate into the analytical model such complexities as yield change and maturity. The more sophisticated the approach, the more possibilities open up to alert risk managers. Besides refining their thinking about cheapest to deliver, more sophisticated models can uncover new opportunities for beneficial handling of short-term money.

There may well be a tide in the affairs of men which leads to fortune. First, one has to recognize the tide, then identify when the flood will be. Basis traders accomplish that through careful charting of the basis.

IV

A Basis Trading Practicum

Short Basis Strategies

Risk managers need to develop a methodical approach as they contemplate hedging strategies. Their thought process needs to include at least these questions:

1. What are the company's business goals?
2. What kind of basis change do I anticipate?
3. What strategy best allows me to
   a. take advantage of that basis change?
   b. achieve the company's business goals?

The business goal is the factor of primary importance.

Speculators can "play the markets." That is really their business. Having established a given amount of risk capital, speculators trade the chance that they can lose their trading stake for the chance that they can make serious money. Risk managers are not in the same business at all. The assets they protect are not risk capital but the lifeblood of their companies.

Accordingly, risk managers only enter the market because it provides a way to achieve an important goal, one that may not otherwise be attainable. Further, the nature of their situation may force them to participate constantly. Speculators can come and go as they please. When the market looks promising, speculators are in—otherwise they are not. Not so hedgers, and forced participation can create quite a problem for them.

Among other things, that means risk managers must develop an extremely disciplined approach to their work. However, discipline has a special sense in risk management. Just as risk managers discipline themselves to be methodical, they must discipline themselves to be flexible. They never allow themselves to trade by habit—to adopt a strategy because that is how they did it last year. After all, the goals may have changed. The market is likely to be very different. Because they have taken the trouble to master all the possibilities the market affords, they can do things that others might hesitate to do—like using long-term instruments for short-term situations.

On the surface, that seems a wrong move. But risk managers who know the rules of the game, who focus resolutely on business goals, and who have taken pains to develop genuine understanding of the markets can rise above conventional wisdom.

Notes on Method

Throughout the discussions of cases that follow, references to T-bond futures implicitly refer to the Chicago Board of Trade contract, which has a $100,000 par value. Also, for a variety of reasons, we use hedge ratios that specify fractional futures contracts. Although that is not always possible in practice, financials hedgers can get close. The Mid-America Commodities Exchange has a half-size T-bond contract which is otherwise equivalent to the CBOT contract. Thus, if a hedge ratio specifies, say, 1.5 contracts, with an implied $150,000 par value, a hedger can use three MidAm bond contracts.

All of the examples of hedging strategy make some assumptions about the way the cash and futures markets operate.

For simplicity, the yield to maturity remains constant in each example. Cash and futures change in equal amounts in opposite directions, except for the basis change. This approach focuses attention on the importance of the basis as the manageable factor in risk management design. To a basis trader, what the prices do matters little. No predicting the markets. The basis is predictable. Since the basis is what makes the difference anyway, that is what hedgers watch.

Anticipation is crucial in hedging. The constant yield assumption plays a role there, too. Prices going in are known. "You could look it up." But what about the cash bond price six months from now? What will the futures price be at the end of the strategy?

Working from what is known, and given the yield assumption, all else follows logically. Imagine, for example, that a hedger plans to trade a 12.5% bond which is exactly 20 years from maturity at the start of the hedge and which has an 8% yield to maturity. The price of that bond is 144.53374, or 144-17. If the hedge unwinds in six months and the yield is stable, then the unwinding price is calculable, using the standard price formula:

$$\frac{1}{(1+.04)^{39}} + .0625 \left[\frac{1 - \dfrac{1}{(1+.04)^{39}}}{.04} \right]$$

Since all that changes is the time to maturity—from 20 years to 19.5—the price at unwinding is 144.06509, or 144-02.

Similarly, on the futures side, imagine that going in, the relevant futures contract is trading at 98-00. In a sense, nobody knows what the futures price might be in six months. Basis traders do know that the basis of the cheapest to deliver bond will converge to zero when the futures contract reaches delivery.

If this 12.5% bond is cheapest to deliver, and its Cf relative to this futures contract is 1.4568, then traders can derive the basis using the bond basis formula:

$$\text{Cash Price} \quad - \quad (\text{Futures x Cf}) \quad = \quad \text{Basis}$$

$$144.06509 \quad - \quad (\text{Futures x } 1.4568) \quad = \quad 0$$

To solve for the unknown futures requires only to divide the cash price by the Cf.

$$\text{Futures} = \frac{144.06509}{1.4568} = 98.891468$$

The futures price on unwinding will be 98-29.

Future futures prices are clearly no more mysterious than future cash prices. If the bond being used is not the cheapest, or is a non-deliverable instrument like a mortgage, the hedger simply locates the cheapest and solves for the prices he needs. This logical foundation makes it possible to *manage* risk.

8

Hedging an Uninvested New CD Issue

Fixed liability, floating asset is a definite problem, until the asset side gets pinned down. Yet financial managers have to cope with just that situation on a regular basis.

Pension managers know what they will have to pay out and when. But they cannot define the asset side until payments arrive and they can invest them. Insurance companies have the same problem. Their actuarial models define their liabilities, but they have to wait to receive and invest the premium stream. Until then, assets float, subject to erosion from yield volatility.

Rising rates are not a problem. If rates rise, the situation improves. But falling rates can be disastrously expensive.

This normal situation does not imply a management lapse. But not having a contingency plan to protect the assets from rate fluctuation is a serious management error. In most cases, the goal of the contingency plan is to maintain a yield spread.

Bankers face an interesting version of this problem. They must issue CDs when customers want to buy them, not necessarily when the bank wants the money. Suppose a banker issues 10% 30-year CDs. The nature of the CD issue defines the liability. Suppose, too, that the banker knows he can invest the money appropriately. Right now the yield from that investment will maintain the two percent spread the banker needs, but he faces a 60-day time lag until he can get the investment in place. In the interim he's vulnerable. It would not be bad if rates went up. His profit would be that much greater. Trouble comes if rates drop. An investment returning less than the required spread profits nothing. The banker wants to protect against that.

To cope, he can hedge his CD issue with T-bond futures. That way he can assure himself the two-point spread and all will be well. His futures trade will move in harmony with the cash market and protect his CD position.

Figure 8-1 summarizes the strategy that will protect him against adverse rate movement.

Figure 8-1

CASH	FUTURES
sell	buy
issue CDs	T-bond futures
buy	sell
invest funds	T-bond futures

There is a tradeoff in this strategy. If rates do rise, the hedged banker will derive no benefit from that market movement. Since the hedge assures the profitability of the deal under any circumstance, that is a reasonable price to pay. After all, if rates fall, the banker will still be in profitable condition.

How it Works

The strategy that will protect this banker closely resembles the forward purchase T-bond hedge (discussed in Chapters 3 and 4). Risk managers need to ask themselves why anyone would engage in a forward purchase.

Here again, suppose the risk manager knows that in two months he will have $40 million to invest. The yield to maturity right now is a satisfactory 8.7%. In 60 days, there is no telling what the rate might be. It could be significantly higher or lower. The risk management goal, then, is to protect against the possibility of falling rates.

The hedger expects the cash to arrive on September 1, 1987. In keeping with that, on July 1, he can forward purchase the 12.5% August 2009-14 bond (which he predicts will be cheapest to deliver) for September 1 delivery and also buy September 87 T-bond futures.

Specifically, the July 1 price of the bond is 137.11142 while the price for September 87 futures is 92-20 (92.625). The Cf for that bond relative to those futures is 1.4623, so the July 1 basis is 53.

$$\text{Cash Price} \quad - \quad (\text{Futures x Cf}) \quad = \quad \text{Basis}$$

$$137.11142 \quad - \quad (92.625 \times 1.4623) \quad = \quad 53.30824$$

Assuming no change in yield to maturity between July 1 and September 1, the cash price will be 136.97011 upon delivery. Given that the 12.5 August 2009-14 bond is cheapest to deliver, the basis will converge to zero. Thus the hedger can price out his futures position at 93-21 (93.667585).

$$\text{Cash Price} \quad - \quad (\text{Futures x Cf}) \quad = \quad \text{Basis}$$

$$136.97011 \quad - \quad (\text{Futures} \times 1.4623) \quad = \quad 0$$

$$\text{Futures} = \frac{136.97011}{1.4623} = 93.667585$$

Figure 8-2 (page 114) summarizes the hedger's forward purchase strategy.

HEDGING AN UNINVESTED NEW CD ISSUE

Strategy 5

A. The Problem
This strategy reiterates #2.

B. Preliminaries

1. *The Basis*

    Cash   − (Futures × Cf)   = Basis

    a. 137.11142 − (92.625 × 1.4623) = 1.6658825 (× 32) = 53.30824

    b. 136.97011 − (Futures × 1.4623) = 0

    $$\text{Futures} = \frac{136.97011}{1.14623} = 93.667585$$

2. *Futures Position Size*

    $$\frac{54,844,568}{1000 \times 137.11142} \times 1.4623 = 584.92$$

C. The Strategy

CASH	FUTURES	BASIS
July 1, 1987		
sell	buy	
forward purchase for	Sep 87 T-bond @92-20	53
September delivery	Cf: 1.4623	
12.5% August 2009-14	HR: 1.4623	
(@137.11142) 8.7% yield	No. of contracts: 584.92	
Par Value: $40,000,000		
Cash Value: (54,844,568)		
September 1, 1987		
buy (take delivery on	sell	
forward purchase)	Sep 87 T-bond @93-21	0
12.5% August 2009-14		
@136.97011, 8.7% yield		
Par Value: $40,000,000		
Cash Value: $54,788,044		
July 1 to September 1: 62 days		

D. Results and Evaluation

1. *Cash Result* (gain)*

    Cash Sale   − Cash Purchase = Cash Result

    54,844,568 − 54,788,044   = 56,524

2. *Futures Result* (gain)

    Futures Change × 31.25 × Contracts = Futures Result
    (in 32nds)

       33.36272   × 31.25 × 584.92   = 609,829

3. *Capital Gain* (not applicable)

4. *Interest Expense* (not applicable)

5. *Interest Income* (not applicable)

6. *Net Hedging Result**

      56,524 Cash Result
  + 609,829 Futures Result

     666,353 Net Hedging Result

8. *Basis Value*

Basis Change × 31.25 × Par Units = Basis Value
53.30824   × 31.25 × 400   = 666,353

9. Basis Value = Net Hedging Result
  666,353   = 666,353

* The cash position, and therefore the cash result and net hedging result, are imaginary figures. The reason to include them in the summary is to provide a basis figure and to provide a means to evaluate the hedge (that is, to provide a net hedging result to balance against the basis value).

Also, notice that since the ending future price is a derived figure (rather than a standard quote), it is actually slightly greater than 93-21, thus the 33.36272 Futures Change.

Figure 8-2

CASH	FUTURES	BASIS
July 1, 1987		

sell
forward purchase for
September delivery
12.5% August 2009-14
(@137.11142), 8.7% yield
  Par Value: $40,000,000
  Cash Value: (54,844,568)
	buy
	Sep 87 T-bond @92-20
	  Cf: 1.4623
	  HR: 1.4623
	  No. of Contracts: 584.92
		53

September 1, 1987		

buy (take delivery on
forward purchase)
12.5% August 2009-14
@136.97011, 8.7% yield
  Par Value: $40,000,000
  Cash Value: $54,788,044
	sell
	Sep 87 T-bond @93-21
		0

July 1 to September 1: 62 days		

The July 1 cash figures are included (in parentheses) simply for ease of reference. The hedger did not make a cash move at that time, but he did need to know what the basis was and how many futures contracts to buy.

On the futures side, there is a 1-01 change in the hedger's favor. That turns out to be a $609,829 gain.

> Futures Change x 31.25 x Contracts = Futures Result
>   (in 32nds)
> 33.36272   x 31.25 x 584.92   = 609,829

Notice that the actual July 1 basis is slightly greater than 53: 53.30824. Using that figure, the cash value of the basis change turns out to be $666,353.

> Basis Change x 31.25 x Par Units = Basis Value
> 53.30824   x 31.25 x   400   = 666,353

The difference between 666,353 and 609,829 is 56,524, the difference between the July 1 and September 1 cash position values. That demonstrates that this basis trader is fully hedged.

The advantage of this strategy should be clear. No one knows for certain what the interest rate market will do even two months in advance. The cash and futures prices float with the market. However, when the hedger buys September futures along with his forward purchase, he establishes a September 1 cash price. He knows that the futures market will move in concert with the cash, and that the basis will converge to zero. That predictable basis move is his protection. In effect, the forward purchase strategy allows the risk manager to invest September 1 funds at July 1 rates.

The banker can do the same thing with his CDs. When the money comes in, he can invest it in T-bills, or some other short-term instrument. What is most important, he can, in effect, make a forward commitment to the investment he will make on September 1. In the meantime, he can protect his yield spread by buying September T-bond futures.

Specifically, when the banker issues $40 million worth of CDs, which is equivalent to selling a cash bond, he makes a commitment to the September 1 investment, which is equivalent to a forward purchase in the sense of the T-bond investment. At that moment, also, he invests the $40 million in T-bills at 6% and buys September T-bond futures at 92-20.

When he is ready to actually make the investment on September 1, he unwinds. He sells the T-bills, invests the money in a 10% 30-year $40 million par loan with a yield to maturity of 10%. Making that loan is equivalent to buying a 10% September 2017 bond. To wrap things up, he sells the T-bond futures at 93-21. Figure 8-3 outlines the details of that trading sequence.

Because of the assumption that the yield will remain unchanged, the cash value of the loan does not change. It is worth noting that any time the coupon is the same as the yield, the cash price is par, 100-00.

Strategy 6

A. The Problem

To shield assets where liabilities are defined but assets are floating, risk managers can use a short basis strategy (sell cash, buy futures), really a variation of the forward purchase, to maintain the yield spread they need for profitability. They give up the gains rising rates might bring to protect against losses from falling rates. The futures position offsets cash movement, and the basis works in the hedgers' favor.

B. Preliminaries

1. *The Basis*

   Cash   − (Futures × Cf)   = Basis
   a. 100 − (92.625 x 1.2262)   = − 13.576775 (x 32) = − 434.4568
   b. 100 − (93.65625 x 1.2262) = − 14.8412938   = − 474.9214016

2. *Futures Position Size*

$$\frac{40,000,000}{1000 \times 100} \times 1.2262 = 490.48$$

C. The Strategy

CASH	FUTURES	BASIS
July 1, 1987		
sell	buy	
make a forward commitment	Sep 87 T-bond @92-20	−434
to an investment	Cf: 1.2262	
10% September 2017	HR: 1.2262	
@100, 10% yield	No. of Contracts: 490.48	
Par Value: $40,000,000		
Cash Value: $40,000,000		
September 1, 1987		
buy	sell	
complete investment	Sep 87 T-bond @93-21	−474
10% September 2017		
@100, 10% yield		
Par Value: $40,000,000		
Cash Value: $40,000,000		
July 1 to September 1: 62 days		

D. Results and Evaluation

1. *Cash Result*

   Cash Sale   − Cash Purchase = Cash Result
   40,000,000 − 40,000,000   = 0

2. *Futures Result* (gain)

Futures Change × 31.25 × Contracts = Futures Result
(in 32nds)

     33   × 31.25 × 490.48   = + 505,808

3. *Capital Gain*

0	Cash Result
+ 505,808	Futures Result
505,808	Capital Gain

4. *Interest Expense* (not applicable)

5. *Interest Income*

40,000,000	CD Proceeds
× .06	Short-term Rate
2,400,000	Annual Short-term Yield
÷ 365	Days
6,575.3425	Daily Yield
× 62	Days in Hedge
407,671	Interest Income

6. *Net Hedging Result*

505,808	Capital Gain
+ 407,671	Interest Income
913,479	Net Hedging Result

7. *Annualized Yield*

913,479	Net Hedging Result
÷ 40,000,000	Cash Value
0.022837	Return
÷ 62	Days in Hedge
0.0003683	Daily Yield
× 365	Days
0.1344435	= 13.44% Annualized Yield

8. *Basis Value*

Basis Change × 31.25 × Par Units = Basis Value
(in 32nds)

  40.4646   × 31.25 × 400   = $505,808

9. Basis Value = Net Hedging Result

  505,808   = 505,808

Figure 8-3

CASH	FUTURES	BASIS
July 1, 1987		
sell	buy	
make a forward commitment	Sep 87 T-bond @92-20	-434
to an investment	Cf: 1.2262	
10% September 2017	HR: 1.2262	
Par Value: $40,000,000	No. of Contracts: 490.48	
Cash Value: $40,000,000		
September 1, 1987		
buy	sell	
complete investment	Sep 87 T-bond @93-21	-474
10% September 2017		
Par Value: $40,000,000		
Cash Value: $40,000,000		
July 1 to September 1: 62 days		

On the futures side, the 1-01 futures change produces a gain of $505,808.

> Futures Change x 31.25 x Contracts = Futures Result
> (in 32nds)
> 33   x 31.25 x 490.48   = +505,808

That futures gain amounts to an annualized yield of 7.44%

Having invested the funds in a short-term instrument, the banker collects $407,671 in interest income for the 62 days.

40,000,000	CD Proceeds
x .06	Short-Term Rate
2,400,000	Annual Short-Term Yield
÷ 365	Days
6,575.3425	Daily Yield
x 62	Days in Hedge
407,671	Interest Income

An unhedged banker could derive this short-term income also. The trouble he would face is that he would be paying out a long-term yield, say 8%, yet he would be earning only a short-term yield, say 6%. The basis gain tends to offset the yield loss. That interest income taken together with the futures gain puts the annualized return of this strategy at 13.44%.

What is of critical importance to the banker is not the return figure, but the fact that this strategy enables him to protect his assets until he can invest them in a suitable long-term loan. Once a strategy like this is in place, the rates can do what they will. His spread, and his profit, is secure.

Why it Works

By being aware that there is far more to hedging than just balancing longs and shorts, this hedger attained his goal. More important, he could predict his positive results from the start. Like all good risk management, this hedge was not a matter of chance.

At the outset, the banker can know a great deal about what will happen to the various components of his hedge. Almost the only thing that he cannot know is what the interest rates will do. No one can predict that. He does know what the cash price is, what the July 1 futures price is, and what the size of his cash position is. He also knows that the basis for the cheapest to deliver T-bond will converge to zero at the delivery date.

Working from all that he does know, the banker can predict all the rest of the information the hedge depends on. For simplicity of exposition, the yield holds constant in this example. Thus the cash side remains unchanged.

Even though the banker does not have a cash bond position, his ability to predict the cheapest to deliver bond is what allows him to determine the September 1 futures price. Once he knows the futures price, he can calculate the ending basis. From that, a hedger can derive the most important fact of all—the basis change. At that point he "knows" what the results of the hedge will be. He knows his position is protected.

Figure 8-4 illustrates the wealth of information that a basis trader has going into his series of trades.

Figure 8-4

CASH	FUTURES	BASIS
July 1, 1987		
sell	buy	
make a forward commitment	Sep 87 T-bond @92-20	-434
to an investment	Cf: 1.2262	
10% September 2017	HR: 1.2262	
@100, 10% yield	No. of Contracts: 490.48	
Par Value: $40,000,000		
Cash Value: $40,000,000		
September 1, 1987		
buy	sell	
complete investment	Sep 87 T-bond @93-21	-474
10% September 2017		
@100, 10% yield		
Par Value: $40,000,000		
Cash Value: $40,000,000		
July 1 to September 1: 62 days		

That basis change information also allow the basis trader to evaluate the hedge design. The value of the basis change is $505,808.

$$\text{Basis Change} \times 31.25 \times \text{Par Units} = \text{Basis Value}$$
$$\text{(in 32nds)}$$
$$40.4646 \quad \times 31.25 \times \quad 400 \quad = \$505,808$$

The fact that the basis value exactly matches the futures change demonstrates that the protection comes from the basis, not from market movement. That would also be true if there were a market movement, a rate change. It is the basis change, the hedge, that provides the protection. Since the basis is predictable, it is possible for the hedger to know what his hedging result will be, even in the planning stage.

The market not only helps a hedger determine the information relevant to his planning, it also tells him what kind of hedge to design. A hedger has two solid indicators concerning what the market wants him to do:

1. Bond basis always widens in a normal yield curve market.
2. Narrow spreads (92-20 to 91-18 to 90-16) reinforce the basis signal.

That kind of basis change, those spreads, tell a basis trader not to store, to design a position short the basis (sell cash, buy futures). How to do it is the difficulty. For that strategy appears to contradict the goal of investing. To buy a thing—a load of steel or a bond—is to hold inventory, to store. Yet, in this kind of market, the hedger knows, a bond is a commodity the longer kept, the less it is worth. This hedger benefitted from his mastery of the markets.

The point to derive from study of this strategy is not that all hedgers should pattern their moves on this one, though it is likely to be consistently useful. Neither is it true that a long position is inevitably a bad idea. Rather, any automatic response to these very complex markets, any copying of an action without a sure grasp of the idea behind the action, is likely to result in losses. It points out how important it is for hedgers to understand the market fundamentals so they can break the bonds of habit and shape hedging strategies to the actual situation.

9

Hedging Against the Forward Sale of a Mortgage Pool

R ate volatility can be especially damaging to mortgage bankers. As rates increase, asset values plunge: yield and price vary inversely. Worse, mortgage bankers' commitments are decades long. There is no easy escape from an adverse market.

For all that, mortgage bankers can achieve a safe position, even in a stormy market. To accomplish that, they either protect their assets or get rid of them. To protect their portfolios, they match their loans with deposits similar in maturity. To get rid of their assets, they can sell their portfolios in the secondary market, packaging them for resale to other banks or to Freddie Mac (FhLB), Fannie Mae (FNMA), or Ginnie Mae (GNMA)—depending on the kind of mortgage.

To resell, lenders have to accumulate a minimum "package"—usually $1 million worth of mortgages. Until they complete the package, the loans accumulating in the "pipeline" are at risk. Rate variation can erode asset value. To protect against that very real danger, mortgage bankers more and more contemplate hedging their pipelines for that critical interim.

The key to a successful mortgage hedge is to sell low, buy high, and still make money. Oddly enough, that can be done—consistently.

The nature of hedging dictates that this counterintuitive situation will occur regularly. A hedger protects against price risk by balancing cash and futures positions. But knowledgeable risk managers know that there is always some slippage in the movement between futures and cash, even in a balanced position. This is a change in the basis, and the hedger's primary objective is to position himself favorably with respect to basis change.

Therefore, mortgage bankers thinking about hedging have to guard against two very natural impulses. They have to look beyond price. And they have to deal in two sides of the market—cash and futures—objectively and with equal vigor.

A Word of Caution

Writing a mortgage is equivalent to buying a cash bond. Mortgage bankers who do not think carefully about hedging and who assume the typical definition of hedging to be inclusive might very well think that having, in effect, bought cash bonds they now need only sell the right amount of futures and the portfolio will be protected. Typically they will be wrong.

Instead, the right strategy for mortgage bankers in most cases is to design a position so they sell cash and buy futures. "*Sell cash? Sell mortgages?*" bankers ask. Bankers are supposed to *write* mortgages, not *sell* them. To them, a position where they buy cash and sell futures seems perfectly natural. A position where they actually sell cash, and buy futures, seems impossible. The trouble with forward-selling mortgages, according to typical mortgage bankers, is that they have to sell at progressively lower forward prices. They resist the associated lower margins, oblivious to the fact that progressively lower futures offset them. The "common sense" position may be natural, but it's wrong. The short position is both possible and preferable.

What a mortgage banker can do is forward sell his mortgage package—or, as bankers say, sell a PC (a participation commitment). Selling a PC locks in a yield. If yields rise, good. The banker's cost of product is less. If yields decline, the spread declines. The banker needs a hedge which will gain on falling rates. For that he uses futures. But he must trade the futures "backwards" from what seems natural. Figure 9-1 summarizes the strategy for mortgage hedging based on the sale of a PC.

Figure 9-1

CASH	FUTURES
Sell a PC	buys futures
Writes mortgages	sells futures

For many bankers, both of these moves are difficult. Selling a PC is unattractive because the agencies—FhLB, GNMA, or FNMA—charge a small fee for the PC which means bankers have to take an even greater discount. Bankers resist the time discounts and the progressively lower forward prices more than the servicing fee. But, good stewards, they resist anything that seems an unnecessary expense. But again, those who hold that view are paying too much attention to price. A closer look at the overall effect of a PC-based strategy shows why price is the wrong focus.

How It Works

Assume that on January 20, 1987, a mortgage banker writes a $10 million 30-year conventional mortgage pool with an underlying average yield of 9.125%, including 3/8% servicing. The pool is valued at par. He plans to sell the package to Freddie Mac on December 1. Meanwhile, to hold himself price neutral, he uses December Treasury bond futures priced at 98-20.

To determine how many futures contracts it will take to balance the cash position, he uses the formula:

$$\frac{\text{Cash Position Value}}{1000 \times \text{Cash Price}} \times \text{Cf} = \text{No. of Contracts}$$

Substituting relevant values, he can determine that he will need 108.96 futures contracts to balance his cash position.

$$\frac{10,000,000}{1000 \times 100} \times 1.0896 = 108.96$$

For the sake of simplicity, assume also that yields remain constant so the cash value doesn't change.

Figure 9-2 shows how all of that comes together in an effective mortgage hedging strategy.

Figure 9-2

CASH	FUTURES
January 20, 1987	

sell
PC discounted to yield 9.65%
yield 9.65%
   Cash Value: $9,631,539
	buy
	Dec 87 T-bond @98-20
	   Cf: 1.0896
	   HR: 1.0896
	   No. of Contracts: 108.96

December 1, 1987	

buy
write a 9.125% coupon mortgage
pool—30-year conventional,
underlying mortgages, average
yield 9.125%, current mortgage
market: 8.75% & 3/8% servicing
   Pool Value: 100-00% par
   Cash Value: $10,000,000
	sell
	Dec 87 T-bond @102-00

January 20 - December 1: 314 days	

This hedger faces a cash loss of $368,431.

Cash Sale	–	Cash Purchase	=	Cash Result
9,631,539	–	10,000,000		= -368,461

However, market forces work to his advantage on the futures side so he manages to protect his pool from value erosion.

Several details of this strategy require attention. The classical hedger, *buying* on the cash side, would think it normal to sell futures to protect his pipeline. Notice that this hedger buys futures to begin with and unwinds by selling them. He reverses the "common sense" order of events.

As a result, on the futures side, this strategy produces a $367,740 gain.

$$\text{Futures Change} \times 31.25 \times \text{Contracts} = \text{Futures Result}$$
(in 32nds)

$$108 \quad \times 31.25 \times \quad 109 \quad = \quad 367,875$$

The sum of the futures gain and the cash loss is the net hedging result.

-368,461	Cash Loss
+367,740	Futures Gain
- 721	Net Hedging Result

For all intents and purposes, this mortgage hedger has achieved a neutral position in the market. His mortgage pool is safe until he can sell it into the secondary market.

Why It Works

This strategy achieves its goal because this hedger understands that, in a normal yield market, financials basis characteristically widens—becomes increasingly negative. He understands that a hedger anticipating that kind of basis change will be most pleased with his hedging results if he is able to design a strategy which renders him short the basis (he sells cash and buys futures).

This banker realized that selling the PC created just such a situation, and that deceptively simple insight allows for an offsetting futures gain sufficient to make this portfolio price neutral.

As mortgage bankers think about how to design a hedge, they must, above all, compare the expected basis gain or loss to the cost of the concession of forward pricing a PC. Having done that, they are in a position to determine the best strategy. Often the basis gain roughly equals the PC forward concession. That allows forward pricing without cost.

Again, the key to the success of this strategy is the widening basis. Figure 9-3 expands on Figure 9-2 by adding basis information. Notice that the basis on January 20 was -227; on December 1, it had become -344. As with bonds, the formula for deriving the basis is

$$\text{Cash} \quad - \quad (\text{Futures} \times \text{Cf}) \quad = \quad \text{the basis.}$$

HEDGING AGAINST THE FORWARD SALE OF A MORTGAGE POOL

Strategy 7

A. The Problem

To safeguard a mortgage "pipeline" from rate volatility, a banker can sell a PC, thus selling mortgages into the secondary market before completing the package. In effect, this forward purchase enables him to design a short basis strategy (sell cash, buy futures) and so capitalize on the basis change he knows a normal yield market will produce. The major benefit: ordinarily, the futures position will offset the PC discount.

B. Preliminaries

1. *The Basis*

   Cash   − (Futures × Cf)   = Basis
   a. $100 - (98.625 \times 1.0896) = -7.4618 \ (\times \ 32) = -238.7776$
   b. $100 - (102 \times 1.0896) \ \ \ = -11.1392 \ (\times \ 32) = -356.4544$

2. *Futures Position Size*

   $$\frac{10,000,000}{1000 \times 100} \times 1.0896 = 108.96$$

C. The Strategy

CASH	FUTURES	BASIS
January 20 1987		
sell	buy	
PC discounted to yield 9.65%	Dec 87 T-bond @98-20	−239
	Cf: 1.0896	
Cash Value: $9,631,539	HR: 1.0896	
	No. of Contracts: 108.96	
December 1, 1987		
buy	sell	
write a 9.125% coupon mortgage pool--30 year conventional, underlying mortgages, average yield 9.125%, current mortgage market: 8.75% & 3/8% servicing	Dec 87 T-bond @102-00	−356
Pool Value:100-00% par		
Cash Value:$10,000,000		
January 20 to December 1: 314 days		

D. Results and Evaluation

1. *Cash Result* (loss)

    Cash Sale − Cash Purchase = Cash Result
    9,631,539 − 10,000,000   = −368,461

2. *Futures Result* (gain)

    Futures Change × 31.25 × Contracts = Futures Result
    (in 32nds)
        108   × 31.25 × 108.96   = +367,740

3. *Capital Gain* (not applicable)

4. *Interest Expense* (not applicable)

5. *Interest Income* (not applicable)

6. *Net Hedging Result*

− 368,461	Cash Loss
+ 367,740	Futures Gain
− 721	Net Hedging Result

7. *Annualized Yield*

- 721	Net Hedging Result
÷ 10,000,000	Cash Value
− 0.0000721	Return
÷ 314	Days in Hedge
− 0.0000002	Daily Yield
× 365	Days
− 0.0000838 = −0.0084%	Annualized Yield

    (in effect this is breakeven)

8. *Basis Value*

    Basis Change × 31.25 × Par Units = Basis Value
    117.6768   × 31.25 × 100   = 367,740

9. Basis Value = Futures Result

    367,740   = 367,740

In this case, the formula

$$100 \quad - \ (98.625 \times 1.0896) \ = \ -7.0835$$

derives -227/32nds as the beginning basis. Similar arithmetic establishes -344 as the end point basis.

These negative basis numbers require comment. Treasury bonds will not maintain a basis below zero. Arbitragers see an opportunity when that happens and immediately force it back up. But mortgages are a different story. The market views them as lower quality, and lower quality causes lower basis. Also, as a nondeliverable product, mortgages are not susceptible to arbitrage, so they can maintain negative basis values. That poses no problems for a hedger. The real issue for him is basis change. What he wants to know is whether the basis is becoming more negative or more positive—widening or narrowing. In this case, the basis widens 117/32nds.

Figure 9-3

CASH	FUTURES	BASIS
January 20, 1987		
sell	buy	
PC discounted to yield 9.65%	Dec 87 T-bond @98-20	-227
yield 9.65%	Cf: 1.0896	
Cash Value: $9,631,539	HR: 1.0896	
	No. of Contracts: 108.96	
December 1, 1987		
buy	sell	
write a 9.125% coupon mortgage	Dec 87 T-bond @102-00	-344
pool—30-year conventional,		
underlying mortgages, average		
yield 9.125%, current mortgage		
market: 8.75% & 3/8% servicing		
Pool Value: 100-00% par		
Cash Value: $10,000,000		
January 20 to December 1: 314 days		

The basis change tells an important part of the story of this hedge. Notice that the basis widens, becomes more negative, 117/32nds. Since each 32nd has a value of $31.25, each futures contract experiences a basis gain of $3,656.25 (117 x $31.25 = $3,658.25). Multiplying that dollar basis change times the number of $100,000 units of par shows that the total basis change has a value of $365,625. The basis change then, is what offsets the adverse cash situation. An important part of this hedging story is that the hedger realized how to design a hedge so the basis change would work in his favor. The basis change allows him to achieve price neutrality.

Achieving such an advantage is not especially difficult, either. All it takes to design a successful hedge is an understanding of the storage fundamentals and what they suggest about hedging strategy. If a mortgage banker understands that, and if he can bring himself to ignore price, he can sell low, buy high, and still protect his pipeline.

10

A Bond Dealer's Hedge

The idea of a "short sale" is hard to grasp. A "short" *sells* something he doesn't have, seemingly a contradiction. Yet farmers have been doing it for years. They regularly sell all or part of a crop that may not even be planted, much less harvested.

Bond dealers do the same thing. Few cash bond customers realize that when they buy a bond, they are often buying something the dealer doesn't have. Indeed, dealers deliver on those sales by borrowing the bond from someone who does have one—usually a big insurance company. Those companies carry a huge inventory of long-term investments, so they can easily supply the dealer's needs.

Dealers handle customer needs by borrowing a bond and turning right around and selling it (it is marginally more accurate to say they sell a bond and turn right around and borrow it). *A reverse repurchase agreement,* or *reverse repo* for short, creates a contract to redeliver the bond at a certain time and price. They protect the insurance company, or whoever provides the bond, by paying cash for the bond. That protects the present value of the bond. The insurance company has some credit risk, though only for value change. But who protects the bond dealer?

Obviously, the dealer has a very real problem. The "repo" agreement specifies a price for returning the bond. At a certain time, the dealer has to go into the open market, buy the relevant bond, and "return" it to the insurance company. That much is straightforward. Trouble can develop in the form of an adverse move in cash bond prices. What if the prices go higher than the agreed-upon price?

Bond dealers routinely hedge that position in the futures market. As a result, they operate unfettered by concerns about what the market will do. Like the grain traders, price is of no concern.

The bond dealer sells cash, to start with, so he buys futures to cover his replacement move. At the appropriate time, he buys a bond in the open market to cover his repo. At that time, too, he sells futures. Figure 10-1 summarizes that sequence.

Figure 10-1

CASH	FUTURES
sells bond (borrowed from insurance company on a repo agreement)	buys T-bond futures to cover replacement
buys bond in open market to cover repo	sells futures

This kind of transaction pleases both sides. The bond dealer covers his risk successfully. The investment manager at the insurance company derives a nice short-term return without really giving up his long-term investment (since he lent the bond rather than sold it).

How it Works

The bond dealer's lack of worry is easy to understand. Assume that on September 1, 1987, the dealer sells $14 million par worth of 12.5% Aug 2009-14 bonds at 150.4099. The total value of the cash-side transaction is $21,057,386.

Assume that he borrowed the bond that he is selling, but the details of the repo need not be of concern here. Suffice it to recognize that he has agreed to return the bond at a set price on December 1, 1987. The emphasis here is on how the dealer covers his risk, not how he borrows the bond.

To offset his cash position, the dealer buys Dec. 87 T-bond futures. The size of his cash position dictates the purchase of 203.952 futures contracts at 98-05.

Then, on December 1, 1987, the dealer unwinds. He buys the 12.5% Aug 2009-14 bonds at market, which is 150.18. At the same time, he sells Dec 87 T-bond futures at 103-00. Figure 10-2 shows the details of that trading sequence.

Figure 10-2

CASH	FUTURES
September 1, 1987	
sell	buy
12.5% August 2009-14	Dec 87 T-bond @98-05
@150.4099, yield 7.68%	Cf: 1.4568
(borrowed on reverse repo)	HR: 1.4568
Par Value: $14,000,000	No. of Contracts: 203.952
Cash Value: $21,057,386	
December 1, 1987	
buy	sell
12.5% August 2009-14	Dec 87 T-bond @103-00
@150.18, yield 7.68%	
(to repay reverse repo)	
Par Value: $14,000,000	
Cash Value: $21,025,200	

September 1 to December 1: 91 days

Because this strategy assumes an absence of yield change, the difference in the cash bond price between September 1 and December 1 is due to the time difference. The Cash Result is an insignificant $32,186 gain.

$$\text{Cash Sale} \quad - \quad \text{Cash Purchase} \quad = \text{Cash Result}$$

$$21{,}057{,}386 \quad - \quad 21{,}025{,}200 \quad = \quad 32{,}186$$

A Bond Dealer's Hedge

Strategy 8

A. The Problem

To accommodate customer needs without the liability of cash inventory, bond dealers "borrow" the bonds they sell their customers. They protect themselves against adverse market action by hedging their position with T-bond futures. At worst, the futures position offsets cash changes so the dealers can return the borrowed bonds without loss. Often, the short basis hedge (sell cash, buy futures) results in enhanced profitability.

B. Preliminaries

1. *The Basis*

   Cash $-$ (Futures $\times$ Cf)   = Basis

   $150.4099 - (98.15625 \times 1.4568) = 7.415875 \, (\times \, 32) = 237.308$

   $150.18 \;\; - (103 \times 1.4568) \;\;\;\;\; = 0.1296 \, (\times \, 32) \;\;\; = 4.1472$

2. *Futures Position Size*

   $$\frac{21{,}057{,}386}{1000 \times 150.4099} \times 1.4568 = 203.952$$

C. The Strategy

CASH	FUTURES	BASIS
September 1, 1987		
sell	buy	
12.5% August 2009-14	Dec 87 T-bond @98-05	237
@150.4099, yield 7.68%	Cf: 1.4568	
(borrowed on reverse repo)	HR. 1:4568	
Par Value: $14,000,000	No. of Contracts: 203.952	
Cash Value: $21,057,386		
December 1, 1987		
buy	sell	
12.5% August 2009-14	Dec 87 T-bond @103-00	4
@150.18, yield 7.68%		
(to repay reverse repo)		
Par Value: $14,000,000		
Cash Value: $21,025,200		
September 1 to December 1: 91 days		

D. Results and Evaluation

1. *Cash Result* (gain)

Cash Sale − Cash Purchase = Cash Result
21,057,386 − 21,025,200   = 32,186

2. *Futures Result* (gain)

Futures Change × 31.25 × Contracts = Futures Result
(in 32nds)
155   × 31.25 × 203.952   = 987,892.50

3. *Capital Gain* (not applicable)

4. *Interest Expense* (not applicable)

5. *Interest Income* (not applicable)

6. *Net Hedging Result*

```
      32,186.00  Cash gain
  + 987,892.50  Futures gain
  1,020,078.50  Net Hedging Result
```

7. *Annualized Yield*

```
    1,020,078.50  Net Hedging Result
 ÷ 21,057,386.00  Cash Value
      0.0484428  Return
           ÷ 91  Days in Hedge
      0.0005323  Daily Yield
          × 365  Days
      0.1943035  = 19.43% Annualized Yield
```

8. *Basis Value*

Basis Change × 31.25 × Par Units = Basis Value
233.1608   × 31.25 × 140   = 1,020,078.50

9. Basis Value = Net Hedging Result
1,020,078.50 = 1.020.078.50

On the futures side, there is a significant result. The 4-27 change in futures prices, given a position of this size, produces a futures gain of $987,892.50.

Futures Change x 31.25 x Contracts = Futures Result
(in 32nds)
    155   x 31.25 x 203.952 = 987,892.50

The net hedging result is the sum of the cash gain and the futures gain, or $1,020,078.50.

32,186.00	Cash Gain
+ 987,892.50	Futures Gain
1,020,078.50	Net Hedging Result

This strategy produces a 19.43% annualized yield. The absence of a yield change in this example suggests an absence of volatility. That may or may not be a good assumption. Often, the yield fluctuates a good bit. In a given three-month period, it is entirely likely to see it return to where it started. This circumstance illustrates the point that, if nothing else, the basis play is good even in relatively flat markets. A yield change, however, would have no impact on trade results.

Why It Works

Also, bond dealers like this approach because it is relatively risk-free—to those who understand how the markets work and why. Even more important than the profit is the fact that the bond dealer has protected himself so he can return the bond at the specified price without suffering a loss. This bond dealer knows that bond basis characteristically deteriorates—widens—to zero. He also knows that a widening basis rewards a short basis position (sell cash, buy futures).

It is that simple. The key to the success of the bond dealer's strategy is the widening basis. Figure 10-3 shows how the predictable basis development contributes to the situation.

Figure 10-3

CASH	FUTURES	BASIS
September 1, 1987		
sell	buy	
12.5% August 2009-14	Dec 87 T-bond @98-05	237
@150.4099, yield 7.68%	Cf: 1.4568	
(borrowed on reverse repo)	HR: 1.4568	
Par Value: $14,000,000	No. of Contracts: 203.952	
Cash Value: $21.,057,386		
December 1, 1987		
buy	sell	
12.5% August 2009-14	Dec 87 T-bond @103-00	4
@150.18, yield 7.68%		
(to repay reverse repo)		
Par Value: $14,000,000		
Cash Value: $21,025,200		

September 1 to December 1: 91 days

Notice that on September 1, 1987, the basis is 237/32nds. The formula for deriving bond basis is

$$\text{Cash} \quad - \quad (\text{Futures} \quad \text{x} \quad \text{Cf}) \quad = \quad \text{Basis}$$

$$150.4099 \quad - \quad (98.15625 \text{ x } 1.4568) \quad = \quad +237$$

On December 1, the basis has widened to 4/32nds. The basis for the 12.5% August 2009-14 bond in relation to the December 87 T-bond futures contract widened 233 points during the time of this strategy. It is a fundamental of the market that the basis has to widen this much just to keep the yield of the bond at a constant storage level. This is not something that requires a favorably volatile market for results.

Since each 32nd is worth $31.25, each contract experiences a basis gain, in dollar terms, of $7,281.25. Multiplying the dollar value of the basis change times the number of $100,000 par cash units, 140, shows that the total basis change roughly equals the net hedging result of $1,020,078. (The trivial $703 discrepancy, only 0.005% error, is due to rounding.)

$$7,281.25 \quad \text{x} \quad 140 \quad = \quad 1,019,377$$

The bond dealer clearly has found a way to take advantage of the anticipated basis change. Further, the fact that bond dealers so ofen borrow bonds to sell them is hardly a chance occurrence. Rather, it follows from a deliberate policy which depends, in turn, on the nature of the bond market.

If the dealer operated his business like an ordinary store, holding inventory until someone bought it, he would be in all kinds of trouble. It isn't just that he would have inventory risk exposure. He would. But the main problem would be that if he sold futures against that cash exposure, it would put him long the basis. That classical hedging strategy is just right for a narrowing basis. Bond basis widens. A widening basis works against the long basis position.

A check of the Federal Reserve bond dealer position reports reveals that all are short. Clearly, those people understand full well that the market rewards the short basis position and punishes those who allow inventory to accumulate. In response, they have devised a business approach that harmonizes with their market.

11

A Pension Manager's Yield Enhancement Strategy

Pension fund managers face an interesting challenge. They have a responsibility to protect the assets placed in their trust. Yet they have a charge to take those funds into the market and make them grow. As a result, it matters a great deal how the managers do that. The financial media often refer to "aggressive fund managers"—always seeming to imply by that term a somewhat reckless, high risk approach. The term hardly seems complimentary, though they laugh that win. Some risk managers may perceive here a divided duty, but really they shouldn't. A basis trader can be aggressive without sacrificing safety.

Consider how a pension fund manager might handle a portfolio of U.S. Treasury bonds. This represents a safe long-term investment. It will earn in the area of eight or nine percent—nothing spectacular, but a good return. Fund managers striving to outperform the market average can significantly improve their returns by engaging in a short basis strategy—maintaining, in the long run, both the safety and the integrity of their portfolios.

To accomplish such a coup, a portfolio manager would begin by selling a cash bond out of inventory and investing the proceeds of the sale in short-term T-bills. At the same time, he buys T-bond futures. When it comes time to unwind, he sells bills and futures, buys back the cash bond, and adds up his gains. All in all, this sequence of events produces the same effect as having held the long-term bond and collected the basis gain. Figure 11-1 summarizes this sequence.

Figure 11-1

CASH	FUTURES
sell cash (buy T-bills)	buy T-bond futures
buy cash (sell T-bills)	sell T-bond futures

Curiously, a fund manager who sets up this kind of strategy is able to be an "aggressive fund manager" without putting the assets of the fund at risk.

How it Works

Assume that on May 15, 1987, a portfolio manager sells $14 million par of the 12.5% August 2009-14 bond at 130.2356 (130-08) and 9.25% yield. At the same time he invests in T-bills which yield 6% and buys December '87 T-bond futures at 87-00.

When it comes time to unwind, on December 31, 1987, he buys $14 million par of the 12.5% bond at 129.9547 and sells the December '87 futures at 89-00. That assumes no change in the yield to maturity of the bond. Figure 11-2 details the trading sequence.

Figure 11-2

CASH	FUTURES
May 15, 1987	
sell 12.5% August 2009-14 @130.2356, 9.25% yield Par Value: $14,000,000 Cash Value: $18,232,984 (buy T-bills)	buy Dec 87 T-bond @ 87-00 Cf: 1.4561 HR: 1.4561 No. of Contracts: 203.854
December 31, 1987	
buy cash (sell T-bills) 12.5% August 2009-14 @129.9547, 9.25% yield Par Value: $14,000,000 Cash Value: $18,193,658	sell Dec 87 T-bond @ 89-00

The $39,326 cash gain from the bond trade is insignificant—less than half a percent of par, annualized.

$$\text{Cash Sale} \quad - \quad \text{Cash Purchase} \quad = \quad \text{Cash Result}$$

$$18,232,984 \quad - \quad 18,193,658 \quad = \quad 39,326$$

The investment in 6% T-bills produces a return of $689,357 during this period. On the futures side, the 2-00 handle gain has a cash value of $2000 a contract, a total of $407,708.

$$\begin{array}{c}\text{Futures Change} \quad x \quad 31.25 \quad x \quad \text{Contracts} \quad = \quad \text{Futures Result}\\ \text{(in 32nds)}\\ 64 \qquad x \ 31.25 \ x \quad 203.854 \ = \ 407,708\end{array}$$

A Pension Manager's Yield Enhancement Strategy

Strategy 9

A. The Problem

To outperform the market average of a Treasury bond portfolio, a pension fund manager can use a short basis strategy (sell cash, buy futures). He sells bonds out of inventory, invests the cash in T-bills, and buys T-bond futures. In a normal yield market, a widening basis (becoming more negative) assures enhanced returns. A basis trader can be aggressive without sacrificing the safety or the integrity of his portfolio.

B. Preliminaries

1. *The Basis*

   Cash   − (Futures × Cf)   = Basis
   a. 130.2356 − (87 × 1.4561) = 3.5549 (× 32) = 113.7568
   b. 129.9547 − (89 × 1.4561) = 0.3618 (× 32) = 11.5776

2. *Futures Position Size*

$$\frac{18,232,984}{1000 \times 130.2356} \times 1.4561 = 203.854$$

C. The Strategy

CASH	FUTURES	BASIS
May 15, 1987		
sell	buy	
12.5% August 2009-14,	Dec 87 T-bond @ 87-00	114
yield 9.25%, @ 130.2356	Cf: 1.4561	
Par Value: $14,000,000	No. of Contracts: 203.854	
Cash Value: $18,232,984		
(buy T-bills)		
December 31, 1987		
buy cash	sell	
(sell T-bills)	Dec 87 T-bond @89-00	12
12.5% August 2009-14,		
9.25% yield, @129.9547		
Par Value: $14,000,000		
Cash Value: $18,193,658		

D. Results and Evaluation

1. *Cash Result* (gain)

   Cash Sale − Cash Purchase = Cash Result
   18,232,984 − 18,193,658   = 39,326

2. *Futures Result* (gain)

   Futures Change × 31.25 × Contracts = Futures Result
   (in 32nds)
       64   × 31.25 × 203.854 = 407,708

3. *Capital Gain*

39,326	Cash gain
+ 407,708	Futures gain
447,034	Capital Gain

4. *Interest Expense* (not applicable)

5. *Interest Income* (6% T-Bill investment)

18,232,984	Cash Value
× .06	T-Bill Rate
1,093,979	Annual Income
÷ 365	Days
2,997.2028	Daily Income
× 230	Days in Hedge
689,357	Interest Income

6. *Net Hedging Result*

447,034	Capital Gain
+ 689,357	Interest Income
1,136,391	Net Hedging Result

7. *Annualized Yield*

1,136,391	Net Hedging Result
÷ 18,232,984	Cash Value
0.0623261	Return
÷ 230	Days in Hedge
0.000271	Daily Yield
× 365	Days
0.0989088	= 9.89% Annualized Yield

8. *Basis Value*

   Basis Change × 31.25 × Par Units = Basis Value
   102.179   × 31.25 × 140   = 447,034

9. Basis Value = Capital Gain
   447,034   = 447,034

The net hedging result is the sum of those three gains.

39,326	Cash Gain
689,357	T-bill Return
407,708	Futures Gain
1,136,391	Net Hedging Result

That is a good result. What a fund manager needs to be able to show, though, is that the result of this strategy improves on the alternative—leaving the bond in inventory and collecting the yield.

Given a yield to maturity of 9.25%, this bond would return $1,062,758 during the period between May 15 and December 31. The hedging strategy netted $1,146,391. That amounts to an annualized return of just under 10%—three-fourths of a percent improvement over leaving the bond in inventory.

Why It Works

Risk managers who have taken the trouble to master the market fundamentals, like the basis, expect results like this. They take it as a given that, in a normal yield market, bond basis widens. They know that a widening basis rewards a short basis strategy. In addition, thoughtful basis traders understand that this strategy allows them to add their basis gain to the short-term yield of the T-bills, which will always produce a return equal to or greater than the long-term rate alone, over time.

Figure 11-3, along with the usual buy, sell, and price information, shows where the gains originate—it's the basis.

Notice that the 12.5% bond produces a 102-point basis change during the period of this strategy.

The price changes on both the cash and futures sides are virtually automatic as well. The cash change, due to the slight change in maturity, is insignificant and will occur in any case. The futures price, too, will change predictably—the change in this case is largely controlled by the implied repo rate.

The implied repo rate defines the rate of return from a hypothetical simultaneous purchase and sale of a debt instrument, with a fixed future price of sale and date of delivery. It will never be higher than the short-term rate. Usually it will be less. That imposes a limit on the returns for just holding a bond. The implied repo rate divided by the short-term rate defines a percent of carry. Full carry, the maximum reward for holding the bond, occurs when the two rates are equal. So it is equivalent to the short-term rate. The lower the percent of carry, the less incentive there is to just hold the bond in inventory. The returns in that case will be mediocre at best.

Figure 11-3

CASH	FUTURES	BASIS
May 15, 1987		
sell	buy	
12.5% August 2009-14	Dec 87 T-bond @ 87-00	114
@ 130.2356, 9.25% yield	Cf: 1.4561	
Par Value: $14,000.000	HR: 1.4561	
Cash Value: $18,232.984	No. of Contracts: 203.854	
(buy T-bills)		
December 31, 1987		
buy	sell	
cash (sell T-bills)	Dec 87 T-bond @ 89-00	12
12.5% August 2009-14		
@ 129.29547, 9.25% yield		
Par Value: $14,000,000		
Cash Value: $18,193,658		

In reality, the risk manager's task is not to puzzle over how the prices, or even the basis, will change. That will take place with or without his concurrence—in a predictable way. His choice concerns whether he will establish a position on the right side of the known changes. If he does, the market will work in his behalf. If he does not, the market will exact its pound of flesh.

When all is said and done, the portfolio is right back where it started. The fund owns $14 million par of the 12.5% August 2009-14 bond. In the meantime, though, the fund manager has significantly improved the performance of the bond portfolio by taking advantage of the predictable market characteristics. Risk managers, at some time, are masters of their own fates.

V

A Basis Trading Practicum
Long Basis Strategies

It is impossible to stress too much the importance of freeing oneself from shallow, conventional thinking. Even the soundest general rules are still only general rules. These strategies offer ample illustration.

The first thing risk managers have to learn about the financial markets is that the only reason to use futures is to take advantage of the basis, the cash-futures relationship. Financial risk managers have many cash alternatives available to them. They must consider their business objectives, and decide whether there is a "basis play" available. If so, they should use futures. Otherwise, they should not.

The second thing risk managers have to learn is that, since financial basis invariably converges to zero, the short basis strategy rewards the hedger. Several earlier examples illustrate that. It is often rewarding to go to considerable trouble to engineer that kind of situation. At the same time, the hedger who unthinkingly adopts a long basis position is likely to be sorry.

Third, risk managers have to learn that that is just a general rule, albeit a good one.

Sometimes a strategy involving a position long the basis is the right one to develop. How do hedgers tell the difference? It isn't always easy. But risk managers know that, while the bond basis tends to widen, there are often short periods of time when it narrows. A methodical risk manager who keeps careful records can reap the benefits of those market variations.

Astute risk managers also know that the basis story is only part of the larger story. The right strategy, in their minds, is the one that helps them achieve some larger business goal. Risk management is not its own reward. Speculation may be. But risk management is subordinate to the policies and goals of the business. It is a way to protect assets and achieve those goals.

Naturally no one objects when a risk manager enhances yields. As hedgers evaluate risk management strategies, asking whether this or that strategy made money is asking the wrong question. Their first concern should be whether they protected assets, held funding costs within acceptable limits, or achieved the goal that originally motivated participation.

All that is to say that the business goal is first. Always. That's not a general rule. That's dogma. And oddly enough, sometimes strategies involving long basis positions are the right ones to accomplish the business goals.

Notes on Method

Several of the strategies in this section involve non-deliverable cash instruments—mortgages and loan commitments. The constant yield assumption creates a situation such that cash price for that kind of instrument remains unchanged. The real question concerns the nature of the basis change. The basis at the outset is calculable given the known cash, futures, and Cf values. But how to determine what the endpoint basis will be?

Basis traders know that the basis for the cheapest to deliver T-bond will converge to zero. That knowledge makes it possible to determine what the future futures price will be. If the cheapest to deliver bond is the (hypothetical) 12% May 2010-15, and its price will be 140-24 at 8% yield to maturity, then the futures price will be 99.506159, or 99-16.

$$\text{Cash Price} - (\text{Futures} \times \text{Cf}) \quad = \text{Basis}$$
$$140.74159 - (\text{Futures} \times 1.4144) = 0$$

$$\text{Futures} = \frac{140.74159}{1.4414} = 99.506159$$

Given that the cash price of some non-deliverable instrument will be par, or 100, the futures price will be 99.506159, and the Cf is 1.5090, a basis trader can derive the basis for that instrument at that time. It will be -1605.

$$\text{Cash} - (\text{Futures} \times \text{Cf}) = \text{Basis}$$
$$100 - (99.506159 \times 1.5090) = -1605$$

Mortgages and other non-deliverables typically have negative basis values. That reflects the fact that they are non-deliverable and that the market considers them lower quality instruments than T-bonds which, in a normal yield environment, cannot sustain negative basis.

In a sense, it is impossible to know just what the future holds. Yet basis trading logic allows risk managers to develop informed opinions. The removal of guesswork is a key feature of good risk management.

12

A Classical Short Futures Hedge

Financial managers can often improve their companies' cash positions significantly by constructing hedges which use U.S. Treasury bonds and T-bond futures—as long as they don't pay too much attention to price. Important as sound cash management has become in this era of fierce international competition and volatile money markets, the idea of ignoring price seems paradoxical, but only on the surface.

Traditionally, hedging involves shifting price risk by establishing balancing cash and futures positions. Thus it might seem wise management, when buying bonds, to protect the cash position against erosion by selling futures. In practice, that strategy will almost inevitably cause distress. Most of the stories about hedges gone awry refer to this kind of hedge.

Figure 12-1 summarizes what seems to be a perfectly logical strategy based on that approach. The hedger, having bought cash bonds, balances his position by selling futures. Later, he unwinds his positions by selling the cash bonds and buying futures.

Figure 12-1

CASH	FUTURES
buy T-bonds	sell futures
sell T-bonds	buy futures

153

How It Works

Consider the case of a would-be hedger who thought, on June 24, 1987, to buy 1000 bonds of the 13.25% May 2009-14 issue which was then selling at 157.35225 and yielding 8%. To protect that position he sold 15.707 contracts of Dec futures at 97-00. Assuming no change in the yield rate, that hedger would next sell the bonds and buy futures on December 1 of that year. Figure 12-2 summarizes that trade sequence.

Figure 12-2

CASH	FUTURES
June 24, 1987	

buy
13.25% May 2009-14
@157.35225, 8% yield
    Par Value: $1,000,000
    Cash Value: $1,573,522
	sell
	Dec 87 T-bond @97-00
	    Cf: 1.5707
	    HR: 1.5707
	    No. of Contracts: 15.707

December 1, 1987	

sell
13.25% May 2009-14
@157.068398, 8% yield
    Par Value: $1,000,000
    Cash Value: $1,570,684
	buy
	Dec 87 T-bond @100-00

June 24 to December 1: 160 days	

On the cash side there is a $2,670 loss—all things considered, a trivial amount.

$$\text{Cash Sale} - \text{Cash Purchase} = \text{Cash Result}$$
$$1{,}570{,}684 - 1{,}573{,}522 = -2{,}838$$

The purpose of a hedge is to protect against principal loss due to rate change by using futures. On the futures side, though, there is a 3-00 change which, because the sale price is lower than the purchase, defines a loss of $47,121.

$$\text{Futures Change} \times 31.25 \times \text{Contracts} = \text{Futures Result}$$
$$\text{(in 32nds)}$$
$$96 \times 31.25 \times 15.707 = -47{,}121$$

Summing the cash loss and the futures loss reveals a capital loss of $49,959.

-2,838	Cash Loss
-47,121	Futures Loss
-49,959	Capital Loss

During the 160 days the strategy was in place, the hedger would have collected interest income because of the bond coupon. Coupon payment is based on the par value, not the actual price.

1,000,000	Par Value
x .1325	Coupon Rate
132,500	Annual Interest Income
÷ 365	Days
363.0137	Daily Interest Income
x 160	Days of Hedge
58,082	Interest Income

The sum of the $58,082 interest income and the $49,959 capital loss is the net hedging result: $8,123. Actually, that amounts to an annualized return of 1%. That hardly provides a strong argument for hedging.

Far more significant than that number is the $49,959 capital loss. After all, any bond holder would have earned the interest income. That has nothing to do with the hedge. The hedge itself produced an annualized return of -7.24%. A return like that calls for some thought about what could have gone wrong.

Why It Doesn't Work

The trouble with that hedge, as with so many that make the news, is that this hedger apparently failed to grasp the market fundamentals the hedge should have taken advantage of.

Financials hedgers, like hedgers in any other market, need to pay attention not to price but to basis change. In order to design effective hedges, they need to develop an appreciation for the factors that cause basis change—in particular, the storage problem.

A CLASSICAL SHORT FUTURES HEDGE

Strategy 10

A. The Problem

Risk managers who for some reason have ignored the role of the basis often think they can protect an investment from value erosion and earn a long-term yield on a short-term investment by selling futures to balance their cash transactions. While they achieve "price neutrality," a major goal in the minds of many, the storage fundamentals work against this long basis position (buy cash, sell futures) in a normal yield environment.

B. Preliminaries

1. *The Basis*

   Cash   − (Futures × Cf) = Basis (in 32nds)
   a. 157.352252 − (97 × 1.5707) = 4.99435 (× 32)   = 159.8192
   b. 157.068398 − (100 × 1.5707) = −0.00161 (× 32) = −0.05152

2. *Futures Position Size*

$$\frac{1,573,522}{1000 \times 157.352252} \times 1.5707 = 15.707$$

C. The Strategy

CASH	FUTURES	BASIS
June 24, 1987		
buy	sell	
13.25% May 2009-14	Dec 87 T-bond @97-00	160
@157.352252, 8% yield	Cf: 1.5707	
Par Value: $1,000,000	HR: 1.5707	
Cash Value: $1,573,522	No. of contracts: 15.707	
December 1, 1987		
sell	buy	
13.25% May 2009-14	Dec 87 T-bond @100-00	0
@157.068398, 8% yield		
Par Value: $1,000,000		
Cash Value: $1,570,684		
June 24 to December 1: 160 days		

D. Results and Evaluation

1. *Cash Result (loss)*

   Cash Sale − Cash Purchase = Cash Result
   1,570,684 − 1,573,522   = −2,838

2. *Futures Result* (loss)

   Futures Change × 31.25 × Contracts = Futures Result
     (in 32nds)
         96   × 31.25 × 15.707   = −47,121

3. *Capital Loss*

$$
\begin{array}{rl}
-\ 2,838 & \text{Cash Loss} \\
\underline{-\ 47,121} & \text{Futures Loss} \\
-\ 49,959 & \text{Capital Loss}
\end{array}
$$

4. *Interest Expense (not applicable)*

5. *Interest Income*

$$
\begin{array}{rl}
1,000,000 & \text{Par Value} \\
\underline{\times\ .1325} & \text{Coupon Rate} \\
132,500 & \text{Annual Interest Income} \\
\underline{\div\ 365} & \text{Days} \\
363.0137 & \text{Daily Interest Income} \\
\underline{\times\ 160} & \text{Days of Hedge} \\
58,082 & \text{Interest Income}
\end{array}
$$

6. *Net Hedging Result*

$$
\begin{array}{rl}
-\ 49,959 & \text{Capital Loss} \\
\underline{+\ 58,082} & \text{Interest Income} \\
8,123 & \text{Net Hedging Result}
\end{array}
$$

7. *Annualized Yield*

$$
\begin{array}{rl}
8,123 & \text{Net Hedging Result} \\
\underline{\div\ 1,573,522} & \text{Cash Value} \\
0.0051623 & \text{Return} \\
\underline{\div\ 160} & \text{Days in Hedge} \\
0.0000323 & \text{Daily Yield} \\
\underline{\times\ 365} & \text{Days} \\
0.0117765 & =\ 1.18\%\ \text{Annualized Yield}
\end{array}
$$

8. *Basis Value*

$$
\begin{array}{lll}
\text{Basis Change} \times 31.25 \times \text{Par Units} & = & \text{Basis Value} \\
159.87072\quad\ \times 31.25 \times 10 & = & 49,959
\end{array}
$$

9. Basis Value = Capital Loss

   49,959   = 49,959

The central idea of the storage problem is that the basis responds to the market's desire to store the commodity in question. In this regard, financials are the same as the grains or anything else. When the market wants to drive the commodity—bonds in this case, of course—into storage, the basis widens. The winning strategy then is to short the basis—to sell cash, buy futures. The hedge just considered is clearly an example of a long basis strategy.

The first thing financials hedgers need to do is to learn to listen to what the basis is telling them. Bond basis is similar to grain or oil basis. The standard formula enables hedgers to discover that the June 24 basis for the 13.25% May 2009-14 bond in relation to December T-bond futures is 160 while the December 1 basis is 0.

$$\text{Cash} \quad - \quad (\text{Futures x Cf}) \quad = \quad \text{Basis (in 32nds)}$$

$$157.352252 - (97 \ \text{x } 1.5707) = 4.99435 \, (\text{x } 32) = 160$$

$$157.068398 - (100 \text{ x } 1.5707) = -0.00161 \, (\text{x } 32) = 0$$

During the term of this hedge, the basis widened 160 points, as Figure 12-3 shows.

Figure 12-3

CASH	FUTURES	BASIS
June 24, 1987		

buy
13.25% May 2009-14
@157.35225, 8% yield
  Par Value: $1,000,000
  Cash Value: $1,573,522
	sell
	Dec 87 T-bond @97-00
	  Cf: 1.5707
	  HR: 1.5707
	  No. of Contracts: 15.707
		160

December 1, 1987		

sell
13.25% May 2009-14
@157.068398, 8% yield
  Par Value: $1,000,000
  Cash Value: $1,570,684
	buy
	Dec 87 T-bond @100-00
		0

June 24 to December 1: 160 days

Figure 12-4

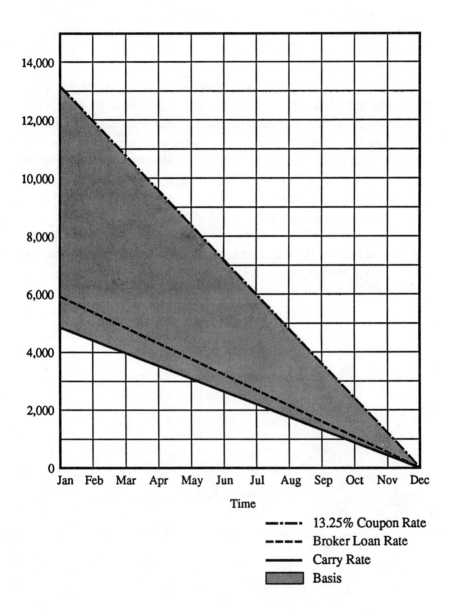

Bond basis generally deteriorates, or widens, given a normal yield curve market. The reason is easy to discover.

In a normal market, the bond basis will be at least enough to keep the position yielding something less than the short term rate, as Figure 12-4 illustrates.

As the futures contract nears expiration, the interplay of the long-term yield and the short-term yield causes the dollar value of the interest accruals to decline. The basis declines as well. That happens because the impending contract expiration requires less and less money to offset the extra yield earnings. The basis widens to maintain storage levels. Knowing what factors control the basis allows a hedger to fit his strategy to the particular situation.

A widening basis calls for going short the basis, not long. That explains the loss. In effect, by going long the basis, this hedger took a position on the wrong side of the basis, as basis traders say. He tried to store bonds when the market told him not to.

Bad luck? Not at all. This hedger's loss is entirely predictable, almost a foregone conclusion—to a student of the basis.

13

A Classical Hedge Is Right, Sometimes

The classical hedge usually comes to grief because of the basis change characteristic of Treasury bonds and other financials. That does not mean that alert financial managers never adopt that position. Situations exist where the trading pattern described in Figure 13-1 (which, at this level of abstraction, repeats Figure 12-1) constitutes good, heads-up risk management.

Figure 13-1

CASH	FUTURES
buy U. S. Treasuries	sell futures
sell cash bonds	buy futures

What such a risk manager has on his mind when he initiates this strategy is that he can earn a yield substantially better than the short-term rate if he stays on top of things. There is nothing untoward about this. This hedger simply takes advantage of a thorough awareness of the bond market, a superior record-keeping system, and articulate goals.

How It Works

This hedger will initiate the strategy at noon on March 30, 1987, by buying 10,000 14% Nov 2011 U.S. Treasury bonds at 172.08722. His total purchase price is $17,208,722. On the futures side he sells 163.74 June T-bond futures contracts at 102-00.

When it comes time to unwind, at 2:00 p.m. on April 3, 1987, he sells the cash bonds at 172.075661 (total proceeds—$17,207,566) and he buys June T-bond futures at 101-29. Figure 13-2 summarizes the details of this strategy.

Figure 13-2

CASH	FUTURES
March 30, 1987 noon	
buy	sell
14% November 2011	Jun T-bond @ 102-00
@ 172.08722, 7.5% yield	Cf: 1.6374
Par Value: $10,000,000	HR: 1.6374
Cash Value: $17,208,722	No. of Contracts: 163.74
April 3, 1987 2:00 p.m.	
sell	buy
14% November 2011	Jun T-bond @ 101-29
@ 172.075661, 7.5% yield	
Par Value: $10,000,000	
Cash Value: $17,207,566	
March 30 to April 3: 4 days	

On the cash side, this hedger sees a $1,156 loss, but the futures side tells quite a different story.

Cash Sale   –   Cash Purchase = Cash Result
17,207,566 –   17,208,722   =   -1,156

Notice that the futures side shows a gain of 3/32nds a contract. That amounts to a $16,374 futures gain.

Futures Change x 31.25 x Contracts = Futures Result
(in 32nds)
32   x 31.25 x 163.74 = 15,350

The sum of the cash loss and the futures gain determines the capital gain of the hedge: $15,218.

-1,156	Cash Loss
+15,350	Futures Gain
+14,194	Capital Gain

That capital gain amounts to an 8% annualized yield for this hedge. The long basis strategy, in this situation, allows the hedger to earn slightly more than the long-term yield on a short-term investment. In fact, it improves on the stated yield to maturity by 6%.

Also, the hedger holds the cash bond for the four days, so he derives interest income. Given the 14% coupon and the $10 million par value, that amounts to $15,342. The sum of the interest income and the capital gain is $29,356, a 17% annualized return for the strategy. Combining the interest income—which any bond holder would earn, hedged or not—this strategy allows the hedger to earn better than the long-term yield on a short-term investment.

Why It Works

The success of this strategy is, again, no mystery. Notice the very short span of the trade—in and out in four days. That seems a superficial factor, but a consideration of Figure 13-3 shows that it is not.

The basis at the outset is 162 over. At the end point it *narrows* to 167 over. The basis moves 5/32nds more positive. Normally, over time, bond basis widens and a classical hedging strategy held in place for three to six months loses. Here, the basis narrowed briefly, and an alert financial manager can take advantage of that situation.

The discussion of the basis in Chapter 3 points out that the basis does not describe a straight line as it converges toward zero. There are variations from the norm. To an alert basis trader who keeps careful records, those variations create opportunities.

Just how much of an opportunity becomes clearer given the fact that interest accrues to a premium bond, like this one, to create a yield near 8%. During the same time period T-bills, the shortest-term U.S. Treasuries, yielded 5.75%. In particular, this strategy allows a financial

A CLASSICAL HEDGE IS RIGHT, SOMETIMES

Strategy 11

A. The Problem

To capitalize on temporary basis narrowings, hedgers can use a long basis strategy (buy cash, sell futures) — the so-called "classical hedge." While the basis typically widens in a normal yield environment, events like Treasury refundings or contract expirations cause "momentary" incentives to storage. These narrowings seldom last more than a few days, but hedgers who track basis carefully and have a plan ready can reap benefits.

B. Preliminaries

1. *The Basis*

   Cash   − (Futures × Cf)   = Basis
   a. $172.08722 - (102 \times 1.6374) = 5.07242 \ (\times \ 32) = 162.31744$
   b. $172.07566 - (101.90625 \times 1.6374) = 5.2143663 \qquad = 166.85972$

2. *Futures Position Size*

   $$\frac{15,778,125}{1000 \times 172.08722} \times 1.6374 = 163.74$$

C. The Strategy

CASH	FUTURES	BASIS
March 30, 1987 noon		
buy	sell	
14% Nov 2011	Jun T-bond @102-00	162
@172.08722, 7.5% yield	Cf: 1.6374	
Par Value: $10,000,000	HR: 1.6374	
Cash Value: $17,208,722	No. of Contracts: 163.74	
April 3, 1987 2:00 p.m.		
sell	buy	
14% Nov 2011	Jun T-bond @101-29	167
@172.075661, 7.5% yield		
Par Value: $10,000,000		
Cash Value: $17,207,566		
March 30 to April 3: 4 days		

D. Results and Evaluation

1. *Cash Result* (loss)

   Cash Sale − Cash Purchase = Cash Result
   $17,207,566 - 17,208,722 \quad = -1,156$

2. *Futures Result* (gain)

   Futures Change × 31.25 × Contracts = Futures Result
     (in 32nds)
          $3 \qquad \times \ 31.25 \times 163.74 \quad = 15,350$

3. *Capital Gain*

$$
\begin{array}{rl}
-\ 1,156 & \text{Cash Loss} \\
+\ 15,350 & \text{Futures Gain} \\
\hline
+\ 14,194 & \text{Capital Gain}
\end{array}
$$

4. *Interest Expense* (not applicable)

5. *Interest Income*

$$
\begin{array}{rl}
10,000,000 & \text{Par Value} \\
\times\ .14 & \text{Coupon Rate} \\
\hline
1,400,000 & \text{Return} \\
\div\ 365 & \text{Days} \\
\hline
3,838.6164 & \text{Daily Yield} \\
\times\ 4 & \text{Days in Hedge} \\
\hline
15,342 & \text{Interest Income}
\end{array}
$$

6. *Net Hedging Result*

$$
\begin{array}{rl}
14,194 & \text{Capital Gain} \\
+\ 15,342 & \text{Interest Income} \\
\hline
29,536 & \text{Net Hedging Result}
\end{array}
$$

7. *Annualized Yield*

$$
\begin{array}{rl}
29,536 & \text{Net Hedging Result} \\
\div\ 15,778,125 & \text{Cash Value} \\
\hline
0.001872 & \text{Return} \\
\div\ 4 & \text{Days in Hedge} \\
\hline
0.000468 & \text{Daily Yield} \\
\times\ 365 & \text{Days} \\
\hline
0.1708162 & =\ 17\%\ \text{Annualized Yield}
\end{array}
$$

8. *Basis Value*

Basis Change $\times$ 31.25 $\times$ Par Units = Basis Value
4.54228 $\quad\times$ 31.25 $\times$ 100 $\quad$ = 14,194

9. Basis Value = Capital Gain
14,194 $\qquad$ = 14,194

Figure 13-3

CASH	FUTURES	BASIS
March 30, 1987 noon		
buy	sell	
14% November 2011	Jun T-bond @ 102-00	162
@ 172.08722, 7.5% yield	Cf: 1.6374	
Par Value: $10,000,000	HR: 1.6374	
Cash Value: $17,208,722	No. of Contracts: 163.74	
April 3, 1987 2:00p.m.		
sell	buy	
14% November 2011	Jun T-bond @ 101-29	167
@ 172.075661, 7.5% yield		
Par Value: $10,000,000		
Cash Value: $17,207,566		
March 30 to April 13: 4 days		

manager—who knows an opportunity when he sees one—to replace that 5.75% with something approaching 8%, which is almost 40% better than the bill rate.

14

A "Common Sense" Mortgage Hedge

A critical problem for mortgage bankers is the fact that the value of their loan commitments can change before they can act on them. The bankers take applications at fixed rates. Processing an application can take several weeks. By that time rates can change enough to erode the value of the portfolio.

Bankers package conventional mortgages for sale to FhLB—colloquially, Freddie Mac—FNMA or GNMA (Fannie Mae and Ginnie Mae, respectively), depending on the kind of mortgages. Those agencies provide absolute protection, in the sense that bankers get rid of the problem by selling the assets. But sometimes it takes weeks or even a month or two to accumulate the package, a period during which the "pipeline" is dangerously exposed.

Further, the loans in the "pipeline" are anticipated but undeliverable, so bankers, as many of them see it, have two alternatives. They can forward sell the Freddie Mac package or hedge the pipeline. Forward sale gives them 120 days or so to build the package.

Freddie Mac requires delivering a higher rate (or taking a greater discount)—as much as half a percent for the forward sale. The forward sale prices go lower the farther out they go, like bond futures. Bankers do not like locking in lower prices, so they find forward sale very difficult to do. What they fail to see is that the futures offset the forward sale discount. Futures move in concert with the cash market. As a result, the correct hedge position counters the discounts. Because they don't understand that, many bankers prefer not to forward sell.

Instead, they hedge. At least they believe they do. The usual textbook definition suggests that, to hedge, a person must simply take equal and opposite positions in cash and futures.

Writing a mortgage is equivalent to buying a cash bond. Bankers who do not think carefully about hedging, who assume the typical definition of hedging to be correct and inclusive, might think that having, in effect, bought cash bonds they need only sell the right amount of T-bond futures and the portfolio will be protected. Figure 14-1 summarizes this "common sense" approach to mortgage hedging.

Figure 14-1

CASH	FUTURES
buy write mortgages	sell T-bond futures
sell sell mortgages into secondary market	buy T-bond futures

How it Works

To see more precisely how such a hedge might work, assume that on July 2, 1986, a banker wrote 10.2% 30-year mortgages (maturity is July 2, 2016) with a total value of $10,000,000 and 10.2% yield. Writing mortgages, to repeat, is equivalent to buying cash. He plans to sell them to Freddie Mac on December 1. Meanwhile, to hold himself price neutral, he wants to hedge his position on the futures market.

Accordingly, he sells December T-bond futures at 96-18. He'll need 124.68 contracts to balance his mortgage position. When he sells his mortgages, he'll buy futures to complete the transaction. Figure 14-2 summarizes these details.

Figure 14-2

CASH	FUTURES
July 2, 1986	
buy	sell
write 10.2% 30-year	Dec 86 T-bond @96-18
mortgages, yield 10.2%	Cf: 1.2468
Par Value: $10,000,000	HR: 1.2468
Cash Value: $10,000,000	No. of Contracts: 124.68
December 1, 1986	
sell	buy
mortgages into secondary	Dec 86 T-bond @99-17
market, yield 10.2%	
Par Value: $10,000,000	
Cash Value: $10,000,000	

July 2 to December 1: 151 days

Because of the assumption that the yield would not change, there is no change in the cash price. That position holds neutral.

Lucky. Because the futures side tells an unhappy story. The 2-31 futures change is a loss, which comes to a total of $370,144.

$$\begin{array}{l} \text{Futures Change} \ \times \ 31.25 \ \times \ \text{Contracts} = \text{Futures Result} \\ \quad \text{(in 32nds)} \\ \qquad 95 \qquad\quad \times \ 31.25 \ \times \ 124.68 \quad = -370{,}144 \end{array}$$

Since the banker actually holds the mortgages, he has to pay something to finance them, but he also collects some interest from the homeowners. If the banker pays a short-term rate of 7% for these funds, the interest expense is $289,589.

10,000,000	Mortgage Value
x .07	Short-Term Rate
700,000	Annual Interest Expense
÷ 365	Days
1,917.8082	Daily Interest Expense
x 151	Days in the Hedge
289,589	Interest Expense

A "COMMON SENSE" MORTGAGE HEDGE

Strategy 12

A. The Problem

To avoid the PC discount, mortgage bankers often try to protect their "pipelines" with a long basis strategy (buy cash, sell futures). Writing a mortgage is equivalent to selling a cash bond, so selling futures seems a reasonable approach. These bankers, having ignored the storage prompts of the basis, will find that the market actually works against them. In most cases their results will be worse than had they not tried to hedge.

B. Preliminaries

1. *The Basis*

   Cash $-$ (Futures $\times$ Cf) = Basis (in 32nds)
   a. $100 - (96.5625 \times 1.2468) = -20.394125 \, (\times \, 32) = -652.612$
   b. $100 - (99.52139 \times 1.2468) = -24.083269 \, (\times \, 32) = -770.66461$

2. *Futures Position Size*

$$\frac{10,000,000}{1000 \times 100} \times 1.2468 = 124.68$$

C. The Strategy

CASH	FUTURES	BASIS
July 2, 1986		
buy	sell	
write 10.2% 30 year	Dec 86 T-bond @96-18	-653
mortgages, 10.2% yield	Cf: 1.2468	
Par Value: $10,000,000	HR: 1.2468	
Cash Value: $10,000,000	No. of Contracts: 124.68	
December 1, 1986		
sell	buy	
mortgages into secondary	Dec 86 T-bond @99-17	-771
market, 10.2% yield		
Par Value: $10,000,000		
Cash Value: $10,000,000		
July 2 to December 1: 151 days		

D. Results and Evaluation

1. *Cash Result*

   Cash Sale $-$ Cash Purchase = Cash Result
   $10,000,000 - 10,000,000 \quad = 0$

2. *Futures Result* (loss)

   Futures Change $\times$ 31.25 $\times$ Contracts = Futures Result
      (in 32nds)
         95      $\times$ 31.25 $\times$ 124.68 $= -370,144$

3. *Capital Loss*

$$
\begin{array}{rl}
0 & \text{Cash Result} \\
+\,370{,}144 & \text{Futures Loss} \\
\hline
-\,370{,}144 & \text{Capital Loss}
\end{array}
$$

4. *Interest Expense*

$$
\begin{array}{rl}
10{,}000{,}000 & \text{Mortgage Value} \\
\times\ .07 & \text{Short-term rate} \\
\hline
700{,}000 & \text{Annual interest expense} \\
-\ 365 & \text{Days in a year} \\
\hline
1{,}917.8082 & \text{Daily interest expense} \\
\times\ 151 & \text{Days in the hedge} \\
\hline
289{,}589 & \text{Interest expense}
\end{array}
$$

5. *Interest Income*

$$
\begin{array}{rl}
10{,}000{,}000 & \text{Par Value} \\
\times\ .102 & \text{Coupon Rate} \\
\hline
1{,}020{,}000 & \text{Return} \\
-\ 365 & \text{Days} \\
\hline
2{,}794.5205 & \text{Daily Yield} \\
\times\ 151 & \text{Days in Hedge} \\
\hline
421{,}973 & \text{Interest Income}
\end{array}
$$

6. *Net Hedging Result*

$$
\begin{array}{rl}
-\,370{,}144 & \text{Capital Loss} \\
-\ 289{,}589 & \text{Interest Expense} \\
+\ 421{,}973 & \text{Interest Income} \\
\hline
-\ 237{,}760 & \text{Net Hedging Result}
\end{array}
$$

7. *Annualized Yield*

$$
\begin{array}{rl}
-\,237{,}760 & \text{Net Hedging Result} \\
\div\ 10{,}000{,}000 & \text{Cash Value} \\
\hline
-\ 0.023776 & \text{Return} \\
\div\ 151 & \text{Days in Hedge} \\
\hline
-\ 0.0001575 & \text{Daily Yield} \\
\times\ 365 & \text{Days} \\
\hline
-\ 0.0574718 & =\ -5.75\%\ \text{Annualized Yield}
\end{array}
$$

8. *Basis Value*

Basis Change $\times$ 31.25 $\times$ Par Units = Basis Value
118.05261 $\times$ 31.25 $\times$ 100   = 368,914

9. Basis Value = Capital Loss
   368,914   = 370,144 (variation: 0.33%)

Net Hedging Results at Other Interest Rates

        0 Cash Result
− 370,144 Futures Loss
− 413,699 Interest Expense (at 10%)
+ 421,973 Interest Income
− 361,870 Net Hedging Result

        0 Cash Result
− 370,144 Futures Loss
− 206,849 Interest Expense (at 5%)
+ 421,973 Interest Income
− 155,020 Net Hedging Result

The banker collects interest at the coupon rate of 10.2%, so the gain there is $421,973.

10,000,000	Par Value
x .102	Coupon Rate
1,020,000	Return
÷ 365	Days
2,794.5205	Daily Yield
x 151	Days in Hedge
421,973	Interest Income

The sum of the cash result, futures loss, interest expense, and interest income is a negative $204,479.

0	Cash Result
-370,144	Futures Loss
-289,589	Interest Expense
+421,973	Interest Income
-237,760	Net Hedging Result

It might be tempting to believe that in certain business contexts this strategy could work after all. The short-term lending rate varies, depending upon the credit-worthiness of the mortgage bank. Banks with low short-term rates might think this a good strategy.

The short-term rate may range between 5% and 10%, but a little more arithmetic shows that this strategy is a loser in any case.

With the short-term rate at 10%, and all else the same, the hedger will have a substantial loss: $361,870.

0	Cash Result
-370,144	Futures Loss
-413,699	Interest Expense (at 10%)
+421,973	Interest Income
-361,870	Net Hedging Result

With the short-term rate at 5%, all else the same, the loss will be smaller, but no less a loss: $155,020.

0	Cash Result
-370,144	Futures Loss
-206,849	Interest Expense (at 5%)
+421,973	Interest Income
-155,020	Net Hedging Result

These numbers demonstrate, if it is not otherwise intuitively obvious, that the problem with this strategy is not the bankers' cost of money. Rather, the futures loss is insurmountable no matter how favorable the short-term funding market. Since even a small mortgage banker sees loan numbers like these, this is clearly not the strategy to use.

Why It Works

It should be no secret by now why this mortgage hedge produces disappointing results. In mortgage hedging, as with other financials, the basis typically works against a position long the basis (buy cash, sell futures). Expanding the analysis of Figure 14-2 to show the basis change during the term of this hedge illustrates exactly what happened. Mortgage hedgers calculate the basis just as they would for bonds. Substituting in the formula shows that the basis going into this strategy is -653 while the ending basis is -771.

Cash	–	(Futures x Cf)	=	Basis (in 32nds)		
100	–	(96.5625 x 1.2468)	=	-20.394125 (x 32)	=	-653
100	–	(99.52139 x 1.2468)	=	-24.083269 (x 32)	=	-771

These negative basis numbers require comment. In a normal yield environment, Treasury bonds cannot maintain a basis below zero. Arbitragers see an opportunity for riskless profits when that happens and immediately force it back up. But mortgages are a different story. The market views them as lower quality, and lower quality means lower basis. Also, as a nondeliverable product, mortgages are not susceptible to arbitrage. As a result, they can maintain negative basis values.

The real issue, here as elsewhere, is basis change. The negative basis numbers are of no importance—merely a quirk of the mortgage instrument. This kind of widening (or negative change) operates just as it would in the case of a bond where the numbers are all positive.

Figure 14-3, which summarizes all of that, thus shows a basis change of -132. That simply says that, during the time this strategy was in place, the basis widened a great deal.

Figure 14-3

CASH	FUTURES	BASIS
July 2, 1986		
buy	sell	
write 10.2% 30-year	Dec 86 T-bond @96-18	-653
mortgages, yield 10.2%	Cf: 1.2468	
Par Value: $10,000,000	HR: 1.2468	
Cash Value: $10,000,000	No. of Contracts: 124.68	
December 1, 1986		
sell	buy	
mortgages into secondary	Dec 86 T-bond @99-17	-771
market, yield 10.2%		
Par Value: $10,000,000		
Cash Value: $10,000,000		
July 2 to December 1: 151 days		

That returns the discussion to the essential hedging consideration—the storage question. The "classical hedge" (buy cash, sell futures, later unwind) was originally invented to protect physical inventories. When an elevator owner accumulates cash grain, he protects himself by selling futures—the classical hedging situation.

No grain trader would hedge this way if the market was issuing a "don't store" signal, though. But, anticipating a narrowing basis, this is the strategy to use, since that is one of the strong "store" signals. Anticipating a widening basis, never. Going long a widening basis tends to be expensive.

Since financial basis normally widens, basis traders would find the unfortunate result of the "common sense" mortgage hedge entirely predictable. It is not a function of chance, something that would be different had the banker acted a few days, or even weeks or months, sooner or later. Rather, it follows from very general—therefore, foreseeable—market phenomena.

Mortgage hedgers need to keep in mind that mortgage points are not subject to basis change. For that very reason, points can play an important role in a mortgage hedger's strategy. He can select either high coupon and low points or low coupon and high points without yield effect.

What that means is that a mortgage hedger can minimize adverse basis change. In the typical case, the basis works against the long basis position. If a mortgage hedger has to be long the basis for some reason, he can charge higher points and set lower rates. The yield effect over the life of the loan will be the same as if he charged lower points and set a higher rate. The advantage is that the low rate means there will be less basis loss.

Mortgage hedgers might keep this in mind for another reason. If rates change, the nature of the mortgage basis (mortgage basis is typically negative) causes a typical mortgage to manifest the effect far more markedly than the cheapest to deliver T-bond. Because of that, mortgage hedgers might wish to lean toward a high point-low rate mix as a general rule. That way, they would always be less subject to adverse basis change. Yet their yield situation would be the same as if they had used a different mix.

15

A Classical
Mortgage Hedge
for Short-Term
Protection

A position long the basis normally will not pay off for a mortgage banker. However, like other risk managers, mortgage bankers must not become prisoners of general rules. Situations occur from time to time that mandate exceptions. Alert risk managers recognize those situations and have strategies ready to take advantage of them.

The classical risk situation for mortgage bankers involves the new loan pipeline—the completed loans which have yet to be packaged and sold into the secondary market. Those loans, like any uninvested funds, are subject to interest rate variation.

Mortgage bankers know that, in general, a position long the basis will not protect their pipeline but positions short the basis will. Yet they also know that sometimes the so-called classical mortgage hedge will do the job if the exposure period will be very short. In the middle of a government refunding, the basis will be abnormally wide. When the market issues a "store" signal like that, bankers know the classical hedge, long the basis, is the right strategy. Yet they also know that sometimes the so-called "classical mortgage hedge" will do the job if the exposure period will be very short. When the market issues a "store" signal like that, bankers know the classical hedge, long the basis is the right strategy. In the middle of a government refunding, the basis will be abnormally wide.

On a given day, the mortgage banker writes a series of loans, which is equivalent to buying a cash bond. To offset the cash risk, he sells bond futures. When he delivers the pipeline into the secondary market, he is selling cash. So he also buys futures. Figure 15-1 summarizes that trade sequence.

Figure 15-1

CASH	FUTURES
write mortgages	sell futures
sell into seconary market	buy futures

If the banker correctly gauges the market situation, that strategy will protect his pipeline from rate volatility.

How it Works

Assume that on April 1, 1987, a mortgage banker writes $10 million worth of 10% 30-year mortgages (maturity, April 1, 2017). They are valued at 112.84%, or $11,284,000. The secondary market yield at that point is 8.78%. To hold himself price neutral, he sells June T-bond futures at 98-00 (Cf, 1.2262). He will need 122.62 futures contracts to balance his mortgage position.

Four days later, on April 5, 1987, he sells his mortgages and buys futures to complete the transaction. Figure 15-2 summarizes this mortgage hedging transaction.

Given the stable yield assumption, the cash side does not change. Had there been a change, the banker had protection in place.

Figure 15-2

CASH	FUTURES
April 1, 1987	
buy	sell
write 10% 30-year mortgages	Jun 87 T-bond @98-00
@112.84, discounted to yield 8.78%	Cf: 1.2262
Par Value: $10,000,000	HR: 1.2262
Cash Value: $11,284,000	No. of Contracts: 122.62
April 5, 1987	
sell	buy
sell mortgages into secondary	Jun 87 T-bond @95-30
market @112.84, 8.78% yield	
Par Value: $10,000,000	
Cash Value: $11,284,000	
April 1 to April 5: 4 days	

On the futures side, that protection produced a $252,904 gain because, happily, this mortgage banker understood the fundamental market features that could affect his hedge. The futures side shows a 2-02 change. Since this hedger started with a "sell" and finished with a "buy," that constitutes a gain. To derive its value, convert 2-02 into 66/32nds. Each 32nd has a cash value of $31.25. And this hedger traded 122.62 contracts, so his futures gain was $284,625.

Futures Change x 31.25 x Contracts = Futures Result
   (in 32nds)
    66   x 31.25 x 122.62   =   252,904

In a "storage" situation like this, the hedger will have both interest expense and interest income. The expense is his cost of funding the mortgages he is holding. If his cost of funds is 7%, the interest expense will be $8,656 for this four-day period.

11,284,000	Mortgage Cash Value
x .07	Short-Term Rate
789,880	Annual Interest Expense
÷ 365	Days
2,164.0548	Daily Interest Expense
x 4	Days in Hedge
8,656	Interest Expense

A CLASSICAL MORTGAGE HEDGE FOR SHORT-TERM PROTECTION

Strategy 13

A. The Problem

To protect a mortgage pipeline from rate variation, bankers can sometimes use a long basis strategy (buy cash, sell futures). In a normal yield environment, the basis ordinarily works against that position. However, from time to time a situation arises which causes an incentive for storage — an oversupply of mortgages, for example. If the period of exposure is very short, the banker who is ready can benefit with the long basis strategy.

B. Preliminaries

1. *The Basis*

   Cash   − (Futures × Cf)   = Basis
   a. 112.84 − (98 × 1.2262)   = −7.3276 (× 32)   = −234.4832
   b. 112.84 − (95.9375 × 1.2262) = −4.7985625 (× 32) = −153.554

2. *Futures Position Size*

$$\frac{11,284,000}{1000 \times 112.84} \times 1.2262 = 122.62$$

C. The Strategy

CASH	FUTURES	BASIS
April 1, 1987		
buy	sell	
write 10% 30 year mortgages @112.84, discounted to yield 8.78%	Jun 87 T-bond @98-00	−234
	Cf: 1.2262	
	HR: 1.2262	
Par Value: $10,000,000	No. of Contracts: 122.62	
Cash Value: $11,284,000		
April 5, 1987		
sell	buy	
sell mortgages into secondary market @112.84, 8.78% yield	Jun 87 T-bond @95-30	−271
Par Value: $10,000,000		
Cash Value: $11,284,000		
April 1 to April 5: 4 days		

D. Results and Evaluation

1. *Cash Result*

   Cash Sale   − Cash Purchase = Cash Result
   11,284,000 − 11,284,000   = 0

2. *Futures Result* (gain)

Futures Change × 31.25 × Contracts = Futures Result
(in 32nds)
     66   × 31.25 × 122.62   = 252,904

3. *Capital Gain*

0	Cash Gain
252,904	Futures Gain
252,904	Capital Gain

4. *Interest Expense*

11,284,000	Mortgage Cash Value
× .07	Short-Term Rate
789,880	Annual Interest Expense
÷ 365	Days
2,164.0548	Daily Interest Expense
× 4	Days in Hedge
8,656	Interest Expense

5. *Interest Income*

10,000,000	Mortgage Par Value
× .10	Coupon Rate
1,000,000	Annual Coupon Payment
÷ 365	Days
2,739.726	Daily Coupon Income
× 4	Days in Hedge
10,959	Interest Income

6. *Net Hedging Result*

+ 252,904	Capital Gain
− 8,656	Interest Expense
+ 10,959	Interest Income
+ 255,207	Net Hedging Result

7. *Annualized Yield* (not applicable)*

8. *Basis Value*

Basis Change × 31.25 × Par Units = Basis Value
80.9292   × 31.25 × 100   = 252,904

9. Basis Value = Capital Gain
252,904   = 252,904

* Annualized Yield is not meaningful in a case like this. This strategy
works because of a short-term basis narrowing. Held in place longer,
it would produce a loss because the basis would widen, given a
normal yield environment, and penalize a long basis position.

The interest income derives from the interest the mortgage holders pay to the bank. Remember, all such coupon payments pay the stated percentage of par, in this case $10,000,000.

10,000,000	Mortgage Par Value
x .10	Coupon Rate
1,000,000	Annual Coupon Payment
÷ 365	Days
2,739.726	Daily Coupon Income
x 4	Days in Hedge
10,959	Interest Income

Finally, the net result of the hedge is the sum of the cash result, the futures gain, the interest expense, and the interest income.

0	Cash Result
+252,904	Futures Gain
-8,656	Interest Expense
+ 10,959	Interest Income
+255,207	Net Hedging Result

Two important points. That $255,207 is not all profit. Transaction costs will take some of it. The interest figures are not really due to the hedging strategy. An unhedged banker would pay for financing and collect coupon payments. The slight interest gain (roughly $2,300) projects to less than 2% annualized return. The real gain in this strategy is from the hedge itself. Also, the goal of this strategy is not to make extra profits, but to protect against value erosion. The fact that the portfolio came through the four days unscathed is the primary recommendation for this strategy.

Why it Works

The general rule says the best way to protect a mortgage portfolio is with a short basis strategy (as Chapter 9 illustrates). That follows from the fact that mortgage basis, like bond basis, characteristically widens. It becomes less positive, more negative. That kind of basis change issues a "don't store" signal. The short basis strategy (where the hedger sells cash at the outset) is the classic non-storage action.

In contrast, a classical hedge is a storage tactic. The hedger goes long the basis—buys cash, sells futures. That is to store the cash commodity—whether it be corn or soybeans, bonds or mortgages. That is why, generally, a widening basis wreaks havoc with the long basis classical hedge.

In general, but not always. Risk managers who chart the basis know that from time to time the basis hits a plateau or even narrows for a short time, say, during a refunding. Alert risk managers have strategies ready so they can quickly shift gears and capitalize on the situation. The idealized basis chart in Figure 15-3 illustrates the possibilities.

From point A to point B, the basis widens 225 points (from -15 to -240). Point B locates the refunding. Finally, between points C and D, the basis narrows from -235 to -154. Both are negative numbers, but that should not obscure the fact that the basis moves 81/32nds more positive. That is the opportunity that this banker anticipated, and took advantage of with his long basis strategy.

Figure 15-4 adds that basis information to the strategy outlined earlier.

Figure 15-4

CASH	FUTURES	BASIS
April 1, 1987		
buy		
write 10% 30-year mortgages		
@112.84, discounted to yield 8.78%		
Par Value: $10,000,000	sell	
Cash Value: $11,284,000	Jun 87 T-bond @98-00	-234
	Cf: 1.2262	
April 5, 1987	HR: 1.2262	
sell	No. of Contracts: 122.62	
sell mortgages into secondary		
market @112.84, 8.78% yield		
Par Value: $10,000,000	buy	
Cash Value: $11,284,000	Jun 87 T-bond @95-30	-154
April 1 to April 5: 4 days		

Figure 15-3 Mortgage Basis

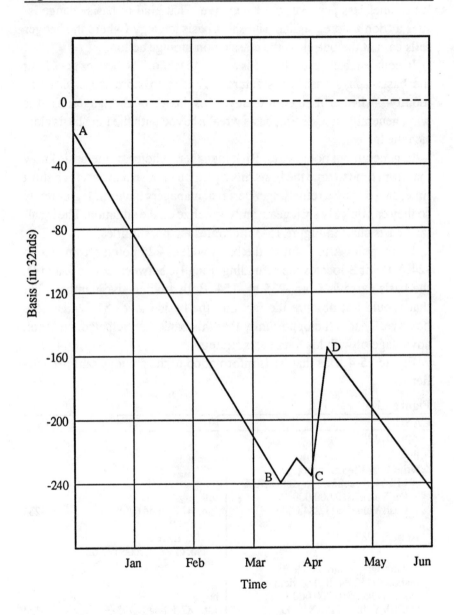

The basis change tells the story here. Hedgers can evaluate their strategies by comparing the basis change with the cash and futures results, for the cash value of the basis change should equal the sum of the cash and futures results. To derive the value of the basis change, financial hedgers find the product of the basis change (in 32nds) times 31.25 times the number of $100,000 par units on the cash side.

$$\text{Basis Change} \times 31.25 \times \text{Par Units} = \text{Basis Value}$$

$$80.9292 \times 31.25 \times 100 = 252{,}904$$

(After rounding, the basis change is 81. Actually, the April 1 basis is 234.4832, the April 5 basis is 153.554, so the change is 80.9292. For illustrative purposes, the extra precision is useful. Hedgers can excuse small variations as the result of rounding.)

That $252,904 exactly matches the futures gain (the cash result was zero, remember). What that says is that the gains are the result of the basis change.

The usual basis trend works against this strategy. More importantly, in a normal market situation, the basis can easily fluctuate 50 to 60 points in a day. Yet situations like this do crop up from time to time.

The negative basis value, impossible in the case of bonds in a normal yield market, is common with mortgages. It results from the fact that mortgages are undeliverable, and it signals the market's perception that mortgages are lower in quality.

When risk managers understand the basis, and keep the kind of records that allow them to harness its energy, their efforts can be especially rewarding.

16

A Banker's Forward Loan Commitment

W hen interest rates are unstable, companies embarking on major capital projects often find planning difficult. Rising interest rates threaten to drive the cost of financing beyond feasibility. Some banks, well aware of the problem, offer a solution in the form of a fixed lending rate.

Imagine that a manufacturing company, USA General Inc., is planning to build a new plant. The project will not require drawing on the funding for about a year and a half. The treasurer of USA General realizes full well what rising interest rates in the interim could mean to the company's feasibility estimates.

With that in mind, the treasurer negotiates with the company's bank to fix a loan rate now for a loan which the two sides will execute a year and a half from now. The bank agrees, specifically, that in 18 months it will loan USA General $100 million with a 30-year amortization at 12%.

The bank's current cost of funds at this maturity is 10.5%. It wants to preserve at least a one percent loan margin. If the loan were being issued right away, that would be no problem. The margin would be 1.5%.

However, the bank faces the very possibility that drove the USA General treasurer to seek out this arrangement in the first place. The possibility of an increasing cost of funds threatens the loan margin. To protect against that eventuality, the bank hedges its loan commitment.

On the cash side of this kind of strategy, the bank does nothing until it disburses the loan funds to USA General. It does make the loan commitment, but the first exchange of funds takes place upon the execution of the loan eighteen months later. It is good risk management procedure to plan strategy in terms of equivalent long and short cash bond actions, as though there were actual cash purchases and sales.

Making a loan commitment is like buying a cash bond. The bank balances that position by selling T-bond futures. When USA General executes the loan, 18 months later, the bank matches the principal amount to deposits, an accounting action equivalent to selling cash bonds, and offsets with a T-bond futures purchase. This is the short of it and the long of it, as Figure 16-1 shows.

Figure 16-1

CASH	FUTURES
buy cash	sell T-bond futures
the bank makes $100,000,000 loan commitment @ 12%, 30 year amortization, to be made on March 1, 1989 Par Value: $100,000,000	
sell cash	buy T-bond futures
USA Gen executes loan and draws funding (bank matches the loan sum to deposits) Par Value: $100,000,000	

This strategy resembles the classical hedge where the hedger establishes a position long the basis (buys cash, sells futures). Typically, because of the characteristic widening of the basis in financials, less alert risk managers think of the long basis strategy only as something to avoid, utterly failing to recognize that often there is some soul of goodness in things evil.

The bank knows that the basis will work against its position to produce a futures loss, but the loss will be for a known amount. In effect, the bank welcomes the known loss to eliminate otherwise unavoidable uncertainty. Uncertainty banished, it can structure its loan agreement to create a secure position.

How it Works

Assume, to review, that on May 15, 1987, the bank agrees to lend USA General $100 million at 12.5% amortized over 30 years, a move equivalent to buying a 12.5% November 2019 bond. The company will execute the loan on January 15, 1989. Assume also a 12.5% yield rate. To protect the cash agreement, the bank buys 1507.4 contracts of December 88 T-bond futures at 88-24.

When USA General executes the loan and draws its funding, the bank will unwind by selling cash, in effect, and buying futures, now at 93-27. Figure 16-2 summarizes the details.

Figure 16-2

CASH	FUTURES
May 15, 1987	
buy	sell

the bank makes $100,000,000 loan commitment, 12.5% 30-year amortization, to be made on December 1, 1988 @100, 12.5%yield
  Par Value: $100,000,000
  Cash Value: $100,000,000
	Dec 88 T-bond @88-24
	  Cf: 1.5074
	  HR: 1.5074
	  No. of Contracts: 1507.4

November 15, 1988	
sell USA Gen executes loan and draws funding (bank matches the loan sum to deposits) Par Value: $100,000,000	buy Dec 88 T-bond @93-27
May 15, 1987 to November 15, 1988: 18 months	

A BANKER'S FORWARD LOAN COMMITMENT

Strategy 14

A. The Problem

To maintain a profitable rate spread when making a loan commitment for "future delivery," a bank can use a T-bond futures position to offset rate increases. The bank knows the basis will work against its long basis position (buy cash, sell futures) — to a known degree — and charges a loan commitment fee (like points) to compensate for the basis effect. That fee amounts to a premium the customer pays to ensure the loan rate in advance.

B. Preliminaries

1. *The Basis*

   Cash $-$ (Futures $\times$ Cf) $=$ Basis
   a. $100 - (88.75 \times 1.5074) = -33.78175 \ (\times 32) = -1081.016$
   b. $100 - (93.84375 \times 1.5074) = -41.460069 \ (\times 32) = -1326.72222$

2. *Futures Position Size*

   $$\frac{100,000,000}{1000 \times 100} \times 1.5074 = 1507.4$$

C. The Strategy

CASH	FUTURES	BASIS
May 15, 1987		
buy	sell	
the bank makes $100,000,000 loan commitment, 12.5%, 30 year amortization, to be made on December 1, 1988 @100, 12.5% yield	Dec 88 T-bond @88-24 Cf: 1.5074 HR: 1.5074 No. of Contracts: 1507.4	−1081
Par Value: $100,000,000 Cash Value: $100,000,000		
November 15, 1988		
sell	buy	
USA Gen executes loan and draws funding (bank matches the loan sum to deposits)	Dec 88 T-bond @93-27	−1327
Par Value: $100,000,000		
May 15, 1987 to November 15, 1988: 18 months		

D. Results and Evaluation

1. *Cash Result*

   Cash Sale   − Cash Purchase = Cash Result
   100,000,000 − 100,000,000   = 0

2. *Futures Result* (loss)

   Futures Change × 31.25 × Contracts = Futures Result
   (in 32nds)
        163   × 31.25 × 1507.4   = − 7,678,319

3. *Capital Loss* (not applicable)

4. *Interest Expense* (not applicable)

5. *Interest Income* (not applicable)

6. *Net Hedging Result* (same as Futures Result)

7. *Annualized Yield* see table of loan commitment costs)

   $$\begin{array}{l} - \ 7,678,319 \quad \text{Net Hedging Result} \\ \div \ 100,000,000 \quad \text{Cash Value} \\ \hline - \ 0.0767832 \quad \text{Return to Hedge} \ = \ -7.67\% \end{array}$$

8. *Basis Value*

   Basis Change × 31.25 × Par Units = Basis Value
   245.7062   × 31.25 × 1000   = 7,678,319

9. Basis Value = Futures Loss
   7,678,319   = 7,678,319

LOAN COMMITMENT COSTS

Commitment Term	Commitment Cost	Yield Effect
3	1.8%	0.25%
6	3.25%	0.325%
9	4.5%	0.625%
12	5.75%	0.8%
18	7.67%	1.0%

Assuming no rate change during the commitment period, the cash side shows no gain or loss since all that really takes place is the delivery of the funds to the company and the bank's matching liability and asset maturities.

On the futures side, the bank sees a futures change of 5-03 or 163/32nds. The value of one 32nd is $31.25, and the bank traded 1507.4 contracts, so the futures result is a loss of $5093.75 a contract or $7,678,319 total.

Futures Change x 31.25 x Contracts = Futures Result
(in 32nds)
163 x 31.25 x 1507.4 = -7,678,319

That futures loss is part of the cost of doing business which the bank will pass on to the company as a commitment fee, much the same as when a mortgage lender charges points to the buyer of a house. In this case, the bank will charge a seven-and-two-thirds percent fee (7.67 points) which will exactly match the futures loss.

Depending on the situation, the bank might feel a need to mitigate the rate-fixing fee. A cash alternative may be better. It could issue some 10% term CDs for 31.5 years and reinvest that money in 6% T-bills. That would create a negative spread of 4% a year, or 6% over the 18 months, and would have the effect of reducing the futures loss by two thirds. The bank would then need to charge only a 6% fee for fixing the rate, which could make the deal somewhat easier to sell. In the end, the banker must weigh the cash alternatives against the futures alternatives in terms of basis expectations.

Why it Works

The bank can fix loan rates because, by doing so, it is dealing with known quantities. No one can predict yield rates this far in advance. Yet the banker, like any good basis trader, knows that the basis for financials will deteriorate, will move in a negative direction. He has a good general idea what futures prices will be also, even as far forward as a year and a half.

Aware of the storage function of the yield rates, basis traders know bond basis will keep the bond position yielding something less than the short-term rate. As the futures contract nears expiration, the dollar difference in interest accruals (the result of interaction between long-term and short-term yields) declines. Therefore, the basis also declines. The nearer the contract's expiration, the less money it requires to maintain the yield level. The widening basis maintains the needed storage level. Because of that, the basis works against the futures side of a long basis position. A trader who sells futures, expecting to buy them back later, will lose.

What is the result of that? Risk managers who know how the bond futures market works can accurately project what the basis will do in a given time period. Figure 16-3 shows what kind of basis picture risk managers would expect to see.

Figure 16-3

CASH	FUTURES	BASIS
May 15, 1987		
buy	sell	

the bank makes $100,000,000 loan commitment, 12.5% 30-year amortization, to be made on December 1, 1988 @ 100, 12.5% yield
    Par Value: $100,000,000
    Cash Value: $100,000,000
	Dec 88 T-bond @88-24
	   Cf: 1.5074
	   HR: 1.5074
	   No. of Contracts: 1507.4
		-1081

November 15, 1988		
sell USA Gen executes loan and draws funding (bank matches the loan sum to deposits) Par Value: $100,000,000	buy Dec 88 T-bond @93-27	-1327
May 15, 1987 to November 15, 1988: 18 months		

The basis here differs superficially from T-bond basis. Bonds will not sustain a negative basis. The negative basis values result from the same factors as the negative numbers in the mortgage strategies. This is a non-deliverable product which the market considers lower in quality than T-bonds. That matters little. What interests basis traders is not whether the numbers are negative or positive, but how the basis changes. As with T-bond basis, the basis in this situation widens in a normal yield curve market.

In this situation, the basis change accounts for the futures change. The value of the basis change is the product of the basis change times 31.25 times the number of $100,000 par cash units.

Basis Change (in 32nds)	x 31.25	x Par Units	= Basis Value
246	x 31.25	x 1000	= 7,687,500
(245.7062	x 31.25	x 1000	= 7,678,319)

The row of figures in parentheses eliminates rounding. It shows that the futures loss and the basis value are equivalent numbers. Thus the basis change accounts for this hedging result.

The rate-fixing fee may trouble some people. It need not. The bank uses the long basis strategy to lock in the loan rate. That works because cash and futures prices move in concert, except for the basis effect. The hedge allows the banker to lock in the spread he needs to make the loan profitable. He is armed against rate volatility.

The banker also knows that, given the fact that the financial basis widens in a normal yield curve market, the basis will work against his position. No guess work here, either. The basis is a predictable factor, so the banker knows what his basis loss will be. He charges a "commitment fee" in exchange for holding the loan rate open for a period of time. These "points" relate to the known basis loss. Given this 12.5% loan structure, Table 16-1 summarizes the situation for periods ranging from 3 to 18 months. This says that if the loan commitment period is 18 months, as in the example here, the banker will need to charge 7.67 points, a 7.67% commitment fee, to compensate for the basis loss. Amortized over the life of the loan, that has a 1% yield effect. The borrower will, in effect, have a 13.5% loan rather than a 12.5% one. The corporate treasurer and the banker can negotiate how to handle that. They have several choices.

Table 16-1 Loan Commitment Costs

Commitment Term	Commitment Cost	Yield Effect
3	1.8%	0.25%
6	3.25%	0.325%
9	4.5%	0.625%
12	5.75%	0.8%
18	7.67%	1.0%

Details aside, the importance of all this has to do with its predictability. Because the basis loss is a known quantity, the cost of borrowing money becomes a definable factor in the corporation's project planning. The interest rate market can do anything—and probably will during as long a period as a year and a half. No matter. The rate for this loan is locked in.

If an effective 13.5% cost of funds falls within the feasibility range the corporation has defined, they can take that price as a given and plan accordingly. Whether they opt to pay the commitment fee up front or amortize it over 31.5 years (the loan period plus the commitment term) matters little. The important thing here is that the cost of financing the factory becomes a concrete detail.

To see how the commitment period affects the fee situation, consider a case in which the same loan goes through in November of 1987 instead of in January '89. The situation would look markedly different. In fact it would not be, except for the time factor. Figure 16-4 shows the same strategy projected over a six month interval.

Strategy 15

A. The Problem

This situation is the same as strategy 14, except the shorter commitment period lowers the fee.

B. Preliminaries

1. *The Basis*

   Cash − (Futures × Cf)   = Basis
   a. 100 − (91.593755 × 1.5115) = −38.443953 (× 32) = −1230.2065
   b. 100 − (93.71875 × 1.5115) = −41.655891 (× 32) = −1332.9885

2. *Futures Position Size*

   $$\frac{100{,}000{,}000}{1000 \times 100} \times 1.5115 = 1511.5$$

C. The Strategy

CASH	FUTURES	BASIS
May 15, 1987		
buy	sell	
the bank makes $100,000,000 loan commitment, 12.5%, 30 year amortization, to be made on December 1, 1988 @100, 12.5% yield	Dec 87 T-bond @91-19 Cf: 1.5115 HR: 1.5115 No. of Contracts: 1511.5	−1230
Par Value: $100,000,000 Cash Value: $100,000,000		
November 15, 1987		
sell	buy	
USA Gen executes loan and draws funding (bank matches the loan sum to deposits)	Dec 87 T-bond @93-23	-1333
Par Value: $100,000,000		
May 15, 1987 to November 15, 1987: 16 months		

D. Results and Evaluation

1. *Cash Result*

   Cash Sale   − Cash Purchase = Cash Result

   100,000,000 − 100,000,000   = 0

2. *Futures Result* (loss)

   Futures Change × 31.25 × Contracts = Futures Result

      (in 32nds)

        68   × 31.25 × 1511.5   = −3,211,938

3. *Capital Loss* (not applicable)

4. *Interest Expense* (not applicable)

5. *Interest Income* (not applicable)

6. *Net Hedging Result* (same as Futures Result)

7. *Annualized Yield* (see table of loan commitment costs)

8. *Basis Value*

   Basis Change × 31.25 × 1000 = Basis Value

      (in 32nds)

      102.782   × 31.25 × 1000 = 3,211,938

9. Basis Value = Futures Result

   3,211,938   = 3,211,938

Figure 16-4

CASH	FUTURES	BASIS
May 15, 1987		
buy	sell	

the bank makes $100,000,000 loan commitment, 12.5% 30-year amortization, to be made on December 1, 1988 @ 100, 12.5% yield
  Par Value: $100,000,000
  Cash Value: $100,000,000
	Dec 87 T-bond @91-19
	  Cf: 1.5115
	  HR: 1.5115
	  No. of Contracts: 1151.5
		-1230

November 15, 1987		
sell USA Gen executes loan and draws funding (bank matches the loan sum to deposits) Par Value: $100,000,000	buy Dec 87 T-bond @93-23	-1333

May 15, 1987 to November 15, 1987: 6 months

The cash side is the same as before except for the different date for exercising the loan.

The futures side creates a very different picture. For one thing, December 87 futures prices would be 91-19 and 93-23 instead of 88-24 and 93-27. The different hedge ratio means that this strategy requires 5111.5 futures contracts, four more than the longer strategy. As a result, the 2-04 futures change reduces the loss to $2,125 a contract—a total of $3,211,938.

Futures Change x 31.25 x Contracts = Futures Result
  (in 32nds)
  68   x 31.25 x 1511.5   = - 3,211,938

As a result, the bank would only need to charge 3.25 points. Again, the basis accounts for the entire change.

Basis Change x 31.25 x 1000 = Basis Value
  (in 32nds)
  102.782   x 31.25 x 1000 = 3,211,938

Clearly, the predictable basis change again accounts for the loss that this hedge incurs.

Notice that the time interval is six months instead of 18. People focus on price and yield. Seldom do they mention, or even notice, maturity or other time factors. Though not actually a maturity issue, this shows just how important the time factor is in this kind of strategy. In changing interest rate markets, a year and a half is a long time to hold a deal. Looked at that way, 7.67 points seems reasonable.

Nor is the futures pricing any mystery to a basis trader, in either the 18 month or the six month case. As a rule of thumb, the deferred futures months range down at the rate of one handle, or one percentage point, each futures month. Figure 16-5 shows a typical spread.

Figure 16-5

Jun87	_Sep_	_Dec_	_Mar88_	_Jun_
89-00	88-00	87-00	86-00	85-00

The actual size of the spreads follows from the implied repo rate which the short-term rate dictates. Brokers, and even newspapers, are able to provide T-bond futures quotes as far forward as two or two and a half years. Eighteen months is no problem.

The predictable nature of these markets enables hedgers to anticipate. Being able to anticipate outcomes makes planning possible. For that reason, bankers and corporate officers can use hedging strategies to make forward loan commitments with assurance.

17

How a Company Can Fix Its Own Rate

When contemplating a plant expansion, or any similar major capital project, a corporation may opt to finance the project itself. It might also decide to create its own rate-protection plan. To finance the project, it would simply issue a corporate bond. While the corporation has to pay a coupon rate to the investors, that just replaces the interest it would pay the bank. There may be some advantage for the company, depending on the bond market. At the very least, it avoids paying the "middleman" costs to the bank. Issuing a bond has much to recommend it.

An alert financial officer will realize that the corporation has now assumed the interest rate risk a bank has to deal with when it fixes a rate. Between the moment the corporation suggests the project to itself and the time it is actually ready to build, the interest rate picture can change and change again. If rates decline by the time the company is ready to issue its bond, so much the better. If rates increase, disaster. Invariably, if the rate passes a certain level, it drives the entire project past the point of feasibility. As a matter of fact, the corporation can design its own strategy for fixing its borrowing rate whether it finances the project through a bank or through its own bond issue.

Almost worse than the possibility of an unfavorable turn of events is the uncertainty. Planning then becomes difficult at best.

A financial officer can protect against those adversities by making use of the futures markets. In essence, he creates a synthetic loan commitment. His strategy will accomplish exactly what the bank's rate fixing agreement did. It is synthetic because no bank is involved. The corporation is fixing the rate and financing the project on its own.

In using a futures strategy, the corporation gives up the possible advantage of falling rates in exchange for protection against the disastrous situation that rising rates would bring about. Once the corporate planners define a feasible cost of financing the project, the hedge that the risk manager designs succeeds as long as it brings in the project at that cost.

Naturally enough, the company will not need the money until all the planning is done and it is ready to begin work on the project. At that point, the treasurer will issue the bond to raise the cash. However, even as the various planning groups get started with their work, the treasurer enters the futures market in anticipation of the day he sells the bond. He sells enough U.S. Treasury bond futures to cover the size of his bond issue. He plans to buy them back when he actually issues his bonds. Figure 17-1 summarizes his trading sequence.

Figure 17-1

CASH	FUTURES
	sells T-bond futures
sells corporate bonds to fund expansion project	buys T-bond futures

The danger the treasurer wants to protect against, as before, is that too high a rate change might make the plant uneconomical to build. This strategy guards against that.

How it Works

Assume that the corporation projects a June 1988 startup for the new plant construction project. In keeping with that timetable, the treasurer plans to put his rate-fixing strategy in place on May 15, 1987 and to unwind it on May 15, 1988 when he will issue his corporate bonds.

He plans to issue a 12.5% January 2019 bond, par value $100 million. Assuming a 12.5% yield to maturity, and assuming no yield change during the term of the hedge, the cash price of the bond will remain unchanged. To fix the "loan rate," he sells 1509.5 June 88 T-bond contracts at 90-00.

When he unwinds on May 15, 1988, he will sell the cash bond to fund the project and buy June 88 futures at 93-25. Figure 17-2 outlines the details of this strategy.

Figure 17-2

CASH	FUTURES
May 15, 1987	
buy	sell
make 12.5% 30-year (Jan	Jun 87 T-bond @90-00
2019) synthetic loan commitment	Cf: 1.5095
@100, 12.5% yield	HR: 1.5095
Par Value: $100,000,000	No. of Contracts: 1509.5
Cash Value: $100,000,000	
May 15, 1988	
sell	buy
12.5% 30-year (January 2019)	Jun 87 T-bond @93-25
corporate bond	
@100, 12.5% yield	
Par Value: $100,000,000	
Cash Value: $100,000,000	

May 15, 1987 to May 15, 1988: 12 months

Because of the unchanging yield assumption, the cash side remains unchanged.

The risk manager sold futures low and bought high. The 3-25 change represents a loss.

How A Company Can Fix Its Own Rate

Strategy 16

A. The Problem

To defend against adverse rate changes, a corporation can create a "synthetic loan agreement." Whether planning to issue a corporate bond or to borrow, the agreement establishes a long basis position (buy cash, sell futures). The futures will offset any adverse rate change. While the basis works against this position, it does so to a known degree — a premium the company willingly pays in exchange for a definable planning situation.

B. Preliminaries

1. *The Basis*

Cash $-$ (Futures $\times$ Cf) $=$ Basis
a. $100 - (90 \times 1.5095)$ $= -35.855 \ (\times \ 32)$ $= -1147.36$
b. $100 - (93.78403 \times 1.5095) = -41.56699 \ (\times \ 32) = -1330.1438$

Deriving End Point Futures Price

(based on the 12.5% August 2009-14 T-bond as cheapest to deliver)

Cash $-$ (Futures $\times$ Cf) $=$ Basis
$136.268202 - ($Futures $\times 1.4530) = 0$

$$\text{Futures} = \frac{136.268202}{1.4530} = 93.78403$$

2. *Futures Position Size*

$$\frac{100,000,000}{1000 \times 100} \times 1.5095 = 1509.5$$

C. The Strategy

CASH	FUTURES	BASIS
May 15, 1987		
buy	sell	
make 12.5% 30 year (Jan 2019)	Jun 87 T-bond @90-00	-1147
synthetic loan commitment	Cf: 1.5095	
	HR: 1.5095	
@100, 12.5% yield	No. of Contracts: 1509.5	
Par Value: $100,000,000		
Cash Value: $100,000,000		
May 15, 1988		
sell	buy	
12.5% 30 year (January 2019)	Jun 87 T-bond @93-25	-1330
corporate bond		
@100, 12.5% yield		
Par Value: $100,000,000		
Cash Value: $100,000,000		
May 15, 1987 to May 15, 1988: 12 months		

D. Results and Evaluation

1. *Cash Result*

   Cash Sale   − Cash Purchase = Cash Result
   100,000,000 − 100,000,000   = 0

2. *Futures Result*

   Futures Change × 31.25 × Contracts = Futures Result
      (in 32nds)
         121   × 31.25 × 1509.5   = −5,707,797

3. *Capital Loss* (not applicable)

4. *Interest Expense* (not applicable)

5. *Interest Income* (not applicable)

6. *Net Hedging Result* (same as Futures Result)

7. *Annualized Yield* (see table of loan commitment costs)

8. *Basis Value*

   Basis Change × 31.25 × Par Units = Basis Value
   182.6495   × 31.25 × 1000   = 5,707,797

9. Basis Value = Futures Result
   5,707,797   = 5,707,797

$$\text{Futures Change} \times 31.25 \times \text{Contracts} = \text{Futures Result}$$
$$\text{(in 32nds)}$$
$$121 \qquad\qquad \times 31.25 \times 1509.5 \qquad = -5{,}707{,}797$$

That loss is entirely predictable. Financial hedgers know that this kind of strategy will suffer a loss. They also know the magnitude of the loss. If a bank were fixing the rate, it would charge a 5.75% commitment fee to hold the rate for 12 months. Amortized over the life of the bond issue, that has a 0.8% yield effect. The corporation has several options concerning how to handle that cost. Ultimately, the crucial fact is that the loss is a known, manageable quantity. Gone is the undefined fear of what the rates will do in the next year.

Why it Works

To see why business people can define the cost of financing this far in advance, review what the financial officer can and cannot know as he contemplates that strategy.

He cannot possibly know what interest rates will do. The track record of economists and other seers of the business world suggests how full of briars is this working-day world.

He does know that the basis will widen. He also knows his initial cash and futures prices and how long the hedge will be in place. He can define or derive the rest of the information.

For simplicity of exposition, the yield holds constant in this example which, in turn, holds cash constant.

Next, it is possible to predict which Treasury bond will be cheapest to deliver. Even though there is no T-bond position in play in this strategy, this is important for deriving futures prices and basis data that does come into play here.

Most important, the basis of the cheapest to deliver T-bond will converge to zero. Say the cheapest to deliver bond is the 12.5% August 2009-14. On May 15, 1988, the basis for that bond relative to the June 88 T-bond futures will be zero. That is a given. Also, the Cf for that bond, and that futures contract, is 1.4530.

The May 15, 1988, price is a predictable function of the change in time to maturity. It will be 136.268202. Since the basis at that time will be zero, the bond basis formula allows the risk manager to derive the May 15, 1988 price for June 88 futures. It will be 93.782848, or 93-25.

$$
\begin{array}{rcl}
\text{Cash} & - & \text{(Futures x Cf)} & = & \text{Basis} \\
136.268202 & - & \text{(Futures x 1.4530)} & = & 0 \\
\\
\text{Futures} & = & \dfrac{136.268202}{1.4530} & = & 93.782848
\end{array}
$$

The cash prices of the synthetic loan agreement and the initial futures price are known. Along with this derived futures price, the risk manager can derive the basis numbers for the end points of the agreement.

$$
\begin{array}{rcll}
100 & - & (90 \times 1.5095) & = & -1147 \\
100 & - & (93.782848 \times 1.5095) & = & -1330
\end{array}
$$

As a result, the risk manager knows he can expect a 183/32nds widening of the basis. Notice also that the value of that basis change is equivalent to the futures result derived earlier.

$$
\begin{array}{lcccccl}
\text{Basis Change} & \times & 31.25 & \times & \text{Par Units} & = & \text{Basis Value} \\
\text{(in 32nds)} & & & & & & \\
183 & \times & 31.25 & \times & 1000 & = & 5{,}718{,}750 \\
182.6495 & \times & 31.25 & \times & 1000 & = & 5{,}707{,}797
\end{array}
$$

Par Units indicates the number of $100,000 units of the par value. The parenthesized string of numbers involves an unrounded basis change value and show an exact match with the futures result figure.

Since the futures result is entirely a basis effect, as is shown, and the basis is predictable, the risk manager can know what the result of his hedge will be from the planning stage. None of that is magic. It only requires working with the givens of the situation to predict the future outcome. That, in turn, allows the risk manager to decide whether it falls within acceptable limits. If it does, the project is doable.

This kind of hedging situation requires some redefinition of what constitutes success in risk management. The common view holds that the goal of hedging in fixing parameters. People who hold that view think that only when a price is fixed is a position hedged. More useful is the view that a risk manager should be willing to use any tools available. He defines a risk and then figures out how to offset that risk in the most effective way. "Matching off" risk is the primary goal, of course. But the possibility of enhanced returns is also important.

This rate fixing strategy suggests yet another kind of hedging goal. It may be worth it to a risk manager to pay a predetermined premium if, in exchange, he can create a defined situation.

No doubt, it would be nice if every risk management strategy produced returns well above even long-term rates. That can happen. But it is really more a speculator's dream than a risk manager's expectation.

A risk management strategy succeeds when it *helps him to achieve his business goals*.

Take this case. The main threat to the corporation planning a major capital expenditure is the unknown. The financial people believe that if the cost of financing the project stays within certain limits, the project is feasible. Perhaps the interest rate on May 10, 1987, is about 11%, and the feasibility threshold is 14%. Given that, the business goal is to keep the financing cost under 14%.

If a risk manager just trusted the cash market, the rates might go anywhere in the next year and a half. They could go as low as 9%, as high as 16%. Pleasant as 9% would be, that kind of uncertainty is untenable. So the risk manager opts for a workable certainty.

In this case, the basis clearly works against the corporation's position. Oddly enough, that is all right.

The corporate treasurer, in planning his strategy, is well aware that the futures market will work against him. But to a *known degree*. This strategy will contain the rate somewhere in the area of 13.5% (given the yield rate plus the "commitment cost"). That makes planning possible.

The basis is a predictable economic force, even when it works against a hedger. When it comes to *managing* risk, that is an important gain. It allows a risk manager to achieve his business goals. Ultimately, that, and not how he did in the markets, defines his risk management success.

VI

A Basis Trading Practicum

Complex Basis Strategies

B esides designing hedging strategies appropriate to various business situations—protecting mortgage pipelines, enhancing portfolio yields, or fixing loan rates—risk managers often confront complex situations having to do with the issue of bond quality, the problem of carry, or the exigencies of the foreign currency markets.

When traders incorporate those considerations into their thinking, they can often refine their hedge placements, make use of financial instruments like reverse repos, or design foreign currency swaps.

These discussions only touch the surface. Yet they do suggest the range of possibilites—the kinds of things risk managers need to be aware of.

An important thing to keep in mind is no matter how exotic an approach seems, these are still basis plays. The storage incentives operate just as they do in the simpler cases. At bottom, the more things change, the more they stay the same.

The foreign currency situation does bring up one interesting ramification. In certain situations, futures are not the right answer. Instead of a cash-futures hedge, cash forwards produce better results. Yet traders decide that question in terms of the basis situation. If the kind of basis change the futures hedge creates is advantageous, then futures are the answer. If not, then cash forwards are at least an alternative to explore.

18

The Role of Bond Quality

B asis traders face a tough question concerning which cash bond to use, the so-called quality issue which is important not to over-simplify. Some traders regard all U.S. Treasury issues to be equal in quality because they assume them to have zero default risk. Given a scale of instruments with "junk bonds" at one extreme, treasuries at the other, and the various mortgage, corporate and municipal instruments ranged in between, that makes sense, in a way.

However, even Treasury bonds vary in quality, and bond quality is a complex issue—depending on factors like yield, which can change, and coupon and maturity which, though fixed, differ for each bond. As a result, bond quality is not fixed but flexible.

Bond Quality Can Change

With physicals, quality is obvious. Traders distinguish different grades of oil, corn, or lumber. To pay a premium for higher quality, or get a discount for lower, seems normal enough.

Premium and discount bond prices reflect traders' thoughts about bond quality in roughly the same way. However, a tank full of #1 oil remains #1 oil start to finish. Users may be willing to pay more for

213

premium grade in January than they are in July, but that does not reflect a quality change.

Not so with bonds. Changing economic conditions alter bond quality itself, not just traders' willingness to pay. If yields plummet, a long maturity bond may lock risk managers into a situation that is no longer advantageous. It is not that they are just unwilling to pay a premium for the long maturity bond. The actual bond quality changes. If yields promise to fall steadily, the long maturity bond may appreciate in both desirability and quality.

Long maturity issues increase in value, or price, in declining yield markets because they initially had higher yields. Price premiums lower the yields of those bonds to current rates. On a given day, the price of the 13.25% May 2009-14 bond is 143-18, which includes a 43-18 premium. That brings the yield down to the 8.73% market level. (Remember that when coupon and yield to maturity are the same, the price of the bond is 100-00, and price and yield vary inversely. Accordingly, exacting a premium for the 13.25% bond drives the yield down.)

More importantly for hedgers, as yields fall, high coupon bonds deteriorate in value because of the "constant reinvestment assumption" which the bond pricing formula embodies. The idea is that bond holders will be able to reinvest the coupon earnings at a constant level, but of course they cannot. In a normal and declining yield market, holders of high coupon bonds suffer because they must reinvest at lower and lower rates. At low levels, the probability of a turnaround increases, making high coupons a good risk. Therefore, in a normal and declining yield market, the prices for low coupon bonds will be fairly accurate, but high coupon bonds will be overpriced. As a result, traders equate high coupon with low quality—in that kind of market. Low coupons gain in quality because there is less coupon to reinvest, which diminishes the negative impact of falling reinvestment rates.

When rates are rising, the situation reverses. Traders regard high coupon as higher quality. With rates rising, they can reinvest coupon earnings at higher and higher rates. Low coupon becomes low quality.

The market adjusts to this reinvestment assumption by demanding higher yield to maturities for the higher coupon issues in failing rate environments. It lowers their yield as rates climb—lower relative to lower coupons.

In sum, a high quality bond today may lose quality in coming days. A low quality bond may improve.

A Pseudo-Issue

To make matters more complex, some quality differences, though real, are irrelevant to the concerns of a risk manager. Take the basis—the difference between cash and futures prices. Some basis-related quality differences are important to risk managers. Others are not.

The basis is a quality factor just as much as yield, coupon, and maturity. Risk managers should distinguish between fixed basis differences and basis change. Academic discussions of the basis, especially those concerning agricultural commodities, emphasize the fixed differences.

Corn basis differs for each delivery point. The basis in Chicago may be "ten under the July" while the Beloit, Wisconsin, basis may be "fifteen under the July." That difference may reflect transportation costs. Concentration on those fixed differences can be misleading. They have no relevance for hedgers, who instead want to know what basis change reveals about storage incentives. If the radiation furor in central Europe is enough to motivate a strong movement of corn, the basis will narrow to prompt a move out of storage, but it will narrow about the same amount in Chicago and Beloit.

In like manner, the financial markets exhibit fixed basis differences. Mortgages and other loans manifest a negative basis, while Treasury bond basis is positive. That fixed difference reflects a quality judgement. The market thinks bonds are higher in quality than mortgages.

To risk managers, those differences matter little. The interesting fact is that bond basis and mortgage basis respond in the same ways to market fundamentals. A narrowing basis creates a storage incentive. A widening basis creates a disincentive. Mortgage basis, like bond basis, characteristically widens (becomes more negative) in a normal yield curve environment. To a hedger, that matters. The bond-mortgage quality difference, though real, is irrelevant.

The Risk Management Perspective

Risk managers also have to recognize that bond quality is in the eye of the beholder. Financial risk management discussions often focus on the "cheapest to deliver" bond, the one which will have the widest (most negative) basis at delivery. The basis of all bonds always converges toward zero, but the basis of only one bond achieves zero. That bond is cheapest to deliver.

In a sense, cheapest to deliver is more a cash market issue than a risk management one. Delivery in the trading of bonds has the same import as it does in the case of physical commodities. A futures contract promises that a short will deliver a specified amount of a commodity to the long—whether it is 5,000 bushels of corn or $100,000 worth of bonds. The "deliverer" has some choice with regard to quality, location, and timing. Obviously, since the corn contract specifies #2 corn (and the #2 specifications delineate what kinds of impurities and imperfections are acceptable, and in what quantity), no grain trader will deliver anything better if he can help it.

Bond delivery is much the same. Roughly three dozen T-bonds are deliverable against the futures contract. The short chooses which one to deliver, and will definitely choose the cheapest to deliver bond. Somewhat paradoxically, the lowest quality bond is the "best" for his purposes.

Quite different motivations impel a hedger's choices. He may want to use the cheapest to deliver bond. He may not. His choice comes down to whether he expects the basis to work for or against his position. If he thinks the basis change will work in his favor, the best bond is the one that will produce the most basis change. If he thinks the basis change will work against his position, the best bond is the one that will produce the least basis change. In either case, that may or may not be the cheapest to deliver bond.

Curiously, no matter which bond the hedger trades, he needs to have a sense of which bond will be cheapest to deliver. For one thing, given that he can predict which bond will be cheapest, he can predict a futures price and that allows a reasonable prediction of the market situation at the time of unwinding. For another, he can predict all other basis values in relation to the basis of the cheapest to deliver bond. For a hedger, the "best" bond is the one that produces the appropriate basis change. The hedger may not choose the cheapest to deliver, but his choice will depend on his being able to predict which bond will be cheapest—no simple decision. Because cheapest to deliver is a quality issue and bond quality can change, cheapest status can change back and forth among several bonds.

A Hedger's Bond Choice

A hedger's bond choice can alter his results dramatically. Assume, for example, that a risk manager, in the process of designing a short basis strategy (sell cash, buy futures), needs to decide between the 7.25% May 2016 bond and the 12.5% August 2009-14 issue. In a normal yield curve market he knows the short basis position will put him on the right side of the basis. Figure 18-1 outlines the essentials of that strategy.

Figure 18-1

CASH	FUTURES	BASIS
May 15, 1987		
sell	buy Sep 87 T-bond @ 89-31 Cf: _____	_____
Par Value: $10,000,000 Cash Value:_____	HR: _____ No. of Contracts: _____	
September 1, 1987		
buy	sell Sep 87 T-bond @ _____	_____
Par Value: $10,000,000 Cash Value: _____		

May 15 to Septembeer 1: 108 days

The figure includes what the hedger knows about the situation before he makes the bond choice. He knows when he wants to begin and finish, whether he wants to buy and sell, what the cash par value will be, and the initial price of the futures contract he wants to trade. Having chosen the cash bond, he will be able to fill in the rest of the blanks. So the pressing question is which bond and how to decide.

Looking only at cheapest to deliver, the hedger would see that on May 15 that was the 7.25% May 2016 bond. Yet by the projected unwinding point he can see the 12.5% August 2009-14 will be cheapest. That narrows the field, but it hardly suggests a choice.

A better line of inquiry would be to consider how much the basis will change relative to each bond. On May 15, the basis for the 7.25% bond is 63/32nds in contrast to the 12.5% August 2009-14 whose basis is 96/32nds.

$$\text{Cash} \ - \ (\text{Futures} \ \text{x} \ \text{Cf}) \quad = \quad \text{Basis}$$

$$7.25\%:\ 84.37849 \ - (89.96875 \ \text{x} \ .9159) \ = ... = 63.23558$$

$$12.5\%:\ 134.37365 \ - (89.96875 \ \text{x} \ 1.4601) = ... = 96.3289$$

The trader can predict that by September 1, the 7.25% will widen to 7/32nds, but the 12.5% will converge to zero—it will become cheapest to deliver.

$$\text{Cash} \ - \ (\text{Futures} \ \text{x} \ \text{Cf}) \quad = \quad \text{Basis}$$

$$7.25\%:\ 84.40933 - (91.9252 \ \text{x} \ .9159) \ = ... = 6.8812582$$

$$12.5\%:\ 134.21999 - (91.9252 \ \text{x} \ 1.4601) = ... = 0.0001754$$

So while the 7.25% widens 56/32nds, the 12.5% will widen 96/32nds. For a trader who knows his strategy will put him on the right side of the basis, the 12.5% is the better choice.

The 40-point difference in basis change significantly alters the hedge performance. Figures 18-2 and 18-3 summarize the strategy using first the 7.25% bond and then the 12.5%.

Figure 18-2

CASH	FUTURES	BASIS
May 15, 1987		
sell 7.25% May 2016 @84.37849, 8.66% yield 　Par Value: $10,000,000 　Cash Value: $8,437,849	buy Sep 87 T-bond @89-31 　Cf: 0.9159 　HF: 0.9159 　No. of Contracts: 91.59	63
September 1, 1987		
buy 7.25% May 2016 @84.40933, 8.66% yield 　Par Value: $10,000,000 　Cash Value: $8,440,993	sell Sep 87 T-bond @91-30	7
May 15 to September 1: 108 days		

Figure 18-3

CASH	FUTURES	BASIS
May 15, 1987		
sell 12.5% August 2009-14 @134.37365, 8.84% yield 　Par Value: $10,000,000 　Cash Value: $13,437,365	buy Sep 87 T-bond @89-31 　Cf: 1.4601 　HF: 1.4601 　No. of Contracts: 146.01	96
September 1, 1987		
buy 12.5% August 2009-14 @134.21999, 8.84% yield 　Par Value: $10,000,000 　Cash Value: $13,421,999	sell Sep 87 T-bond @91-30	0
May 15 to September 1: 108 days		

The net hedging result is positive in either case, yet the higher coupon bond produces a stronger gain. The greater basis change produces an advantage to a basis trader who is on the right side of the basis.

At times, basis traders have to take positions where the basis will work against them. In that case, the right choice is the bond that will produce the least basis change. If the same hedger were to go long the basis (buy cash, sell futures), the 7.25% would be the better choice. Essentially, all that is required is to reverse the order of the buys and

THE ROLE OF BOND QUALITY

Strategy 17

A. The Problem

Besides designing the right strategy, hedgers must also choose the right cash bond. Many people insist that the cheapest to deliver is the right choice. Hedgers must be able to predict cheapest, but often that is not the bond to use. If the hedger is on the right side of the basis, he should trade the bond that will produce the most basis change. Otherwise, he should look for the least change. In either case, that may be cheapest, but it may not.

B. Preliminaries

1. *The Basis*

   Cash   − (Futures × Cf)   = Basis

   7.25% May 2016 issue

   a. $84.37849 - (89.96875 \times .9159) = 1.9761119 \, (\times 32) = 63.23558$
   b. $84.40933 - (91.9252 \times .9159) = 0.2150393 \, (\times 32) = 6.8812582$

   12.5% August 2009-14 issue

   a. $134.37365 - (89.96875 \times 1.4601) = 3.0102781 = 96.3289$
   b. $134.21999 - (91.9252 \times 1.4601) = 0.0000055 = 0.0001754$

2. *Futures Position Size*

   7.25%

   $$\frac{8,437,849}{1000 \times 84.37849} \times .9159 = 91.59$$

   12.5%

   $$\frac{13,437,365}{1000 \times 134,37365} \times 1.4601 = 146.01$$

C. The Strategy (the 7.25% May 2016 issue)

CASH	FUTURES	BASIS
May 15, 1987		
sell	buy	
7.25% May 2016	Sep 87 T-bond @89-31	63
@84.37849, 8.75% yield	Cf: 0.9159	
Par Value: $10,000,000	HR: 0.9159	
Cash Value: $8,437,849	No. of Contracts: 91.59	
September 1, 1987		
buy	sell	
7.25% May 2016	Sep 87 T-bond @91-30	7
@84.40933, 8.75% yield		
Par Value: $10,000,000		
Cash Value: $8,440,933		
May 15 to September 1: 108 days		

D. Results and Evaluation (the 7.25% May 2016 issue)

1. *Cash Result* (loss)

   Cash Sale − Cash Purchase = Cash Result
   8,437,849 − 8,440,933 = −3.084

2. *Futures Result* (gain)

   Futures Change × 31.25 × Contracts = Futures Result
   (in 32nds)
   63 × 31.25 × 91.59 = 180,318

3. *Capital Gain* (not applicable)

4. *Interest Expense* (not applicable)

5. *Interest Income* (not applicable)

6. *Net Hedging Result*

− 3,084	Cash Result
+ 180,318	Futures Result
177,234	Net Hedging Result

7. *Annualized Yield* (not applicable)

8. *Basis Value* (not applicable)

9. (not applicable)

C. The Strategy (the 12.5% August 2009-14 issue)

CASH	FUTURES	BASIS
May 15, 1987		
sell	buy	
12.5% August 2009-14	Sep 87 T-bond @89-31	96
@134.37365, 8.84% yield	Cf: 1.4601	
Par Value: $10,000,000	HR: 1.4601	
Cash Value: $13,437,365	No. of Contracts: 146.01	
September 1, 1987		
buy	sell	
12.5% August 2007-12	Sep 87 T-bond @91-30	0
@134.21999, 8.84% yield		
Par Value: $10,000,000		
Cash Value: $13,421,999		
May 15 to September 1: 108 days		

D. Results and Evaluation (the 12.5% August 2009-14 issue)

1. *Cash Result* (gain)

   Cash Sale − Cash Purchase = Cash Result
   13,437,365 − 13,421,999 = 15,366

2. *Futures Result* (gain)

Futures Change × 31.25 × Contracts = Futures Result
  (in 32nds)
      63   × 31.25 × 146.01   = 287,475

3. *Capital Gain* (not applicable)

4. *Interest Expense* (not applicable)

5. *Interest Income* (not applicable)

6. *Net Hedging Result*

      15,366 Cash Gain
  + 287,475 Futures Gain
     302,841 Net Hedging Result

7. *Annualized Yield* (not applicable)

8. *Basis Value* (not applicable)

9. (not applicable)

sells. Then hedging the 12.5% bond produces a $302,841 loss instead of that much gain. In contrast, the 7.25% bond produces only a $177,234 loss.

Whether establishing a long or a short position, these examples make it clear that the correct focus for a hedger is not the cheapest to deliver question but the expectation concerning basis change. If the hedger knows he will be on the right side of the basis, he wants the bond that will produce the greatest basis change. If he knows he will be on the wrong side of the basis, he wants a bond that will produce the smallest possible basis change. Again, cheapness enters into the consideration only tangentially.

Why it Works

To understand why it works this way, risk managers need to keep in mind the role of the basis. In a normal market, the bond basis will be enough to maintain the storage level, usually at a point somewhat below the standard short-term rate. Figure 18-4, a version of the by-now-familiar schematic, illustrates the situation with three bonds—the 7.25% May 2016, the 10.375% May 2007-12, and the 12.5% August 2009-14.

The solid line nearest the bottom defines carry—the net yield of buying and holding a bond for a short period. The dashed line defines the short-term lending rate. The three varied lines represent the coupons of the three bonds. In this idealization, all three converge to zero. (In reality, only one will actually achieve zero basis.)

With the passage of time the dollar amounts diminish. If someone holds the 12.5% bond for a year, the coupon payments will be $12,500 for each $100,000 par, but it will pay only $6,250 for half a year. So it is with all bonds. Also, at approximately 90% of carry (the short-term rate defines full carry, so the carry rate divided by the short-term rate defines the percent of carry), the market will pay $5,500 for $100,000 par held a year. That return diminishes just as the coupon does, though at a different rate, of course.

Figure 18-4

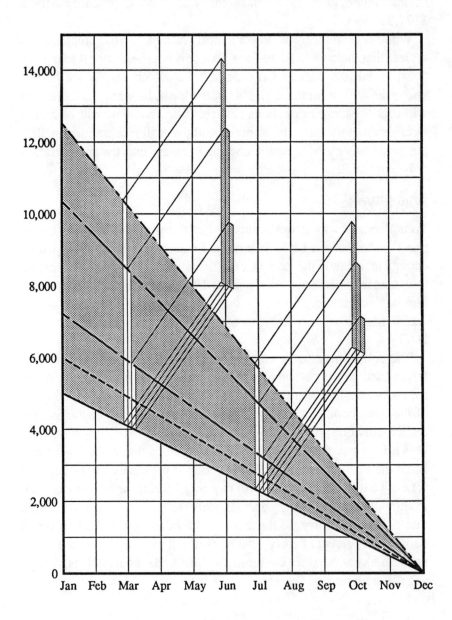

Notice that at the start of February, the coupon of the 12.5% bond has reached $10,400 and the carry level has declined from $5,500 to $4,600. As a result, the basis has to "take away" $5,800 to maintain the storage level. At the same point, the 7.25% bond reached the $6,000 level, so the basis only has to "take away" $1,400 in that case. (Since a 32nd is worth $31.25, dividing the basis values by 31.25 derives the basis in the more usual 32nds.)

By the first of June, just four months later, the coupons and the carry rate have declined more. Accordingly, the basis for all bonds widens, and so maintains a constant yield level. Table 18-1 shows the basis relationship for all three bond at the starting point, February 1, and June 1. It also show how much the basis widens for each bond.

Table 18-1

		Start	Feb 1	June 1	Basis Change
7.25%	Coupon Value	7,250	6,000	3,600	
	Basis Value	1,750	1,400	800	
	Basis (32nds)	56	45	26	19
10.375%	Coupon Value	10,375	8,600	5,200	
	Basis Value	4,875	4,000	2,400	
	Basis (32nds)	156	128	77	51
12.5%	Coupon Value	12,500	10,400	6,300	
	Basis Value	7,000	5,800	3,500	
	Basis (32nds)	224	187	112	75

Clearly, while this schematic obscures the cheapest to deliver question, it does show why a higher coupon bond will tend to experience a larger basis change than a lower coupon bond.

Acknowledging Complexity

In reality, the situation is even more dramatic than the schematic indicates. The high coupon bond approaches zero the soonest, because, as the schematic illustrates, the high coupon bonds need greater basis reduction to bring the yield of their long-term investment to less than the rate of short-term alternatives like T-bills. Consequently, higher coupon bonds normally exhibit the sharpest rate of convergence. That basis principle explains both the difference in rates of convergence and the direction of basis change in a normal yield market. Yet that kind of representation cannot show the changing relationships among the various issues.

Figure 18-5 adds significant information to the picture. This figure assumes a stable yield to maturity. The x axis indicates the amount of convergence in 32nds. The y axis indicates the basis in 32nds. Notice that cheapest to deliver status changes during the time represented on this graph. On the day symbolized at the left edge of the graph, the 7.625% bond is cheapest to deliver. By the day symbolized by the right edge of the graph, the highest coupon bond is cheapest to deliver. Traders have come to consider it the lowest quality issue of the three.

A variety of other factors influence bond quality in significant ways. While an introductory discussion like this is not the place to undertake a full analysis of those issues, risk managers need to be aware of the kinds of possibilities that exist.

To cite but one example, the imperfections of the bond contract affect the rates of convergence. Given a stable 8% yield, the 12.5% issue converges far more sharply than the 7.625% issue. An analytical model which incorporates different yield levels, however, reveals that at different yields not only does cheapest to deliver status change but also the relationship among different issues varies.

These changes are predictable. Given the assumption that all issues have the same yield to maturity, this model allows risk managers to predict which issue will be cheapest to deliver solely on the basis of the mathematics of pricing and basis change. It does not require use of such imponderables as where the market is headed.

Incorporating yield variations (and abandoning the uniform yield assumption) opens up further possibilities. Because of the variety of factors that enter into bond quality considerations, risk managers do well to analyze quality from several points of view. An analyst who develops models of portfolio structure and performance for a major bond house

Figure 18-5 Static Basis Convergence

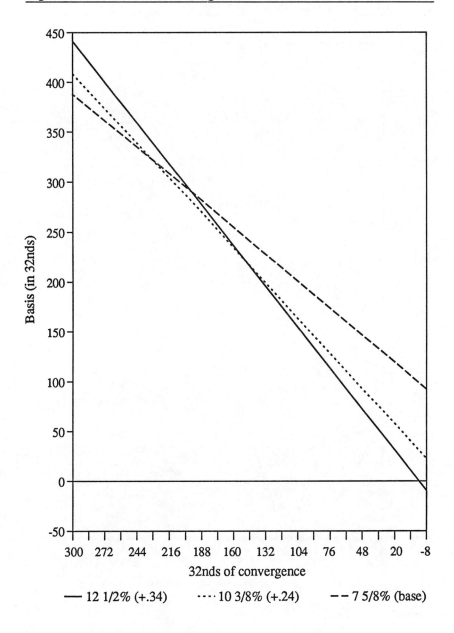

Figure 18-6 Basis with Respect to Yield

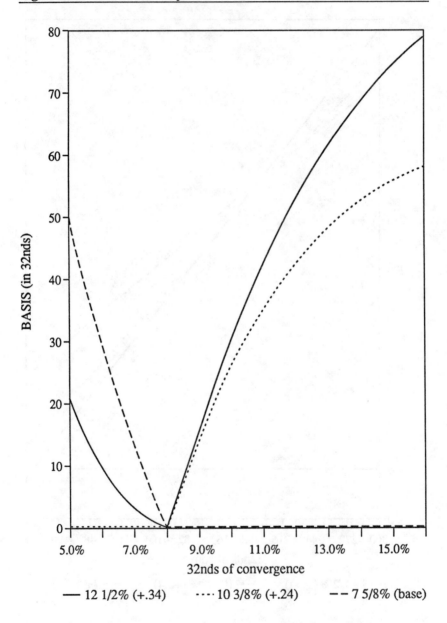

BASIS (in 32nds)

32nds of convergence

—— 12 1/2% (+.34)   ···· 10 3/8% (+.24)   –– 7 5/8% (base)

claims that the more sophisticated the model the greater the reality and usefulness of the results. People can work with simplified models as long as they only need to solve certain limited problems. Those models achieve their simplicity by assuming away numerous quirky details which do not conveniently disappear in real life. While it is not appropriate to enter into those complexities here, in point of fact, even a personal computer can handle the various models adequately. The real impact of better models for a risk manager is that the greater the reality of the analysis, the more opportunities it is likely to uncover.

19

Basis, Spreads and Hedge Placement

Hedge placement refers to the basis trader's choice of which futures month to trade. Consider a typical short basis hedging strategy, where the risk manager will sell cash and buy futures. He plans to initiate this hedge on April 1, 1987 and unwind in early December. Figure 19-1 outlines the general plan.

Figure 19-1

CASH	FUTURES
April 1, 1987	
sell 10.375% May 2009-14	buy _____ T-bond
December 1, 1987	
buy 10.375% May 2009-14	sell _____ T-bond

On April 1 he will buy futures, but the question remains: Which futures month? Many hedgers automatically choose the contract closest to the end point of the strategy—in this case, the December 87 futures. If the hedger has done everything else correctly, that is a sound move.

231

However, depending on what the market is doing, there may be hedge placements that would produce even better results. In some situations, "bringing his hedge forward" to June 87s or September 87s might enhance returns. So might placing it farther out to March 88s or even June 88s in certain other cases.

In making those choices, basis traders have to consider the tradeoff between profit potential and risk. If the extra risk falls within acceptable limits, given predetermined business goals and policies, the extra profit may make taking on extra risk worthwhile. In some cases, the level of risk is significant.

Besides the risk decision, risk managers also must consider the storage incentives, or "what the market wants them to do." Basis traders most often judge the storage incentive and decide the hedge placement question in terms of what the spreads indicate. However, a trader's ability to read the spreads depends on his understanding of what the basis is for and how it operates in the market.

How the Basis Works

All else being equal, the basis keeps the return constant at a level at or below the short-term rate. Assume a bond with a $100,000 principal amount and an 8% yield. If the time from purchase to sale is one year, the long-term yield will be $8,000 and the short-term, assuming a 6% rate, will be $6,000, a $2,000 difference.

Reduce the carry period to six months and the long-term yield will be $4,000 (at 8%), the short-term will be $3,000 (at 6%). The difference between the two drops from $2,000 to $1,000. The long-term and short-term rates holding constant, the spread between them remains 2%.

The basis is the force that keeps the yield difference in place. At one year, the basis has to "take away" $2,000. At six months it has to "take away" only $1,000. If the basis at the start of the year were 64 (in 32nds, of course), it would have to widen to 32 just to maintain the yield at the level of the short- term rate. Figure 19-2 illustrates this essential situation, and shows how the basis widens even when the rate remains unchanged.

Figure 19-2

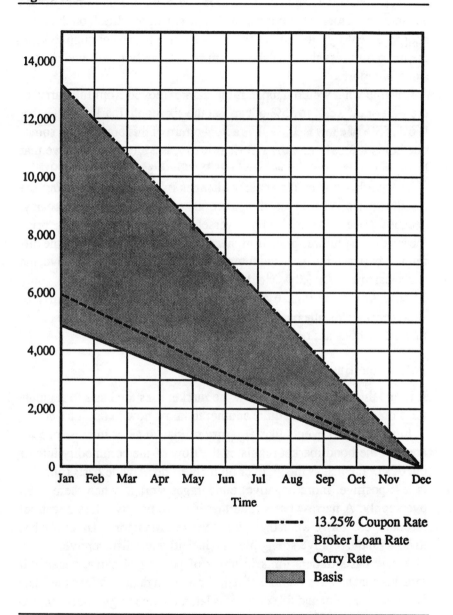

13.25% Coupon Rate
Broker Loan Rate
Carry Rate
Basis

Since the short-term rate is the most the bond can pay (the laws of economics, remember, impose a full carry upper limit on holding hedged inventory), the bond basis has to widen at least enough to keep the net return less than the short-term rate. Usually it will widen considerably more.

Imagine what would happen if the market moved from full carry, at the start of the year, to 55% of carry at the six month mark. If full carry is 6%, 55% of carry is 3.3%. The actual return of this bond, when someone holds it for six months at 55% of carry, is $1,100. To achieve that level, the basis would have to widen 35/32nds, say from 64 to 29.

The market makes those carry changes by raising or lowering the reselling price. A lower reselling price "takes away" more, lowers carry, because price and yield vary inversely. Raising the reselling price means that the futures price is higher relative to the cash. When the difference between the cash and futures prices becomes more positive, the basis narrows. At 3.3% yield, it is necessary to "take away" only $1,100. At 6%, $3,000. Even when there was no change in carry or short-term yields, the basis had to widen 35 points in six months just to maintain a constant return level.

Putting the Basis to Work

It is one thing to understand how the market uses the basis to regulate the storage impulse, and quite another to know how to put it to work.

In response to events like Treasury refinancings or interest rate increases, the bond market regulates the flow of the commodity into or out of storage just as the grain or oil markets do. A wide basis (one that is less positive, more negative) encourages storage when there is an oversupply. A narrow basis (one that is more positive, less negative) discourages storage when there is a shortage. An important question has to do with the relative strength of the incentive, or disincentive.

Astute basis traders think in terms of percent of carry, because it remains constant in situations that differ in other details. When the basis is 120 at one point and 88 six months later, anyone might think the two situations very different. Yet they are closely parallel. Both times the market may be paying 100% of carry. Percent of carry is the relevant fact. It tells basis traders just how the market feels about the storage question. Further, working with percent of carry allows historical comparison of facts from all markets. Regardless of changes in yield, and even yield curve relationships, percent of carry provides a reliable indicator.

Spreads are the same as the basis in that they provide a gauge of the store-don't store message the market is issuing. They differ in that while the basis is microeconomic—unique to each coupon, maturity, and dealer—spreads are macroeconomic, generic to the entire market. This is a typical spread display for U.S. Treasury bonds:

Jun	Sep	Dec	Mar88	Jun
100-13	99-14	98-17	97-21	96-27

Succeeding futures months always show lower prices in T-bond spreads.

The Implied Repo Rate and Percent of Carry

Partly because of their background in banking and finance, traders in the financial commodities use special terminology when they discuss spreads. Where basis traders in other commodities refer to the "cost of carry," or just "carry," those in financials tend to refer to an "implied repo rate." A repo (short for "repurchase agreement") is a conventional arrangement in which someone contracts to sell a bond and buy it back at a given time and price. This difference in terms obscures the view of some risk managers, though it shouldn't.

By way of background, when anyone stores a physical commodity there is a cost, the "cost of carry." That is easy to visualize. If a grain trader is storing corn, he has to pay a storage fee. Shrinkage and spillage will cost something. And a person storing grain pays an interest charge for financing his holdings. Each physical market has a "full carry" rate, the full cost of storing the commodity from one contract month to the next. An economic law limits return to storage. No such limit applies to noncarry, or inverted, markets.

This matter of storage seems not to apply to the financial markets. Bonds do not shrink like corn does. There is no spillage during transfer as with oil. But risk managers should not let financial terminology obscure the realities of the situation.

In fact, the bond spreads allow the definition of storage incentives in similar terms to those used by traders in other markets. The short-term benchmark is typically the T-bill rate. The so-called *repo rate* is closely related to that. If the T-bill rate is 6%, the repo rate might be 6.25%, the small premium motivated by accounting effort and a slight repurchaser default risk, on market value change only—if it is correctly documented.

The rate of decline between bond futures months defines an *implied repo rate* which establishes the short-term return to buying a cash bond and delivering it. Thus the implied repo rate is equivalent to the return to storage in the physicals.

The implied repo rate will be less than or equal to the short-term benchmark. If the T-bill rate is 6%, the implied repo rate might be 3%. Bankers usually use a dollar figure for the implied repo rate, but risk managers should get used to thinking in terms of percent of carry. Where the implied repo rate equals the T-bill rate (6% and 6%, say), then the market is paying 100% of carry. In traditional terms, that defines full carry. Where the T-bill rate is 6% and the implied repo rate is 3%, the market is paying 50% of carry. If the T-bill rate defines full carry, a basis trader who knows the implied repo rate can easily determine the percent of carry and gauge the storage incentive.

Clearly, just as with the basis indicator, the lower the percent of carry, the less inclination to storage. The spreads offer a clue to a basis trader concerning what he should do. In general, very wide spreads signal a high implied repo rate. That means the percent of carry is also high which creates a strong incentive to store, to buy cash. Narrow spreads signal a low implied repo rate, and a lower percent of carry means less return to storage and less incentive to store.

Remember, thinking in terms of percent of carry allows comparison of situations where prices vary. Dollar-based figures might seem to differ from situation to situation. Prices, after all, can range far. The differences the dollar term suggest often turn out to be illusory.

Using the Spreads

T-bond spreads normally approximate one of three general configurations. The spreads, or price intervals, might be relatively small, as in Figure 19-3.

Figure 19-3

	Jun	Sep	Dec	Mar88
	88-00	87-16	87-00	86-16

"Wide" spreads like these indicate a high implied repo rate, a high percent of carry.

Normally, T-bond spreads resemble those in Figure 19-4 where the intervals are one point.

Figure 19-4

	Jun	Sep	Dec	Mar88
	88-00	87-00	86-00	85-00

Sometimes the intervals are even larger, as in Figure 19-5.

Figure 19-5

	Jun	Sep	Dec	Mar88
	88-00	86-16	85-00	83-16

These "narrow" spreads in Figures 19-4 and 19-5 indicate low implied repo rates and so lower percentages of carry. Clearly, the lower the percent of carry, the less inclination to storage.

To summarize, if a basis trader looking at the spreads sees a small down interval, he knows that indicates a higher implied repo rate and so a high percent of carry. That is a wide spread which encourages storage. If he sees a large down interval, he knows it indicates a lower implied repo rate and a low percent of carry. That is a narrow spread which discourages storage.

STORAGE SIGNALS FROM SPREADS

Store	*Don't Store*
1. small down interval	1. large down interval
2. high implied reepo rate	2. low implied repo rate
3. high % of carry	3. low % of carry
4. wide spread	4. narrow spread

Notice that the narrow and wide signals of the spreads correspond with those of the basis. Given that, it is often enough just to look at the spreads.

Hedging a Carry Market

Returning to the case of the risk manager who is planning to initiate a short basis strategy (sell cash, buy futures) on April 1, 1987, assume that he will sell $1 million par of the 10.375% November 2007-12 bond at 122-28 and buy futures. Given that the spreads are wide (the intervals between months are about 16/32nds), he can make the conservative choice and buy Dec 87 futures. Figure 19-6 summarizes this limited benefit but relatively safe strategy.

Having sold the cash bond for more than he had to pay upon buying it back, this hedger realized a $8,750 cash gain. The price change follows largely from the fact that December 1 is seven months nearer the bond's maturity date. All else being equal—and there's an assumption here of stable yield—bond price moves toward par as maturity approaches.

The hedger also gains on the futures side. He buys Dec 87 futures at 96-24 and sells them at 98-28, a 2-04 gain. That translates into $26,214.

The net hedging result, the sum of the cash and futures gains, is $34,864—a 4.25% annualized return.

Figure 19-6

CASH	FUTURES	BASIS
April 1, 1987		
sell	buy	
10.374% November 2007-12	Dec 87 T-bond @96-24	113
@122-28, 8.06% yield	Cf: 1.2336	
Par Value: $1,000,000	HR: 1.2336	
Cash Value: $1,228,750	No. of Contracts: 12.336	
December 1, 1987		
buy	sell	
10.375% November 2007-12	Dec 87 T-bond @98-28	
@122-00, 8.06% yield		
Par Value: $1,000,000		
Cash Value: $1,220,000		
April 1 to December 1: 244 days		

During the term of the hedge, the basis trader would no doubt invest the cash from the bond sale in T-bills. At 6% yield, that would earn $49,284.

The sum of net hedging result and the T-bill yield is $84,248. Altogether, this strategy produces a 10.25% annualized return.

More aggressive risk managers would think about why the spreads were so wide. One obvious reason would be that there was a major Treasury refinancing going on just at that time. The sudden over-supply of bonds would cause the market to create a storage incentive in the form of a wide basis and wide spreads. The risk manager might reasonably conclude that to be a temporary condition, and expect the spreads to narrow markedly in subsequent months.

Normally, the basis widens just enough to maintain the yield level somewhere below the short-term rate. That will happen whether there is any change in the market or not. But if the risk manager thinks the narrowing will be great enough to significantly lower the implied repo rate and decrease the percent of carry, then he has a choice of tactics.

He can still place the hedge on December futures, although that will not allow him to take advantage of the narrowing. If he buys June 87s instead, then he can capitalize on the narrowing spreads he expects to see. Accordingly, instead of the trade just outlined, he buys the June 87 futures at 97-24.

BASIS, SPREADS, AND HEDGE PLACEMENT

Strategy 18

A. The Problem

In a normal yield curve market, a short basis positi‚n (sell cash, buy futures) produces benefits to the hedger. A normal climate entails a widening basis, and the short position puts the trader on the "right side of the basis." While this strategy does not eliminate price exposure, it does lock in the cash bond purchase price. The futures gain will at least make up for the change in cash prices; more often it results in enhanced yields.

B. Preliminaries

1. *The Basis*

Cash   − (Futures × Cf)   = Basis
a. $122.875 - (96.75 \times 1.2336) = 3.5242 \, (\times 32) = 112.7744$
b. $122 \quad - (98.875 \times 1.2336) = 0.0278 \, (\times 32) = 0.8896$

2. *Futures Position Size*

$$\frac{1,228,750}{1000 \times 122.875} \times 1.2336 = 12.336$$

C. The Strategy

CASH	FUTURES	BASIS
April 1, 1987		
sell	buy	
10.375% Nov 2007-12	Dec 87 T-bond @96-24	113
@122-28, 8.06% yield	Cf: 1.2336	
Par Value: $1,000,000	HR: 1.2336	
Cash Value: $1,228,750	No. of Contracts: 12.336	
December 1, 1987		
buy	sell	
10.375% Nov 2007-12	Dec 87 T-bond @98-28	1
@122-00, 8.06% yield		
Par Value: $1,000,000		
Cash Value: $1,220,000		
April 1 to December 1: 244 days		

D. Results and Evaluation

1. *Cash Result* (gain)

   Cash Sale − Cash Purchase = Cash Result
   1,228,750 − 1,220,000   = 8,750

2. *Futures Result* (gain)

   Futures Change × 31.25 × Contracts = Futures Result
       (in 32nds)
       68   × 31.25 × 12.336   = 26,214

3. *Capital Gain* (not applicable)

4. *Interest Expense* (not applicable)

5. *Interest Income* (not applicable)

6. *Net Hedging Result*

   | | 8,750 | Cash Gain |
   | + | 26,214 | Futures Gain |

       34,964 Net Hedging Result

7. *Annualized Yield*

           34,964 Net Hedging Result
   ÷ 1,228,750 Cash Value

     0.0284549 Return
        ÷ 244 Days in Hedge

     0.0001166 Daily Yield
       × 365 Days

     0.0425658 = 4.25% Annualized Yield

8. *Basis Value*

   Basis Change × 31.25 × Par Units = Basis Value
   111.8848   × 31.25 × 10   = 34,964

9. Basis Value = Net Hedging Result
   34,964   = 34,964

The decision to trade June 87 futures instead of Decembers imposes a series of additional moves. No matter what else happens, the hedger has to roll over his futures position before the first of June. Rolling over involves trading out of one position, in order not to have to take delivery, and immediately establishing a parallel position in a subsequent month. In this case, the hedger will trade out of the Junes and trade into either Septembers or Decembers.

If the market has recovered from the oversupply caused by the refinancing by the end of May, and the spreads have narrowed a good deal, the basis trader will probably roll directly into the December futures.

The cash side of his strategy is the same as in the earlier, more conservative one. He sells the 10.875% November 2007-12 cash bond at 122-28 on April 1, 1987 and buys it at 122-00 on December 1.

On the futures side, he starts by buying June 87 T-bond futures at 97-24. Then on May 27, he sells the Junes at 98-00 and buys Decembers at 94-24. Finally, on December 1 he sells the Decembers at 98-28.

Figure 19-7 summarizes the revised strategy.

Calculating the cash-side result is no problem. The basis trader sold cash at a higher level than when he bought it back. Therefore, he enjoys a cash gain of $8,750.

The futures side operates in two stages in this situation. Between April 1 and May 27, there is a small gain as a result of the price rising 8/32nds, a total of $3,090. Between May 27 and December 1, the futures difference is 4-04, or 132/32nds, which generates a $50,886 gain.

The net hedging result is the sum of the cash gain and the two futures gains, or $62,726. This hedge produces a 7.64% annualized return. The hedger would probably also invest the proceeds of the cash bond sale in T-bills at 6%. The entire package would produce a 13.64% annualized return—an excellent result.

If everything happens as expected. (Much virtue in an *If*.)

It is important to realize what else could happen. The spreads could narrow more slowly. Then the percent of carry would not change enough to create an advantage. If that happened, the basis trader would still have to roll over the futures from June to September or December. Taking delivery on June futures is not part of the plan.

Figure 19-7

CASH	FUTURES	BASIS
April 1, 1987		
sell	buy	
10.375% November 2007-12	Jun 87 T-bond @97-24	66
@122-28, 8.06% yield	Cf: 1.2360	
Par Value: $1,000,000	HR: 1.236	
Cash Value: $1,228,750	No. of Contracts: 12.36	
May 27, 1987		
(121.270)	sell	
	Jun 87 T-bond @98-00	5
	buy	
	Dec 87 T-bond @94-24	
	140	
	Cf: 1.2336	
	HR: 1.2336	
	No. of Contracts: 12.336	
December 1, 1987		
buy	sell	
10.375% November 2007-12	Dec 87 T-bond @98-28	1
@122-00, 8.06% yield		
Par Value: $1,000,000		
Cash Value: $1,220,000		

April 1 to May 27: 57 days
May 27 to December 1: 187 days
April 1 to December 1: 244 days

April 1 to May 27 (57 days)
Futures Gain: 8 x 31.25 x 12.36 = 3,090
(Cash Gain: 1,228,750 - 1,212,700 = 16,050)

May 27 to December 1 (187 days)
Futures Gain: 132 x 31.25 x 12.336 = 50,886
(Cash Loss: 1,212,700 - 1,220,000 = 7,300)

8,750	Cash Gain
3,090	Futures Gain, April 1 to May 27
+ 50,886	Futures Gain, May 27 to December 1
62,726	Net Hedging Result

Strategy 19

A. The Problem

To turn a wide spread situation to advantage, a basis trader can "bring his hedge forward." The expectation is that the spreads will narrow significantly after the market responds to the refunding, or whatever caused the widening. The hedger must "roll over" his futures as contract expiration approaches, but that move is likely to "pick off" an extra yield. This is a relatively safe strategy which can markedly improve the returns.

B. Preliminaries

1. *The Basis*

Cash   − (Futures × Cf)   = Basis
a. $122.875 - (97.75 \times 1.2360) = 2.056 \ (\times \ 32) = 65.792$
b. $121.270 - (98.00 \times 1.2360) = 0.142 \ (\times \ 32) = 4.544$
c. $121.270 - (94.75 \times 1.2336) = 4.3864 \ (\times \ 32) = 140.3648$
d. $122.000 - (98.875 \times 1.2336) = 0.278 \ (\times \ 32) = 0.8896$

2. *Futures Position Size*

$$\frac{1,228,750}{1000 \times 122.875} \times 1.2360 = 12.36$$

$$\frac{1,212,700}{1000 \times 121.270} \times 1.2336 = 12.336$$

C. The Strategy

CASH	FUTURES	BASIS
April 1, 1987		
sell	buy	
10.375% Nov 2007-12	Jun 87 T-bond @97-24	66
@122-28, yield 8.06%	Cf: 1.2360	
Par Value: $1,000,000	HR: 1.236	
Cash Value: $1,228,750	No. of Contracts: 12.36	
May 27, 1987		
(121.270)	sell	
	Jun 87 T-bond @98-00	5
	buy	
	Dec 87 T-bond @94-24	140
	Cf: 1.2336	
HR: 1.2336	No. of Contracts: 12.336	
No. of contracts: 12.336		
December 1, 1987		
buy	sell	
10.375% Nov 2007-12	Dec 87 T-bond @98-28	1
@122-00, yield 8.06%		
Par Value: $1,000,000		
Cash Value: $1,220,000		
April 1 to May 27: 57 days		
May 27 to December 1: 187 days		
April 1 to December 1: 244 days		

D. Results and Evaluation
April 1 to May 27 (57 days)

1. *Cash Result* (gain)*
   Cash Sale − Cash Purchase = Cash Result
   1,228,750 − 1,212,700   = 16,050

2. *Futures Result* (gain)
   Futures Change × 31.25 × Contracts = Futures Result
     (in 32nds)
         8   × 31.25 × 12.36   = 3,090

3. − 7. (not applicable)

8. *Basis Value*
   Basis Change × 31.25 × Par Units = Basis Value
   61.248   × 31.25 × 10   = 19,140

9. Basis Value = (Cash Result) + Futures Result
   19,140   = 19,140

May 27 to December 1 (187 days)

1. *Cash Result* (loss)*
   Cash Sale − Cash Purchase = Cash Result
   1,212,700 − 1,220,000   = −7,300

2. *Futures Result*
   Futures Change × 31.25 × Contracts = Futures Result
     (in 32nds)
       132   × 31.25 × 12.336   = 50,886

3. − 7. (not applicable)

8. *Basis Value*
   Basis Change × 31.25 × Par Units = Basis Value
   139.4752   × 31.25 × 10   = 43,586

9. Basis Value = (Cash Result) + Futures Result
   43,586   = 43,586

April 1 to December 1 (244 days)

1. *Cash Result* (gain)
   Cash Sale − Cash Purchase = Cash Result
   1,228,750 − 1,220,000   = 8,750

6. *Net Hedging Result*
          8,750 Cash Gain
          3,090 Futures Gain (April 1 to May 27)
    + 50,886 Futures Gain (May 27 to December 1)
       62,726 Net Hedging Result

7. *Annualized Yield*

	62,726	Net Hedging Result
÷	1,228,750	Cash Value
	0.0510486	Return
÷	244	Days in Hedge
	0.0002092	Daily Yield
x	365	Days
	0.0763637	= 7.64% Annualized Yield

If the basis trader has reason to believe the spreads will narrow enough by September to create a solid gain, rolling over into Septembers makes sense. Risk managers need to remember that each rollover adds to the transaction costs. With that in mind, he might decide to roll directly into Decembers. If he does that, all else remaining the same, the hedging result will be roughly the same as it was for the conservative strategy.

That rather neutral situation creates more of a nuisance than a problem. Other possibilities, like increasing interest rates, are decidedly negative. When rates rise, the spreads have to widen just to keep the percent of carry constant. In fact, any event that causes the percent of carry to increase will have an adverse effect. What justifies the aggressive approach is the expectation of a decrease in the percent of carry. An increase is a major disappointment.

That risk is real.

At the same time, remember that widening spreads signal a carry market. The downside potential is limited. If the market is paying 85% of carry going in, the worst that can happen is that it will go to full carry—that the trade will go 15% against the risk manager. There is an absolute limit on the risk in a carry market.

As a result, this remains a relatively safe strategy which is capable of earning excellent returns.

To summarize, the limited risk strategy in carry markets is to bring the long hedges forward, the short hedges back.

Hedging a Non-Carry Market

Instead of being very wide on April 1, 1987, the spreads could have been narrow, like these:

June87	Sep	Dec	Mar88	June	Sep	Dec
97-23	96-07	94-24	93-08	91-24	90-07	88-24

The market is making sure no one tries to move into storage. A risk manager, planning a short basis strategy for the period between April 1 and December 1, could still play it safe and place his hedge on the December futures.

But he could use his knowledge of the market to go beyond a defensive hedge like that and seek extra profit. Come December, he knows the spreads should widen. Where they are now roughly 48/32nds, they are likely to widen to 32. If that happens, a basis trader could gain significantly by hedging the June 88 spread instead of the December 87.

The idea of extra profit is so compelling that it is hard to see the element of risk. But suppose that in late October or early November interest rates do not perform as the risk manager expects, or a foreign exchange flap precipitates a financial crisis. All the carry will go out of the market. The disincentive to store will increase instead and the spot month (traders' jargon for the current month) will go up the most. If the December 87 price rises more than the June 88, the risk manager can lose a fortune because the futures will not offset the cash risk. There is no limit on a non-carry market. A carry market cannot pay more than full carry—the short-term rate. Going the other way the pit is bottomless. The spreads compound the problem, much as leveraged loans can accelerate losses. A hedger who played safe with December futures would emerge from such a disaster in relatively good shape.

To summarize, the strategy for noncarry markets is to place long hedges nearby and short hedges out to deferreds. Because there is no economic limit on where the noncarry market can go, this strategy involves a significant element of risk.

In Summary

From this outline of strategic refinements, it should be apparent that the basis creates opportunities. Risk managers who understand this dynamic market factor will see possibilities that others cannot see or even conceive of. Some of the strategies are almost perfectly safe. Others introduce an element of risk. Every risk manager has to decide how to balance risk and opportunity according to general business goals.

A manager who simply wants to protect against risk might well stick with a relatively rudimentary trading program. For such a person balancing risk is essential. Creating profit opportunities matters little. Other managers might want to go farther. They may think they can handle a degree of risk exposure if the chance for gain is sufficient. A good basis strategy can create rewards in either case. The market is available to both. The decision has to come from the individual company's sense of its long term goals.

An understanding of the basis allows planners to arrive at decisions on principled, rather than whimsical, grounds. The beauty of it all is that both conservative and aggressive strategies can come out ahead. It is just a matter of degree.

20

High Powered Short-Term Investing

Having learned how to profit from the eminently predictable cash-futures relationship rather than the prices themselves, knowledgeable risk managers routinely develop short-term returns that improve on the T-bill yield by as much as 80% of the short- term yield. If short-term yields are 6.25%, these risk managers can routinely earn 11.25% on their short-term money.

Performance like that is eye-opening, but hardly a chance result. These risk managers use a strategy—technically, a matched reverse repurchase short sale—which is little more than a regulation basis play. The safety, like the earnings, comes from the inherently predictable basis change. To a veteran basis trader, there is no question whether this kind of strategy will make money. The only question is how much.

A universal challenge for financial managers these days is how to find safe places to put short-term money so it earns worthwhile returns.

Safety alone is no problem. T-bills are safe. Curiously, risk managers can earn much better returns with little loss of safety. Of course they have to realize that the short-term instrument of choice is the long-term U.S. Treasury bond.

Indeed, risk managers operate in a world of apparent contradiction. Their use of long-term instruments for short-term investments is only one example. As a matter of course, they embrace rigorous discipline yet must be free thinkers. Risk managers operate amid the whirlwind of the contemporary financial climate and reap the benefits of its inherent order.

That order derives from the basis, the difference between cash and futures prices.

The Components

The heart of this strategy is the short sale of a cash bond. The other components enable the short sale and establish the foundation of a financial structure that allows risk managers to enhance short-term yields with assurance. The components include

- the short sale of a cash bond
- a reverse repurchase agreement
- long-term U.S. Treasury bonds
- T-bond futures
- a short basis hedging strategy

These elements have stood the test of time.

The short sale is a good example. In simplest terms, *a short* sells something he does not own. When a farmer sells a crop not yet grown, that is a short sale. A risk manager selling a bond he does not own is a short, as is a commodities trader who orders the sale of silver, soybeans, or crude oil futures—when he has no position.

That a person can sell something he does not own seems a paradox to newcomers to commodity trade. For some reason, most "common sense" investors think only in terms of buying. They believe investing involves buying securities, holding them, and gaining from interest or dividend yield and capital appreciation.

True, as far as it goes, but only part of the story. But that view makes it easy to see why so many market veterans consider the typical investor perpetually bullish. The bullish psychological set makes the short sale seem decidedly odd. Yet it is a time-proven and useful investment approach—one which some markets demand.

Neither is there anything new about hedging, though recent attempts to apply it in new areas sometimes create that impression. Also, good basis traders have known for generations that hedging success depends on more than balancing cash and futures positions. Risk managers know they must design their hedges so they will wind up on the right side of the known basis change. The reverse repurchase agreement is the key to getting that done in this case.

Repurchase tools have a long history, too. Banks often use them to cope with short-term liquidity needs. To acquire extra funds when customers draw heavily on loan agreements, bankers can use a *repurchase agreement* (or "repo") in which they contract to sell a bond and buy it back at a given time and price. A *reverse repurchase agreement* (or "reverse repo"), in which bankers first buy the bond and then sell it back, allows them to protect excess cash until they can invest it or loan it out. The cost of these transactions is usually near the Fed funds or interbank rate.

Secured by U.S. Treasuries and with effective yields closely approximating federal fund rates, repurchase agreements provide an alternative to interbank loans. *Federal Reserve System reports of major bond dealers' positions inevitably show them to have negative inventory, which suggests they routinely use repo tools when they sell bonds to customers.* Proper ducumentation assures the safety of the securities. The Federal Reserve controls the money supply this way. Wishing to temporarily add to the money supply, it buys bonds. It reduces the money supply by selling them.

Using cash and futures together, balancing positions, taking advantage of repurchase tools—all of that is common enough. The novelty of this approach to short-term money management is the patterning of a sequence of trades that usefully combines these components.

To begin with, the risk manager borrows a bond, using a reverse repurchase agreement, and short sells it. He immediately invests the proceeds in T-bills or pays them to the "repoing" insurance company as collateral. At the same time, he buys T-bond futures sufficient to balance the cash position. The meaning of the rather clumsy technical designation—matched reverse repurchase short sale—should be clear. The risk manager short sells a bond acquired by means of a reverse repo and matches his cash transaction with futures.

Because the resale of the cash bond is instantaneous, and the T-bill investment finances the reverse repo fee, this is a self-financing transaction. -

When the time comes to unwind this strategy, the risk manager reverses his initial actions. He goes into the market to buy back the cash bond and sell futures. He delivers the cash bond to fulfill the reverse repurchase agreement. Figure 20-1 outlines the sequence of trades.

Figure 20-1

CASH	FUTURES
Sell T-bond acquired through reverse repo	buy T-bond futures
Buy T-bond to fulfill reverse repo	sell T-bond futures

All that remains is to reap the inherently predictable basis gain. Again, predictability assures safety.

How it Works

More specifically, assume that on May 1, 1987, a risk manager acquires $5 million par of the 12.5% August 2009-14 bond at 136-08 on a reverse repo and immediately short sells it at that price. Also, he invests in T-bills and buys 73 contracts of September '87 T-bond futures at 90-27.

Then, on August 1, 1987 he unwinds by buying back $5 million par of the 12.5% August 2009-14 bond at 135-25 and selling the 73 contracts of September T-bond futures at 92-28. That done, he returns the cash bonds to the source. Figure 20-2 summarizes the details of the trade.

Figure 20-2

CASH	FUTURES
May 1, 1987	
sell 12.5% August 2009-14 @136.250, 8.77% yield Par Value: $5,000,000 Cash Value: $6,812,500	buy Sep 87 T-bond @90-27 Cf: 1.4601 Hedge Ratio: 1.46 No. of Contracts: 73.005
August 1, 1987	
buy 12.5% August 2009-14 @135.79429, 8.77% yield Par Value: $5,000,000 Cash Value: $6,789,714	sell Sep '87 T-bond @92-28

May 1 to August 1: 92 days

On the cash side, the result is the difference between the selling price and the purchase price. There is a $22,786 gain.

Cash sale – Cash purchase =   Cash result

6,812,500 –   6,789,714   =   22,786

That is a trivial amount taken by itself. The futures side is what primarily interests the risk manager. There is a gain of 65/32nds, or $2,031.25 a contract, which amounts to a total futures result of $148,281.

Futures Change x 31.25   x Contracts = Futures Result
(in 32nds)
65   x 31.25 x   73 .005 = 148,291

T-bill interest earnings of $103,027 make the reverse repo self-financing, but otherwise do not come into play in evaluating results. The net result of this strategy is the sum of the cash and futures gains, or $171,077.

HIGH POWERED SHORT-TERM INVESTING

Strategy 20

A. The Problem

To create a high yielding short-term investment from cash reserves, money managers can use a reverse repo instrument in conjunction with a short basis strategy (sell cash, buy futures). The reverse repo allows them to borrow a bond for resale and makes the basis work in their favor. The result is a short-term yield which is 66% better than the 6% short-term benchmark and 14% better than the yield to maturity of the bond.

B. Preliminaries

1. *The Basis*

Cash	− (Futures × Cf)	= Basis
a. 136.250	− (90.84275 × 1.4601) = 3.6090406	= 115.4893
b. 135.79429	− (92.875 × 1.4601) = 0.1875025	= 6.00008

2. *Futures Position Size*

$$\frac{6,812,500}{1000 \times 136.25} \times 1.4601 = 73.005$$

C. The Strategy

CASH	FUTURES	BASIS
May 1, 1987		
sell cash	buy	
12.5% August 2009-14	Sep 87 T-bond @90-27	116
@136.250, 8.77% yield	Cf: 1.4601	
Par Value: $5,000,000	HR: 1.4601	
Cash Value: $6,812,500	No. of Contracts: 73.005	
August 1, 1987		
buy cash	sell	
12.5% August 2009-14	Sep 87 T-bond @92-28	6
@135.79429		
Par Value: $5,000.000		
Cash Value: $6,789,714		
May 1 to August 1: 92 days		

D. Results and Evaluation

1. *Cash Result* (gain)

   Cash Sale − Cash Purchase = Cash Result
   6,812,500 − 6,789,714   = 22,786

2. *Futures Result* (gain)

   Futures Change × 31.25 × Contracts = Futures Result
   (in 32nds)
      65   × 31.25 × 73.005   = 148,291

3. *Capital Gain* (not applicable)
4. *Interest Expense* (not applicable)
5. *Interest Income* (not applicable)
6. *Net Hedging Result*

$$\begin{array}{rl} 22,786 & \text{Cash Result} \\ + 148,291 & \text{Futures Result} \\ \hline 171,077 & \text{Net Hedging Result} \end{array}$$

7. *Annualized Yield*

$$\begin{array}{rl} 171,077 & \text{Net Hedging Result} \\ \div 6,812,500 & \text{Cash Value} \\ \hline 0.0251122 & \text{Return} \\ \div 92 & \text{Days in Hedge} \\ \hline 0.000273 & \text{Daily Yield} \\ \times 365 & \text{Days} \\ \hline 0.09963 & = 9.96\% \text{ Annualized Yield} \end{array}$$

8. *Basis Value*

Basis Change $\times$ 31.25 $\times$ Par Units = Basis Value
109.48922 $\times$ 31.25 $\times$ 50 = 171,077

9. Basis Value = Net Hedging Result
171,077 = 171,077

22,786	Cash Gain
+ 148,291	Futures Gain
171,077	Net Hedging Result

That hedging result improves on the T-bill result for the same 92 days by more than $68,000. It amounts to a 9.96% yield, on an annualized basis. That is almost four percentage points better than the short-term rate and almost one percentage point better than the 9% long-term yield of May 1.

Why it Works

To the casual observer, this complex strategy complicates an otherwise simple matter. It's just common sense, to him, that a bond owner can earn the long-term rate while holding a cash bond. Selling futures against that bond creates a riskless situation with regard to the influence of interest fluctuations on prices. As a result, a bond owner collects the long-term yield on a short-term investment. If that were true, the matched reverse repo strategy would be extra work for no reason. Sad to say, it never works that way.

Casual observers characteristically overlook several important facts:

- coupon and yield are not the same
- yield, in U.S. Treasury bond quotes, means yield to maturity
- the basis keeps short-term returns at a level below the short-term rate

People who should know better forget that coupon is not the same as yield, that coupon relates to par not price. The 12.5% August 2009-14 bond pays a holder 12.5% a year, but 12.5% of par. The one year coupon payment would be $125.000 for $1 million par. If the bond cost 131-22 (the June 2, 1987 price), that is 9.5% of $1,316,875, the actual purchase price.

Also, these people forget for some reason that bond yield is actually "yield to maturity." The full yield accrues to him who waits—in this case until August 15, 2009—and involves not only the coupon earnings but also assumes reinvestment of them at a constant yield rate—over time. So the person who holds a bond for a year or less is unlikely to realize even the stated yield.

Arbitragers seize opportunities like this. Buying cash and selling futures, they force the return of holding fixed yield long-term instruments without price risk to the short-term yield, at best. To get a better sense of the actual possibilities, people need to remember that the short-term yield defines full carry for a bond—the full return to a person who buys a bond, holds it for a time, and resells it.

A Law of Hedging: The return to a long basis position will never exceed full carry.

Full carry is the most a bond holder can earn. Most of the time the market pays less than full carry, something between 30% and 60% of carry. If the short-term rate is 6%, and the bond market is paying 40% of carry, the actual return to the bond holder is 2.4%. To anyone who naively expected the 12.5% coupon rate, or even the 9.4% long-term yield, 2.4% is a sobering prospect. Reality often is.

This strategy is safe because it leaves little to chance. It is a given that the basis will decline, or widen. Each time-proven component produces a predictable result or has a well-motivated function in the larger strategy. The complexity serves a purpose and illustrates the premise that basis trading does not offer savings in amount of work. It only offers to make that work more rewarding.

21

Foreign
Currency Swaps
How to Save 40% of
Your Borrowing Costs

Foreign currency swaps grew from nothing in 1977 to an estimated $130 billion activity by 1986. Swaps have emerged as a major force in the financial world. Why? Curiously, the interest in foreign currency swaps has as much to do with borrowing rates and investment yields as with exchange rates. After all, few financial managers can resist swapping a 7.5% prime rate for a 4.5% actual interest and gaining a 40% interest cost savings in the process.

Swaps emerged out of necessity in a climate of rapidly growing international trade. A U.S. business whose international division produces profits of one million Deutsch marks, for example, must repatriate them as dollars. A swap transaction allows structuring of the exchange so the firm can fix its currency rates. That way the balance sheet and profit and loss statement (including that of the foreign subsidiary) is a known factor, not a variable. Also, the stockholders gain profit and loss protection. Perhaps that is enough to account for the interest companies engaged in sizeable foreign trade have shown in swaps.

Since international traders introduced these foreign currency tools just a few years ago, the use of cash forwards and currency futures markets to match international cash flows, and profit from interest rate differentials, has grown phenomenally, a growth which far exceeds what international exposure appears to justify. Because a funny thing happened on the way to the bank.

The inventors of swaps found that, besides matching cash flows in international currencies, they could create substantial interest rate savings or earnings enhancements. An important part of the phenomenal growth in swaps, then, is due to the fact that foreign traders are far from the only beneficiaries of this kind of low risk endeavor. Virtually any business can gain.

How it Works

To understand the enormous potential of swaps, consider an ordinary business situation—borrowing funds. When a business needs money, it normally taps an established line of credit at a bank, most likely at a prime rate which will be somewhere in the neighborhood of 7.5%.

Or the business might engage in foreign currency swaps. That is, instead of borrowing in the usual way, it would enter the foreign debt markets. To borrow $100 million in December, it could borrow 70 million British pounds (these figures being roughly equivalent, though obviously they vary as the currencies fluctuate) at the British prime rate of 12.5%. Then it buys and immediately sells the pounds at $1.42, becoming in effect short pounds. Also it buys June British pound futures at $1.36.

At first glance, it might seem odd to be buying foreign currency futures when the goal is actually to borrow money. It might seem odder to be paying the extra 5% interest (the British 12.5% minus the U.S. 7.5% equals 5%).

The oddity evaporates on closer consideration. The futures purchase offsets the foreign currency exchange rate risk—much as a traditional hedge uses futures to offset cash-side risk. That is, this company borrowed British pounds. It has to repay British pounds some time in the future. At the moment, though, they do not have them. Therefore, they must repurchase those pounds at the then-current market which can change. Clearly, this company faces a risk similar to the one facing the company planning an expansion or the one facing a mortgage banker. However, the futures transaction offsets the possible change in the exchange rates.

The reason for accepting the extra interest (that is, the British 12.5% prime) becomes clear when the company completes the sequence. In May the company unwinds its position by buying pounds back at $1.42 (to simplify the example, assume that the price is unchanged—ultimately that assumption makes no difference) and selling futures—also at $1.42. Notice that the futures price has increased six cents to equal the cash price. This is not happenstance. Basis traders know that cash will equal futures, so they know what this price will be. As a result of that six cent futures gain, the business can more than offset the British borrowing rate and achieve a major savings on the cost of borrowed funds. A 40% interest savings ($3,000,000 in the case of a $100 million loan) is routine.

Looked at this way, the motive for "swapping" seems clear enough. And this is only one of several situations in which a version of this strategy can produce substantial benefits for a business.

While business people aware of the price volatility of the currencies may greet such claims with skepticism, they shouldn't. These benefits are relatively easy to achieve for those who master the fundamental market factors which apply, such as the basis. As Christopher Linden, a California-based money manager, has said in another context, "you don't have to be the first guy to think of an idea; you have to be the first person to understand the dynamics of the situation."

Reviewing Foreign Currency Basis

The currency trader aware of the basis and how it responds to the storage problem in this kind of market will find that he can control market volatility and turn it to his advantage because he does understand "the dynamics of the situation." The trader who does not will wonder where the money went.

The British pound basis is 0.06 over (1.42 - 1.36 = .06). That is, it costs six cents more to buy a pound on the cash market than on the futures market. Were futures prices higher than cash, the basis figure would be negative (for example, 1.36 - 1.42 = -.06). What is crucial is not the basis level at any moment, but how the basis is changing. As the basis becomes more positive, it is a narrowing basis. As it becomes more negative, it widens.

The basis for the German, Swiss, and Japanese currencies typically narrows while the basis for the British and Canadian currencies typically widens. That is because the German, Swiss, and Japanese interest rates are typically lower than the U.S. while the British and Canadian are typically higher.

The storage problem provides the key to understanding why these changes occur and how to take advantage of them. As with any supply and demand sequence, the currency market encourages storage at some times and movement at others. In general, when the market wants to move a currency, the basis narrows. When it wants to store it, the basis widens. As with other financials, currency basis essentially converges toward zero as contract delivery approaches. Currency basis converges to zero because of delivery.

All of this affects the risk manager's choice of strategy. Assuming for the moment that he will simultaneously establish cash and futures positions, the choice is between a long basis position (where the trader buys cash and sells futures) or a short basis position (where the trader sells cash and buys futures). A narrowing basis will reward the long basis position and severely punish the short basis position. Conversely, a widening basis will reward the short basis position and penalize the long basis position.

Why it Works

This brief review of how the basis works helps to explain why a British pound swap to reduce interest costs works as it does. Reiterating, that

Figure 21-1

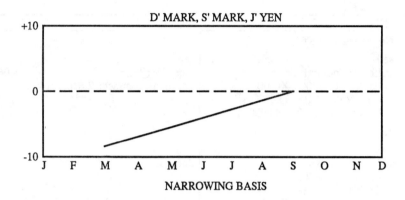

D' MARK, S' MARK, J' YEN

NARROWING BASIS

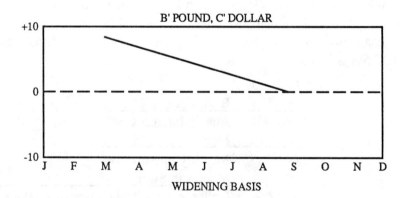

B' POUND, C' DOLLAR

WIDENING BASIS

trader first borrowed British pounds at 12.5% and then engaged in the trade sequence of Figure 21-2.

Figure 21-2

CASH	FUTURES	BASIS
November 1, 1987		
sell	buy	
British pounds @ 1.42	Jun BP @ 1.36	+.06
Par Value: $100,000,000	No. of Contracts: 2,816.9014	
Cash Value: $100,000,000		
Pound Value: £70,000,000		
June 1, 1987		
buy	sell	
British pounds @ 1.42	Jun BP @ 1.42	0
Par Value: $100,000,000		
Cash Value: $100,000,000		
Pound Value: £70,422,535		

November 1, 1986 to June 1, 1987: 7 months

   To see in more detail just how that kind of trading activity can benefit a business whose ultimate goal is to borrow money at a lower than prime rate, consider that, overall, borrowing $100 million worth of British pounds for seven months (November to June) at the British rate of 12.5% will cost $7,291,666.

$100,000,000	
x .125	British Prime Rate
$12,500,000	Annual Interest Cost
÷ 12	Months
$ 1,041,666	Monthly Interest Cost
x 7	Months in Swap
$ 7,291,666	Dollar Interest Paid on Borrowed Pounds

The futures trade used to protect against price risk resulted in a substantial basis gain.

70,422,535	Pounds ($100,000,000 1.42)
x .06	Dollar per Pound Basis Gain
$4,225,352	Total Basis Gain

That gain offsets part of the original interest cost.

$7,291,666	Gross Interest Cost
- $4,225,352	Basis Gain
$3,066,314	Net Interest Paid for Seven Months

Annualizing that net interest allows calculation of the effective interest rate for the loan.

$3,066,314	Net Interest
÷ 7	Months in Swap
$ 438,045	Monthly Interest
x 12	Months
$5,256,540	Effective Annual Interest

As a result, the actual rate this business pays to borrow money is 5.25%. Of course, transaction costs use up part of that gain. Still, this particular swap results in exchanging the 7.5% prime rate for an effective 5.5% rate, and that 2% rate shift amounts to an interest savings which exceeds 26%.

The most important feature to notice in this situation is that the basis converged to zero during the period of this swaps transaction, a completely predictable event. In anticipation of that predictably widening basis—from +.06 to zero—this trader adopted a short basis strategy. That is, on December 15 he sold cash and bought futures. His knowledge of how basis change rewards various strategies made it practically a foregone conclusion that this would be beneficial to his ultimate position. The only thing that can vary, in fact, is the matter of just how beneficial the transaction will be. That depends—on how soon the basis changes during the period of the swap.

Some Additional Considerations

The various swaps approaches succeed given correct choices among several principal variables. For one, the trader has to decide whether it is to his advantage to structure a long basis or a short basis position. He

Foreign Currency Swaps

Strategy 21

A. The Problem

To effect substantial interest rate savings, businesses can design advantageous foreign currency swaps. They can borrow money by borrowing British pounds at British prime, immediately selling them and buying pound futures which creates a short basis postion (sell cash, buy futures). The futures offset the foreign exchange risk. The basis change balances the British borrowing rate and produces a major interest rate savings.

B. Preliminaries

1. *The Basis*
   Cash − Futures = Basis
   a. 1.42 − 1.36 = +0.06
   b. 1.42 − 1.42 =   0

2. *Futures Position Size*
   Cash Position ÷ Contract Size = Futures Position Size (in Pounds)
   70,422,535   ÷ 25,000   = 2,816.9014

3. *Cash Position Size — Pounds*
   Dollar Par Value ÷ Pound Price = Cash Position Size — Pounds
   $100,000,000   ÷ 1.42   = 70,422,535

C. The Strategy

CASH	FUTURES	BASIS
November 1, 1986		
sell	buy	
British Pounds @1.42	Jun 87 BP @1.36	+.06
Par Value: $100,000,000	No. of Contracts: 2,816.9014	
Cash Value: $100,000,000		
Pound Value: £70,422,535		
June 1, 1987		
buy	sell	
British Pounds @1.42	Jun 87 BP @1.42	0.00
Par Value: $100,000,000		
Cash Value: $100,000,000		
Pound Value: £70,422,535		

November 1, 1986 to June 1, 1987: 7 months

D. Results and Evaluation

1. *Cash Result*
   0

2. *Futures Result* (gain)

Futures Change × Contracts   × Contract Size = Futures Result
0.06   × 2,816.9014 × 25,000   = 4,225,352

3. *Capital Gain*

0	Cash Result
4,225,352	Futures Result
4,225,352	Capital Gain

4. *Interest Expense*

$100,000,000	
×.125	British Prime Rate
$12,500,000	Annual Interest Cost
÷ 12	Months
× 7	
$7,291,666	Dollar Interest Paid on Borrowed Pounds

5. *Basis Value*

70,422,535	Pounds ($100,000,000 ÷ 1.42)
×.06	Dollar per Pound Basis Gain
$4,225,352	Total Basis Gain

6. *Net Interest Payment*

$7,291,666	Gross Interest Cost
−$4,225,352	Basis Gain
$3,066,314	Net Interest Paid for 7 Months

7. *Actual Interest Payment*

$3,066,314	Net Interest
÷ 7	Months in Swap
$438,045	Monthly Interest
× 12	Months
$5,256,540	Effective Annual Interest

8. *Annualized Interest Rate*

5,256,540	Effective Annual Interest
÷100,000,000	Cash Value
0.0525654	= 5.25% Effective Annual Rate

9. Basis Value = Capital Gain
   4,225,352   = 4,225,352

has to select the appropriate currency for his trade. And he has to decide whether to use futures or cash forwards.

Futures or Cash Forwards

A "cash forward" market is simply a market in which a dealer—in currencies in this case, so a bank—sets a future cash price for a currency. He agrees that he will, at this moment, sell a British pound or other currency at a given rate for delivery at some future time. As is the case with all the cash markets, the newspaper quotations for currencies state only the spot, or present, month. The cash forward quotes are similar in form to the futures quotes which list several "future" months in addition to the spot month. On October 22, 1987, the forward prices for the British pound may have been something like Figure 21-3.

Figure 21-3

Pound Cash Forwards

	Bid	Ask
Spot	1.6790	1.6885
1 month	1.6763	1.6861
3 month	1.6748	1.6847
6 month	1.6600	1.6705
9 month	1.6505	1.6615
1 year	1.6410	1.6515
3 year	1.5650	1.5805
4 year	1.5270	1.5445
5 year	1.4890	1.5085
7 year	1.4130	1.4365
10 year	1.2990	1.3285
30 year	0.5390	0.6085

October 22, 1987 quotations from J. L. McKinzie and Company, Inc.

Major banks will routinely quote cash forwards for all currencies. In essence, these operate in ways analogous to futures in that they create a basis (spot cash − forward cash = basis). An important difference, though, is that the cash forward market typically produces less dramatic basis change over a given time period than the futures market. That can become extremely important in planning swaps strategy.

Business Goals

To start with, a financial manager must decide on general business goals—to reduce interest expenses, to enhance return on investment, to fix balance sheet values from an off-shore division, to provide P&L protection for the stockholders. Then he must determine what kind of basis change he thinks will occur and whether it will work for his position or against it. Notice that at no time in this deliberation does the swaps strategist concern himself with price. Rather, whatever those may be from moment to moment, he focuses on the crucial cash-futures, or spot-forward, relationship—the basis.

Which Currency

Having settled the general questions, the swaps planner can decide on some of the particulars. If interest savings is the goal, then he is probably better off trading a currency with a low percent of carry. If investment earnings enhancement is the goal, the choice will be among the currencies with a high percent of carry.

The choice of which currency to swap is a function of basis convergence. Currencies with higher-than-U.S. rates will usually have a positive basis—widening to zero. That is illustrated by successively lower deferred foreign currency prices. The spreads in the futures quotes offer a good example.

	Dec	Mar	Jun	Sep
British pound	1.4090	1.3920	1.3760	1.3635

The lower replacement costs serve to offset the higher borrowing rate and reduce the investment yield. Thus the British pound example.

Currencies with lower-than-U.S. rates always have a negative basis—narrowing to zero. In these cases, the successively higher deferred currency prices of the quoted spreads serve as illustration.

	Dec	Mar	Jun	Sep
D' mark	.4867	.4883	.4901	.4919
S' franc	.5846	.5873	.5902	.5930
Yen	.006110	.006130	.006153	.006169

Thus in the case of currencies like the yen, Swiss franc, and Deutsch mark, the basis change serves to increase the investment yield and the borrowing rate.

The law of full carry says that cash positions offset by futures (long cash, short futures—that is, long the basis) will never return more than the short-term interest cost. This is an economic function limited by arbitrage. In short, an investor could not expect to buy British pounds, invest them at 12.5%, and sell British pound futures to protect against exchange rate fluctuations, to create a riskless yield enhancement of 5%. The basis insures an offsetting loss. In fact, the markets usually provide something less than 100% of full carry—say, 50%. Since full carry is the U.S. prime rate, 7.5% in this example, 50% of carry is 3.75%. Accordingly, the advantage goes to a trader who establishes a position short the basis (short cash, long futures), picking up on the lack of carry or "excess" basis convergence.

Basis convergence is well motivated. By definition cash will equal futures on delivery, so at that point the basis equals zero. The relationship between U.S. and foreign interest rates determines whether the basis is positive or negative for a given currency. It should be clear why it narrows or widens to zero. This motion to zero is called basis convergence.

Financial basis, unlike the basis in the case of physical commodities, converges in predictable ways. If the currency rate differential remains constant—say, 12.5% British against 7.5% U.S.—the dollar amount needed to overcome the yield difference declines with time, as Figure 21-4 shows.

Again, if the basis change will reward the trader's position, he wants to maximize the basis change. Futures usually produce more basis change than forwards. On the other hand, if, as sometimes happens, he finds himself in a position where the basis may work against his posi-

Figure 21-4 Foreign Currency Basis Convergence

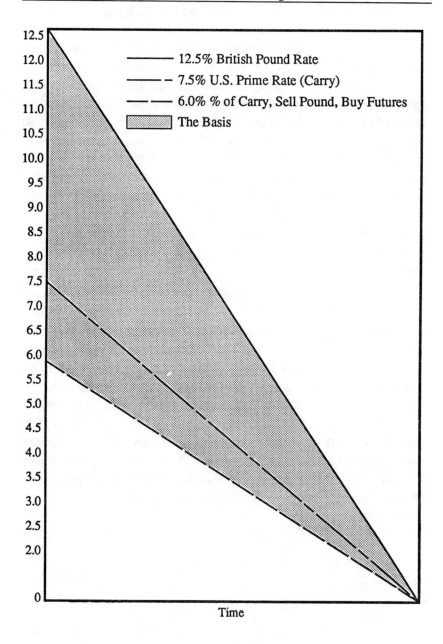

tion, he wants to minimize its impact. Using cash forwards often minimizes the basis change and helps to salvage the situation.

Several additional considerations underscore the importance of entering into a swaps transaction with a highly developed sense of business goals and with an awareness of market fundamentals. Project length and delivery flexibility can affect the choice of futures or cash forwards. Exchanges normally quote futures about 18 months in advance while many banks quote forwards for from one month to one year and negotiate outward as much as 30 years. Longer periods can be handled by rolling futures if the interest rate differential remains constant. Where the rate spread between countries changes, the spread of currency futures will also; and the rollover results would not be constant. Futures rollover exposes the user to greater transaction cost too, but as often as not cash forwards include a rollover premium.

Summing Up

The swaps decision is a basis decision with regard to which strategy to use, how to structure the transaction, and whether to use cash forwards or futures. And it is a basis question not to be taken lightly. Too many say that cash and futures have a high correlation and thus the basis can be ignored. While it may be that the basis will only change 3% to 6% of the total currency value—that 3% to 6% might amount to 50% or 80% of the interest amount. That is not an amount to be casual about.

Swaps strategies offer incredible flexibility of approach. So business people who think carefully about their basic goals and strive to understand the basis dynamics will find swaps to be extremely useful tools which produce highly predictable results. The crucial point is that the choice of swaps strategy is strictly a basis question.

VII

Keeping Track,
Two

22

Accounting for Basis Trades

Record keeping plays an vital role in basis trading. Risk managers often have several strategies in place at one time, each involving large positions—millions, even hundreds of millions, of dollars.

Because of the size of those positions, and what they mean to the companies, it is imperative that risk managers remember that the only reason ever to use futures is for the basis. Also, the only way to evaluate the hedging department is in terms of the basis result. Yet no one can judge the level of basis control unless they monitor and measure the total basis trading outcome.

Trying to keep track of all that without a "basis book" is impossible. Those who try are, in effect, speculating. They may have taken both cash and futures positions at roughly the same time. Yet in the absence of a basis book, that only means that they are speculating in both cash and futures instead of only one or the other. A basis book is especially crucial in financial risk management because the matter of cash-futures balance is so much more complex, even though the essentials of position accounting are the same for all commodities.

Any hedger strives for a balanced position. Yet most traders are always a little out of balance. It is not hard to see why that is the case. To begin with, the hedger carefully calculates hedge ratios, but even those

Figure 22-1 A Basis Trader's Position Sheet

1	2 Settlement Date	3 Run Date (Coupon) Rate	4 Maturity Date	5 Ending Balance	6 Principal Amount	7 Conv Fac	8 Futures	9 Basis	10 Conv Fac	11 Value	12 Basis
						INITIAL			MARKET		
						16-Aug-87 08:37:53 PM					
-1	07/27/87	8.750%	05/15/2017	15,000,000	96.21	1.0841	87.28	44.5	1.0841	99.18	31.3
-1	07/27/87	7.250%	05/15/2016	5,000,000	81.02	0.9163	87.28	17.4	0.9163	84.10	31.6
-1	07/27/87	9.250%	02/15/2016	119,000,000	102.07	1.1389	87.28	68.4	1.1389	104.08	21.8
-1	07/27/87	9.875%	11/15/2015	12,000,000	107.22	1.2076	87.28	50.2	1.2076	110.20	25.9
-1	07/27/87	10.625%	08/15/2015	55,000,000	115.19	1.2902	87.28	71.0	1.2902	118.18	39.5
-1	07/27/87	11.250%	02/15/2015	15,000,000	121.19	1.3574	87.28	74.0	1.3574	124.24	42.0
-1	07/27/87	11.750%	11/15/2014	65,000,000	123.28	1.3833	87.28	74.2	1.3833	127.15	53.6
-1	07/27/87	12.500%	08/15/2014	9,000,000	130.24	1.4583	87.28	83.3	1.4583	134.08	52.3
-1	07/27/87	13.250%	05/15/2014	2,000,000	136.30	1.5320	87.28	74.0	1.5320	140.28	49.9
-1	07/27/87	12.000%	08/15/2013	3,000,000	125.00	1.3999	87.28	63.5	1.3999	128.24	46.3
-1	07/27/87	10.375%	11/15/2012	5,000,000	110.16	1.2336	87.28	67.1	1.2336	113.26	52.2
-1	07/27/87	14.000%	11/15/2011	1,000,000	142.03	1.5773	87.28	111.6	1.5773	146.04	86.1
-1	07/27/87	12.750%	11/15/2010	15,000,000	130.00	1.4459	87.28	94.1	1.4459	133.24	72.4

	1,000,000
Futures	90.30
Updated	08/14/87

Weighted Average Basis

Initial	Market
69	37

Figure 22-1 (continued)

Futures/ Contract	Futures/ Position	Futures Dollars	CHANGE Cash Value	Basis/ Unit	Basis/ Position	Basis Dollars	Hedge Position
13	**14**	**15**	**16**	**17**	**18**	**19**	**20**
98.00	15936	498,008	(435,938)	−13.24	1,986	62,071	162.62
98.00	4490	140,308	(162,500)	14.20	(710)	(22,192)	45.82
98.00	132819	4,150,579	(2,417,188)	−46.61	55,469	1,733,391	1355.29
98.00	14201	443,793	(352,500)	−24.34	2,921	91,293	144.91
98.00	69542	2,173,181	(1,632,813)	−31.44	17,292	540,368	709.61
98.00	19954	623,556	(473,437)	−32.03	4,804	150,118	203.61
98.00	88116	2,753,632	(2,335,938)	−20.56	13,366	417,694	899.15
98.00	12862	401,944	(315,000)	−30.91	2,782	86,944	131.25
98.00	3003	93,835	(78,750)	−24.14	483	15,085	30.64
98.00	4116	128,616	(112,500)	−17.19	516	16,116	42.00
98.00	6045	188,895	(165,625)	−14.89	745	23,270	61.68
98.00	1546	48,305	(40,312)	−25.58	256	7,992	15.77
98.00	21255	664,210	(562,500)	−21.70	3,255	101,710	216.89

	Futures		Bond	Basis Net			Hedge
	(in 32nds)	(dollars)	Net	(in 32nds)		(dollars)	Position
	393,884	12,308,861	(9,085,000)	(288)		3,223,861	4019.22

do not always result in perfect matching of cash and futures. When it comes time to unwind the hedge, the trader has to deal with very different cash and futures prices though his par values on both sides are the same as they were at the start.

Management should establish a policy concerning balance. A good policy might specify that the basis trader must never be more than half a contract out of balance. That is, he must be fully hedged. The purpose of a policy like that is to prevent speculation, intentional or unintentional. Otherwise, a risk manager might inadvertantly speculate and win big a time or two. Such heady "success" often encourages another try. But eventually speculators lose—in amounts to inspire headlines like "Anatomy of a Staggering Loss." A basis trader is not subject to those risks. It is impossible to imagine why a proper basis trader should not always achieve his business goals—especially if he maintains a basis book.

A well-kept position sheet provides more than just information about position balance. It supplies useful progress reports. A basis trader can use it to help time his moves in the market as well as to develop an accurate overall sense of where he is in the market.

Figure 22-1 displays a typical financial position sheet. This trader is keeping track of a portfolio involving thirteen bonds.

Position Identification

A record of this kind groups information in several blocks. The first block, which includes the first six columns, identifies the transactions.

The first column contains a series of positive or negative ones. A 1 indicates a cash purchase and a -1 a cash sale. The inverse will be true on the futures side (notice that here, all the cash transactions are shorts, so all the futures trades will be longs). The second column indicates the day the transaction took place. Columns 3 and 4 identify the bond in terms of coupon rate and maturity date. The fifth column states the size of the position in terms of "transaction par value." Since an individual bond has $1,000 par value, the ending balance divided by 1,000 indicates the number of bonds in the position. The sixth column states the bond price on the settlement date. Keep in mind that these prices

Figure 22-2 Position Sheet Columns 1-6

	Settlement Date	Run Date (Coupon) Rate	16-Aug-87 08:37:53 PM Maturity Date	Ending Balance	Principal Amount
1	**2**	**3**	**4**	**5**	**6**
-1	07/27/87	8.750%	05/15/2017	15,000,000	96.21
-1	07/27/87	7.250%	05/15/2016	5,000,000	81.02
-1	07/27/87	9.250%	02/15/2016	119,000,000	102.07
-1	07/27/87	9.875%	11/15/2015	12,000,000	107.22
-1	07/27/87	10.625%	08/15 /2015	55,000,000	115.19
-1	07/27/87	11.250%	02/15/2015	15,000,000	121.19
-1	07/27/87	11.750%	11/15/2014	65,000,000	123.28
-1	07/27/87	12.500%	08/15/2014	9,000,000	130.24
-1	07/27/87	13.250%	05/15/2014	2,000,000	136.30
-1	07/27/87	12.000%	08/15/2013	3,000,000	125.00
-1	07/27/87	10.375%	11/15/2012	5,000,000	110.16
-1	07/27/87	14.000%	11/15/2011	1,000,000	142.03
-1	07/27/87	12.750%	11/15/2010	15,000,000	130.00

represent a percentage of par, so at 96-21 a bond ($1,000 par) would actually cost $966.56.

For example, the first line says that on July 27, 1987, this trader sold the 8.75% May 2017 bond at 96-21. The par value of his transaction was $15 million which means that he sold 15,000 of that bond (each bond has a $1,000 par value, so 15,000 x 1,000 = 15,000,000). The fourth line says that on July 27, 1987, he sold 12,000 of the 9.875% November 2015 bond at 107-22.

The Intitial Futures Situation

The second block of information specifies the futures market situation at the time of the transaction.

Figure 22-3 Position Sheet Columns 7, 8 and 9

	INITIAL	
Conv Fac	**Futures**	**Basis**
7	8	9
1.0841	87.28	44.5
0.9163	87.28	17.4
1.1389	87.28	68.4
1.2076	87.28	50.2
1.2902	87.28	71.0
1.3574	87.28	74.0
1.3833	87.28	74.2
1.4583	87.28	83.3
1.5320	87.28	74.0
1.3999	87.28	63.5
1.2336	87.28	67.1
1.5773	87.28	111.6
1.4459	87.28	94.1

Column 7 lists the conversion factor for each bond traded. Column 8 gives the nearby futures price for the transaction day. Since these transactions all take place on the same day, the futures price is the same. The ninth column shows the basis for each bond on its settlement date (the day of purchase).

Reading across the fifth line, where the trader has sold 55,000 of the 10.635% August 2015 bond at 115-19, the conversion factor is 1.2902, the futures price is 87-28, and the basis, as of July 27, is 71 (basis values are in 32nds). The ninth line, where the trader sold 2,000 of the 13.25% May 2009-14 bond at 136-30, shows that the conversion factor here is 1.5320, the futures price 87-28, and so the basis is 74.

The Updated Cash and Basis Situation

The third block of information, columns 10 through 12, updates the market situation as of August 14, 1987.

Figure 22-4 Position Sheet Columns 10, 11 and 12

	MARKET	
Conv Fac	Value	Basis
10	11	12
1.0841	99.18	31.3
0.9163	84.10	31.6
1.1389	104.08	21.8
1.2076	110.20	25.9
1.2902	118.18	39.5
1.3574	124.24	42.0
1.3833	127.15	53.6
1.4583	134.08	52.3
1.5320	140.28	49.9
1.3999	128.24	46.3
1.2336	113.26	52.2
1.5773	146.04	86.1
1.4459	133.24	72.4

On that day, the nearby futures price was 90-30. Since it is the same for each bond, the position sheet lists it below (where it says Futures Updated) to avoid a redundant column. Column 10 repeats the conversion factor. Column 11 lists the August 14 cash price for each bond and column 12 the updated basis.

The eighth line, for instance, shows that from July 27 to August 14 the price of the 12.5% August 2009-14 bond has changed from 130-24 to 134-08, and the basis for that bond has changed from 83.3 to 52.3. Similarly, according to line 11, the price of the 10.375% May 2007-12 bond has changed from 110-16 to 113-26, and the basis has changed from 67.1 to 52.2.

The Futures and Cash Value Changes

The fourth block of information, columns 13 through 16, shows the change in the futures and cash values between the settlement date and the day of the update.

Figure 22-5 Position Sheet Columns 13-16

		CHANGE	
Futures/ Contract	Futures/ Position	Futures Dollars	Cash Value
13	14	15	16
98.00	15936	498,008	(435,938)
98.00	4490	140,308	(162,500)
98.00	132819	4,150,579	(2,417,188)
98.00	14201	443,793	(352,500)
98.00	69542	2,173,181	(1,632,813)
98.00	19954	623,556	(473,437)
98.00	88116	2,753,632	(2,335,938)
98.00	12862	401,944	(315,000)
98.00	3003	93,835	(78,750)
98.00	4116	128,616	(112,500)
98.00	6045	188,895	(165,625)
98.00	1546	48,305	(40,312)
98.00	21255	664,210	(562,500)

Column 13 indicates the change in futures prices for one contract in 32nds (the difference between 90-30 and 87-28 is 3-02, or 98/32nds). Column 14 is the product of the single contract change in 32nds and the futures position size. Column 15, the product of column 14 and $31.25 (the cash value of one 32nd), defines the dollar value of the futures change. Column 16 specifies the dollar value of the change in cash prices for the total cash position in a particular bond.

In every position on this sheet, the futures change represents a gain, the cash a loss. While this is a perfectly normal example, there are other possibilities. A hedger might initiate and unwind strategies at the same time. Were that the case, then the values in column 1 would vary as would the matter of whether the cash and futures changes would represent gains or losses.

Because all the futures prices are the same, each contract changed 98/32nds. Beyond that, the second line shows that the futures position which balances the sale of 5,000 7.25% May 2016 bonds changed a total of 4,490/32nds (column 14) and that change has a dollar value of $140,308 (column 15). Meanwhile, the dollar value of the cash position change is $162,500 (column 16). The seventh line shows that the futures position which balances the sale of 65,000 11.75% November 2014 bonds changed a total of 88,116/32nds and that change has a dollar value of $2,753,632. The dollar value of the cash position change here is $2,335,938. Again, the futures changes are gains. The cash changes are losses.

The Basis Value Change

The fifth block defines the nature of the basis change for all of these positions.

Figure 22-6 Position Sheet Columns 17, 18 and 19

Basis/ Unit	Basis/ Position	Basis Dollars
17	18	19
-13.24	1,986	62,071
14.20	(710)	(22,192)
-46.61	55,469	1,733,391
-24.34	2,921	91,293
-31.44	17,292	540,368
-32.03	4,804	150,118
-20.56	13,366	417,694
-30.91	2,782	86,944
-24.14	483	15,085
-17.19	516	16,116
-14.89	745	23,270
-25.58	256	7,992
-21.70	3,255	101,710

Column 17 specifies the basis change (the difference between columns 9 and 12) in 32nds. Column 18 defines the basis change in terms of the number of 100,000 units of par. And column 19 assigns a dollar value to that change.

The sixth line shows that the basis for the 11.25% February 2015 bond widened 32.03 (negatives indicate widening while positives, as in line 2, indicate narrowing). That amounts to a 4,804/32nds for the entire position, and the basis change has a cash value of $150,118. The thirteenth line shows that the basis for the 12.75% November 2010 bond widened 21.7. The total change is 3,255/32nds for a cash value of $101,710.

The Hedge Position

The final column of the position sheet lists the number of futures contracts it takes to balance the cash position.

Figure 22-7 Position Sheet Column 20

Hedge Position
20
162.62
45.82
1355.29
144.91
709.61
203.61
899.15
131.25
30.64
42.00
61.68
15.77
216.89

These range from the 1355.29 contracts required to balance the 9.25% February 2016 bond position (line 3) to the 15.77 contracts required to balance the position in the 14% November 2011 issue.

Futures, Cash, and Basis Sums

All of this is basically data gathering. The numbers across the bottom of the sheet help to interpret the data, turning it into useful information.

Under blocks 4 through 6 are a series of sums. These define position totals. For example, the total hedge position here involves 4019.22 contracts. The total futures position has changed (between July 27 and August 14) 393,884/32nds. The dollar value of that change is $12,308,861. The cash change has a dollar value of $9,085,000, and the value of the basis change is $3,223,861. Notice that the sum of the futures and cash changes equals the value of the basis change. That tells this trader that he is fully hedged. Each position is in balance and so is the entire portfolio.

Weighted Averages

Even more important are the Weighted Average Basis figures toward the center of the sheet which indicate that the average basis for the initial date is 69 and for the update, 37. The basis, of course, is essentially the difference between the cash and futures prices, and differs for each bond. However, when a risk manager trades positions which vary between 1,000 and 119,000 cash bonds, as these do, the total position of the portfolio depends on the average of the basis changes weighted according to the sizes of the positions.

The biggest position here (line 3) also exhibits the biggest basis change. The basis for one position narrows (line 2) and works against the strategy, but it is also one of the smallest positions. Weighted averages allow hedgers to balance all of those factors in a useful way.

These averages can tell risk managers what the basis is doing to them and what they can expect it to do. If risk managers expect the basis to widen, they want to be short the basis. This portfolio experiences a 32-point narrowing according to the weighted averages. This hedger established a short basis position across the entire portfolio, and the 32-point

Figure 22-8

1	2 Settlement Date	3 Run Date (Coupon) Rate	4 Maturity Date	5 Ending Balance	6 Principal Amount	7 Conv Fac	8 INITIAL Futures	9 Basis	10 Conv Fac	11 MARKET Value	12 Bas
-1	07/27/87	8.750%	05/15/2017	15,000,000	96.21	1.0841	87.28	44.5	1.0841	99.18	31
-1	07/27/87	7.250%	05/15/2016	5,000,000	81.02	0.9163	87.28	17.4	0.9163	84.10	31
-1	07/27/87	9.250%	02/15/2016	119,000,000	102.07	1.1389	87.28	68.4	1.1389	104.08	21
-1	07/27/87	9.875%	11/15/2015	12,000,000	107.22	1.2076	87.28	50.2	1.2076	110.20	25
-1	07/27/87	10.625%	08/15/2015	55,000,000	115.19	1.2902	87.28	71.0	1.2902	118.18	39
-1	07/27/87	11.250%	02/15/2015	15,000,000	121.19	1.3574	87.28	74.0	1.3574	124.24	42
-1	07/27/87	11.750%	11/15/2014	65,000,000	123.28	1.3833	87.28	74.2	1.3833	127.15	53
-1	07/27/87	12.500%	08/15/2014	9,000,000	130.24	1.4583	87.28	83.3	1.4583	134.08	52
-1	07/27/87	13.250%	05/15/2014	2,000,000	136.30	1.5320	87.28	74.0	1.5320	140.28	49
-1	07/27/87	12.000%	08/15/2013	3,000,000	125.00	1.3999	87.28	63.5	1.3999	128.24	46
-1	07/27/87	10.375%	11/15/2012	5,000,000	110.16	1.2336	87.28	67.1	1.2336	113.26	52
-1	07/27/87	14.000%	11/15/2011	1,000,000	142.03	1.5773	87.28	111.6	1.5773	146.04	86
-1	07/27/87	12.750%	11/15/2010	15,000,000	130.00	1.4459	87.28	94.1	1.4459	133.24	72

Run Date 16-Aug-87 08:37:53 PM

	1,000,000
Futures	90.30
Updated	08/14/87

Weighted Average Basis

Initial	Market
69	37

Figure 22-8 (continued)

			CHANGE				Hedge
Futures/ Contract	Futures/ Position	Futures Dollars	Cash Value	Basis/ Unit	Basis/ Position	Basis Dollars	Position
13	**14**	**15**	**16**	**17**	**18**	**19**	**20**
98.00	15936	498,008	(435,938)	−13.24	1,986	62,071	162.62
98.00	4490	140,308	(162,500)	14.20	(710)	(22,192)	45.82
98.00	132819	4,150,579	(2,417,188)	−46.61	55,469	1,733,391	1355.29
98.00	14201	443,793	(352,500)	−24.34	2,921	91,293	144.91
98.00	69542	2,173,181	(1,632,813)	−31.44	17,292	540,368	709.61
98.00	19954	623,556	(473,437)	−32.03	4,804	150,118	203.61
98.00	88116	2,753,632	(2,335,938)	−20.56	13,366	417,694	899.15
98.00	12862	401,944	(315,000)	−30.91	2,782	86,944	131.25
98.00	3003	93,835	(78,750)	−24.14	483	15,085	30.64
98.00	4116	128,616	(112,500)	−17.19	516	16,116	42.00
98.00	6045	188,895	(165,625)	−14.89	745	23,270	61.68
98.00	1546	48,305	(40,312)	−25.58	256	7,992	15.77
98.00	21255	664,210	(562,500)	−21.70	3,255	101,710	216.89

Futures		Bond	Basis Net		Hedge
(in 32nds)	(dollars)	Net	(in 32nds)	(dollars)	Position
393,884	12,308,861	(9,085,000)	(288)	3,223,861	4019.22

widening confirms the wisdom of that strategy. The $3.2 million difference between cash loss and futures gain offers further corroboration.

Basis traders know that as delivery nears, the basis of all bonds converges toward zero. The relevant date here is the delivery point for the September futures contract. Since this update is only that, and not an unwinding date, the hedger should be thinking about how much more the basis can narrow. The weighted averages suggest that it can only go about 32 farther. Then he either has to roll over his futures positions or unwind.

A position sheet like this one conveys two important messages. This hedger has protected all of his cash positions. He is fully hedged. Also, the weighted averages confirm the wisdom of the general short basis plan. In this situation, this postion sheet says that the hedger who is short the basis is making money.

VIII

Establishing a Basis Trading System

Effective risk management requires effort and discipline. Risk managers have to understand the way the basis works. They must keep meticulous records so they can track the basis and their own positions. And they have to master the strategic possibilities so they can put their knowledge to work for them.

To accomplish all that, they must somehow overcome the limitations of common sense and a variety of temptations. The strategies often seem counterintuitive. The futures markets are as enchanting as any siren song. Ultimately, more risk management efforts fail because the risk manager just couldn't overcome his price fixation than for any other reason.

Risk managers can triumph if they add to their basis knowledge an awareness of how the markets work. A thorough appreciation of how the markets process trades leads to an understanding of the costs trading entails. Aware of that, risk managers can design risk management systems that overcome the pitfalls and temptations inherent in the "common sense" approach.

Risk managers should remember, too, that risk management requires equal acumen on both the cash and the futures sides. For many businesses, involvement in the futures market is a new adventure. The futures trade has unusual allure. Basis traders need to guard against that. They need not to lose track of the cash alternatives. As a matter of fact, thorough grounding in basis principles helps them handle even such apparently simple matters as buying a cash bond more shrewdly. Also, as the swaps discussion suggests, they can recognize situations where "cash forwards" might be preferable to futures.

All in all, risk managers' basis sense gives them immense flexibility. Their comprehensive bag of tricks allows them to scrutinize each situation on its own terms and choose the approach best suited to protect their assets and take advantage of extra profit opportunities.

23

Working with the Markets

To the uninitiated eye, the "open outcry auction" of the commodities pits appears chaotic. Appearances are deceiving. There's order in that madness. Risk managers need to understand how these markets operate, what their role should be, and what the costs are. Only when they comprehend these things can they make sure they reap rewards in keeping with their efforts.

The Players

Recall the earlier distinction between hedgers and speculators and the identification of risk managers with hedgers—which in no way disparages the speculator's role. However, in thinking about establishing a risk management system, the hedger-speculator distinction established earlier is not the important distinction. Both are likely to be off-floor traders. Floor traders, in contrast, hold exchange seats and so can trade in the pits. They may be floor brokers or locals.

Floor brokers trade customer accounts. Neither speculators nor hedgers, their role is to serve off-floor customers—individual and commercial alike. The terms floor broker and paper trader are interchangeable. Paper trader derives from the fact that the floor broker trades customer paper—the half-sheets that customer orders are written on. At any moment, a paper trader may have hundreds of those in his deck. (A *deck* is the stack of customer paper the floor broker has waiting for action.)

Locals, speculators who trade their own accounts in the pits, are key players in filling the customer orders. A customer can only buy if someone else wants to sell—and only sell if there is a buyer. Locals take those positions and so "make a market" for customers. They may be position traders or scalpers.

Position traders hold positions more than one day in the hopes of profiting from some major market movement.

Scalpers, sometimes called day traders because they seldom carry positions over from one day to the next, count on mental agility to benefit from every little twist and turn of the market. Their tactic is to trade in and out of the market, starting a position ahead—with the edge—and getting out even or with a profit. For example, if a local's last bond trade in the pit was 100-00, then a customer will have to sell a little lower—buy a little higher. The bid, that is, will be at least 100-31, and the ask will be 101-01. In active or thin markets, the spread may well be wider. The 32nd which the local tries to gain on each trade is "the edge." The scalper's goal is to accumulate that edge in a series of trades. A rule of thumb holds that he will make the edge about half the time, break even about a fourth, and lose about a fourth.

Often, too, this tactic leaves the local opposite the market direction. What saves him is that he always starts with the edge. As the market rallies, the local sells. When enough traders are selling, the market dips a bit and the scalper buys. Back and forth, throughout the day, he "scalps" off the edge and so makes money. In this way, he makes the market until permanent position holders take the trade.

The Edge, the Bid-Ask, and Ticks

A surprising number of people, some a long time in the markets, confuse the bid-ask spread with the edge, and the edge with a tick.

A typical line in the daily quotations of Treasury securities includes two prices and looks like this:

Rate	Mat.	Date	Bid	Asked	Chge.	Yld.
15.75	Nov	2001	171-24	172-00	+.12	7.66

The bid is the price at which a trader can immediately sell the bond. The ask is the price at which he can immediately buy. Only brokers can provide usefully current bid-ask quotations.

That spread is not the same as the edge. Actually, the edge is the difference between the last trade and the bid or the ask. If the last bond trade went at 100-00 and the bid is 99-31 while the ask is 101-01, then the edge in either case will be one 32nd. If there is much selling going on, the edge can increase to double that or more. In effect, the edge is the premium that floor traders charge for making the market. It is not a set amount but it is made by the market, and the floor trader has some leeway in what he can do. A bullish local may give up the edge so he can buy all the bonds he can get his hands on. In such a case, he is willing to give up the edge because he expects to profit from a price increase.

There are those who confuse the edge with a tick. The minimum price increment, a tick varies from market to market. Generically, it is one of the smallest price increments. In the grains, a tick is a fourth of a cent a bushel. In financials it is one 32nd. Even though these seem like tiny amounts, multiplied across the size of a typical transaction, they can result in huge dollar amounts. For example, if a corn trader loses the edge on a trade involving 100,000 bushels of corn, he has lost $250. A bond trader who loses a 1/32nds edge on a thousand bonds would lose $31,250.

Often the traders refer to the edge as a tick, or as two ticks. They are describing the size of the edge, not equating the two ideas. Though a tick itself is always a very small number, the edge represents the local's profit. To him, the difference between a one tick and a two tick edge is a big one.

Making the Trade

Trading regulations specify that a floor broker cannot directly match customer orders within his deck. In the jargon of the pits, he cannot "cross" his own paper. There must be a local between all trades. A floor broker can trade with another broker. After all, a floor broker is a kind of local trader.

If that rule were not in place, the floor trader could look through his deck of customer paper and cross orders. For example, finding an order to buy one T-bond contract at market and another to sell one at market, the paper trader could simply mark the current price on each order and send them back to the phone desk as fulfilled.

Since the rules prevent that, the floor broker has to offer the paper to the pit and wait for one of the locals to "make a market" for each of those customers.

One advantage the locals enjoy over other kinds of traders is in the area of transaction costs. At the Chicago Board of Trade, for example, a local pays a very low cost for each trade—on the order of 80 cents for a scratch trade and $1.50 for a nonscratch. In effect, that very minor participation fee is what allows locals to make the market.

The Traditional Trade Sequence

The trade sequence starts when a customer calls his broker. The broker seldom can make the trade himself. Typically he is hundreds or thousands of miles from the city where the relevant "pit" is. He probably does not belong to an exchange, so even if he is in Chicago or New York, where the major exchanges are, he cannot trade on the floor.

Rather he must go through a "clearing firm," a company which handles trades for just such brokers. Smaller volume brokers call the clearing firm's "order desk" to place their customers' orders. Larger volume brokers may be able to call direct to the "phone desk" which is located adjacent to the pits on the trading floor. Trading volume determines a pecking order among the clearing firms. Those who handle the largest volume of trades earn desk positions nearer the pits. Surprisingly, the well-known firms are often not the big volume ones. Rather, those who clear the local traders are.

Either way, the order ultimately reaches the phone desk at the exchange where a phone clerk takes the order, writes a "ticket," and hands it to a runner who takes it to the the pit where a floor broker will execute the trade.

In the pit, the floor broker checks the order and decides whether he can execute it immediately or if it will have to wait for the market to develop. He makes the trade right away if he can. Otherwise he adds the sheet to the deck He might sort buys on top of his deck, sells at the bottom.

He also might have several orders to buy or sell at a given price. Obviously he can't treat each order separately. Say he had 10 orders to buy 2 contracts, all at the same price. Working through the paper one at a time would allow the market to move past the limit. Some of the orders would remain unfilled.

Typically, the floor broker notes the number of orders at that price and writes it on the back of the top ticket. When that ticket surfaces, he will buy 20 contracts (10 orders for 2) at once, note the fill on the back of the first sheet, and catch up on his paper work during the next lull in pit action. That way all 10 customers "get a fill."

Busy brokers have assistants who handle much of that kind of paper work. Also, many trades are "arbed" or signaled into the pit from a phone desk. An assistant "endorses" the paper for the broker in those cases.

The trade filled, the floor broker gives the executed order to a runner who takes the fill back to the phone clerk, who relays it to the broker, who in turn informs the customer of his position.

Transaction Costs—Hidden and Apparent

Risk managers have to recognize the costs of trading. As off-floor traders, they have to pay hefty brokerage fees, compared with what the locals pay. Those commissions are not large amounts when the risk manager sticks to his plan. But if he loses track of the fact that he is not in the same game as the scalpers, this cost can become a significant one. Obviously, each step in that process adds overhead for which the customer pays. For one thing, each person who handles the order gets a salary or a commission. Also, the more people who handle an order, the more chance for error.

Figure 23-1   Traditional Travels of a Trade

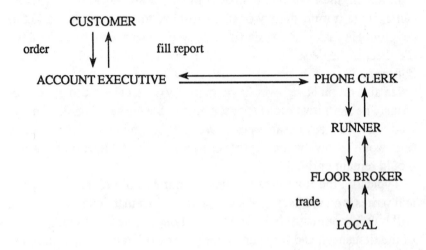

Since the locals are betting they can gain the edge, risk managers should assume that giving it up is part of their cost of doing business.

Another very real cost for risk managers is their lack of feel for the market. Since they are not able to be on the floor to sense the moods and trading tides that tip off the scalpers, risk managers also have to concede that there are details of fine tuning that they will miss—to their cost.

Taken all together, that means customers pay a significantly larger transaction cost than locals do, which is important to bear in mind when planning trading strategy.

Risk managers who do plan carefully find they can reduce those costs significantly. Besides making good use of a basis book, they can take out corporate memberships at the exchanges they use the most. Most of the major exchanges provide such memberships for a nominal fee. The corporate member does not gain floor trading priviledges, but it does get a reduction in transaction costs. The Chicago Board of Trade, to cite just one example, charges $500 a year. Corporate members then pay ten cents for each transaction as opposed to the usual nonmember clearing fee. Risk managers can also use new trading approaches to limit costs.

A Streamlined Trade Sequence

Recent changes in the way both brokers and customers do business together have motivated changes in that trade process. The advent of inexpensive market data transmission equipment, for example, has made it possible for many customers to do their own research and plan their own trades. The current nature of the markets puts an extra premium on rapid execution and on minimizing overhead.

Thus, in the near future, customers more and more can expect to trade through introducing brokers (IBs) who work right on the exchange floor. These people, themselves floor traders, are constantly in touch with what is happening in the market—what the majors are doing, what opportunities are developing.

In this kind of setup, the customer calls direct to the exchange floor. A trader takes the order. Strategically located, he can often signal a trader in the pit directly. In that case, the customer may receive his fill without ever having left the phone. This method creates important benefits for the customer.

The customer gets faster execution and immediate news about his order. Since the contact person in this case is himself a trader, the customer has a more direct connection to the market with people who have a better feel for what is happening and what to look for than non-trading personnel can possibly have. This approach also cuts overhead. The phone clerk and runner are no longer necessary, nor, in many cases, is the second phone call. With overhead reduced, the broker can achieve a reasonable margin and still slash transaction costs. It follows that customers can achieve profits more easily and trade more flexibly.

That streamlined mode of trading can significantly reduce costs. Every step in that regard is important. Still, the most costly mistake would-be risk managers make is to think they can trade the markets like speculators.

Figure 23-2   Streamlined Travels of a Trade

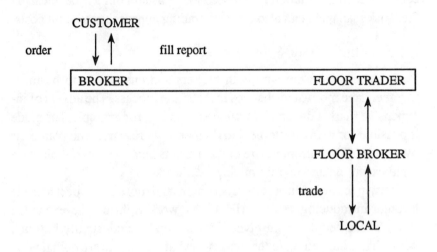

Additionally, where commercial hedgers are making cash exchanges, they can do what is called an "ex pit trade." To make such a trade, the two hedgers simply call their brokers, and instruct them to receive and give up futures at a specific price within the day's range. The ex pit trade protects against market slippage, including giving up the edge. It does not eliminate commissions.

Resisting Temptation

Risk managers must, at all costs, avoid the impulse to become scalpers. To succumb to that urge is a sure way to lose money.

Pursuing the edge in the pits takes steel nerves, split-second timing, and the intuition bred of long, intense experience in the pits. Pure reflex is the scalpers' rule. If they have to think what to do next, it's already too late. It should be obvious that no risk manager can trade that way, nor can anyone not actually on the floor and acting on his own.

Risk managers can profit from careful basis trading, from taking advantage of larger movements in the market. Granted, there may at times be variations within these general patterns that can create opportunities for traders. But even these are gross movements compared to the market flutters to which locals respond.

Trouble comes when risk managers start tracking prices. They are intriguingly volatile. If they weren't, there wouldn't be a market. Then, insidiously, these fluctuations begin to look like opportunities. Worse, they seem opportunities they ought not miss. Before they know it, they're hooked.

Commodities trading can be addictive. And a synonym for a market addict is loser. Basis trading can be a big winner for a careful, disciplined risk manager. The possible gains far outweigh the costs. Certainly there is no point in trying to be a scalper and putting the entire program in jeopardy.

Looking Ahead

In the effort to limit costs, people in all areas invariably think about computers these days. The commodities markets are no exception. As a result, an even more streamlined alternative is emerging in some markets. NASDAQ, for example, uses a system of computer-matched trades. In a system of that kind, customers telephone their buys and sells directly to the computer. The computer matches positions and automatically executes the trades, reporting the results to the exchange.

The great advantage of this approach is that with buys and sells matched by the computer, there is no edge to give up, the transaction costs are minimal, and the mistake rate low. A serious problem arises in illiquid markets. If no customer takes the other side of a position—that is, if everyone wants to sell, or buy—then trading comes to a halt. Traders refer to that as a lack of market efficiency. In the traditional pit, where a local is almost always willing to make a market, the markets are extremely efficient. Many traders think that the traditional markets' efficiency far outweighs any advantage a computerized market might be able to offer at this point.

**Figure 23-3 A Graphic Summary of a Computer-Assisted Trade
Sequence**

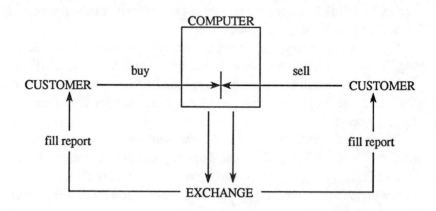

At present, then, it appears to many market experts that the advantages of computer-matched trading are more a promise for the future, if they exist at all, than a present benefit.

Relating Compensation to Services

A further way of managing the costs of a risk management program has to do with the kind of business structure the risk manager establishes to deal with his basis trading needs. He may well conceive of his trading and planning as separate functions to be separately paid for.

On the one hand, since the risk manager is likely to make his own trading decisions and provide much of his own research, he hardly needs a full service broker. Therefore, he might well choose a discount broker to handle his buying and selling so his commissions are minimal.

He should pay separately for basis advice—which is unavailable through most flat price trading brokers.

The reason for distinguishing the two functions—which may, in fact, be performed by the same person as well as by two people—is that if the commission is the broker's only compensation, he will see to it that there is turnover in the account. Risk managers should willingly pay a commission for necessary transactions, compensation should depend on basis returns, not turnover. Thus a separate annual fee for basis advice makes sense.

In sum, the basis trader has to plan his activities so that he is reasonably certain the gains will more than offset the transaction costs as well as provide the protection and the profit opportunities which are the ultimate goals.

24

Buying Cash Bonds

Nothing in the world of finance should be easier than buying a U.S. Treasury bond. The wonder is that so many people botch the job.

In the common view, the process is simple. A buyer solicits quotes for a bond with a satisfactory yield to maturity, finds the highest yield, and places the order. Several problems inhere in that approach. Volatile as the bond market is, a price quote has relevance for a few seconds at most. Worse, to consider only yield is to overlook important quality differences among the various bonds.

Typically, portfolio complexity obscures the error so management does not identify it. It is possible that by the time the error becomes significant, enough time has passed that the effect on the portfolio's performance is devastating.

There is no need to let myopic inattention to details like unstated costs imperil cash side performance.

Use Bid-Ask Spreads

To begin with, the shrewd bond buyer shops carefully. Only if the buyer requests it will dealers give quotes in terms of a "bid-ask spread." The norm is for the dealer to give only a "bid yield" or an "ask yield," but not both. A customer who lets it be known that he wants to buy a bond gets only the selling price from the dealer.

The dealer will state as little additional information as possible. The bid is the price for which the customer can sell the bond. The ask is what the customer must pay. The spread differs from bond to bond, ranging getween one and sixteen 32nds. Figure 24-1 shows bid-asks ranging from eight thirty-seconds to 16 thirty-seconds.

Figure 24-1

Bond			Bid	Ask	Spread (in 32nds)
15.750%	2001	Nov	166-08	166-16	08
11.625%	2002	Nov	132-10	132-18	08
7.625%	2002-07	Feb	97-20	98-04	16
10.375%	2007-12	Nov	123-22	123-30	08
12.500%	2009-14	Aug	145-27	146-03	08

For principal transactions over $1 million, the bid-ask spread should usually not exceed one 32nd. Also, active or high quality securities often have low bid-ask spreads.

Obviously, different bonds have different prices, but it is also the case that the price of a given bond can differ from dealer to dealer—for a variety of reasons. For one, dealers often try to skew the spread to their advantage. Thinking a customer plans to buy, for example, the dealer might skew the spread high to pick off an extra margin. Do not blame *him* for that: *caveat emptor*.

To guard against such tactics, the savvy bond buyer never reveals his intention—whether to buy or to sell. Rather, he asks for a "tradable bid" *and* a "tradable ask." To that, a dealer might reply: "The new issue is 99-01 bid, 99-02 offered, with size of 20 million." Size is the amount tradeable at that price. Doing so makes the spread apparent and makes it difficult for the dealer to skew his price away from the market. Should he think the customer wants to buy and so shade his prices high, without widening the spread, then the customer should sell him securities. That keeps dealers honest.

Use Basis Quotes for Comparability

Dealers routinely give these bid-ask quotes in terms of the price of the moment. The trouble with that, given the nature of the bond market, is the price, like the moment, is fleeting. By the time the buyer gets a quote and dials another dealer, the market has probably moved. As a result, no useful comparison is possible. Fortunately, there is a simple solution.

Knowledgeable bond buyers ask for quotations in terms of the basis. Since the basis quotation relates to the moving market benchmark, it holds good for at least several hours, if not all day. That allows useful comparison of several dealers' quotes.

Further, since only the most astute traders deal in basis pricing, or know to ask for "tradable" bids and asks, the buyer who does so positions himself as a professional and issues a clear "don't tread on me" signal to the dealers. He has taken the first steps toward minimizing transaction costs as well.

Aware of the various dealers' prices, the buyer can now watch the futures market and choose a low point to buy or a high point to sell. Since dealers normally hedge their holdings, a buyer's successful pricing choice will neither affect the dealer's results nor offend him. It may well earn the buyer respect. In any case, the buyer who operates in terms of basis and futures can leave an open order with the dealer to buy at a given basis and a specified futures price, saying something like: "I'm 88 over the Dec bid for 13 million par of 12.5% August 2009-14, good till noon."

Master the Quality Issue

Having created a good impression, the buyer must back it up with a substantial understanding of bond quality. Few bond buyers make the mistake of assuming that equal default risk makes U.S. Treasury bonds equal in quality. For some reason, most buyers pay attention to maturity but overlook the role of coupon. Both are important quality issues.

Yield changes cause variations in bond prices which differ according to maturity and coupon. A given yield change will affect a longer maturity bond more than it will a bond with a shorter maturity. Bonds with different coupons also respond differently to yield changes, the price of a high coupon bond changing more in dollar terms but that of a low coupon more in percentage terms.

As a result a bond buyer's choice of a particular bond is also a choice concerning how his portfolio will respond to a volatile yield environment. He can make that choice unconsciously, or he can make it consciously and so maintain control over portfolio performance.

It is interesting to recall, in this context, that the regulatory agencies have imposed on banks and thrifts an asset-liability sensitivity ratio which often limits them with regard to what maturities they can hold in their portfolios.

The regulators sought, through this device, to ensure that no bank would excessively mismatch its securities portfolio in terms of when it might have to pay out funds. Since Treasuries are easily negotiable, surely the regulators intended by this means to protect the banks and thrifts from the possible value changes that would follow from a major yield change.

That concern is helpful—as far as it goes. But ignoring coupon leaves those institutions exposed to changes which can be every bit as great as those due to different maturities, though an easy remedy is available. An institution can define an acceptable risk level, and the securities trader can increase or decrease portfolio exposure, depending on his expectations about yield change, by taking both maturity and coupon into consideration. Awareness of what factors to consider makes adequate planning possible.

Basis provides a convenient quality indicator. The less positive—that is, the wider—the basis, the lower the quality of the bond. Of all deliverable bonds, the so-called cheapest to deliver has the widest basis. The basis of that issue will converge to zero as delivery approaches. The other bonds will converge toward, but not to, zero.

It is also the case that higher coupon bonds converge more sharply than lower coupon issues. As a result, cheapest to deliver status can change. For example, on a given date a 9.375% bond may be cheapest to deliver, but three months later the 12.5% bond may overtake it.

A further quality variation stems from a weakness in the definition of the bond futures contract. The conversion factors are fixed, yet security prices change at everchanging rates with respect to yield changes. The actual value changes, that is, differ in time and in terms of the other issues.

Figure 24-2 The Cheapest to Deliver Bond Converges to Zero

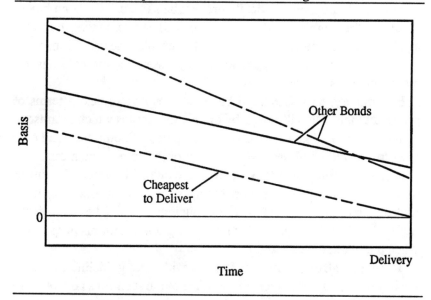

Figure 24-3 The 12.5% Bond Overtakes the 9.375% Bond to Become Cheapest to Deliver

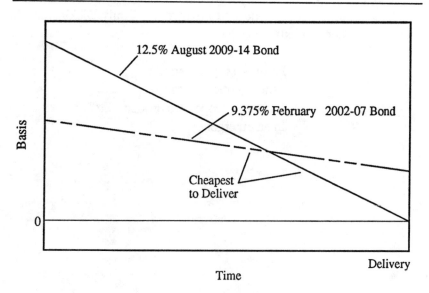

For all that apparent complexity, most of the quality variations among bonds are mathematically predictable. The careful bond buyer, if he takes the trouble, can thus make reasoned choices among the bonds available. Furthermore, that predictability enables the careful manager to review his portfolio systematically, reassessing his holdings for quality changes and risk exposure.

In summary, an astute bond buyer will buy securities in terms of price, not yield. He will select, by price, those issues which promise to earn the best yield given the quality differences. Should the bond ever need to be sold or turned over, transaction costs become a matter of greater importance than they otherwise would. Therefore, the buyer, masking his intention to buy or sell, asks for basis quotes in terms of tradeable bids and asks. After comparing those quotes, he executes the trade when he thinks the market is at the right point for his purposes—when the market feels right.

The payoff? Buying smart, in keeping with these guidelines, can save the buyer up to half a percent of the value of the securities portfolio just from careful trading in and out. Perhaps more important, careful management can control what could otherwise be enormous exposure to quality risks. Attention to detail when buying bonds can result in especially satisfying portfolio performance. As Emily Dickinson said in quite another context:

> Faith is a fine invention
> When gentlemen can see,
> But microscopes are prudent
> In an emergency.

25

A Two-Trader System

B asis trading is an involved and complicated process. In no sense does it lighten anyone's load. But it can make bearing that load more rewarding.

The difficulty comes from the variety of demands on the basis trader. He must understand the basis and the storage imperatives that drive it. He must constantly evaluate current events in terms of what they mean to the drive into or out of storage. He must maintain charts and records to keep track of basis developments and to maintain awareness of his positions and of the results of his strategies. And he must achieve mastery of the strategic repertoire sufficient to be able to match strategy to situation effectively.

That is a tall order. The more so because basis trading often flies in the face of conventional wisdom. Basis traders often act in ways that cash traders simply cannot comprehend. What seems natural and well-motivated to a basis trader often seems counterintuitive to a cash trader.

Because that is true, it is probably safe to say that almost never can the same person handle both tasks. What's more, extensive background as a cash bond trader may well render a person unable to become a basis trader. There is just too much habit to overcome.

That need not deter anyone from embarking on a risk management program. It simply requires that risk managers give as much thought to matters of business structure and staffing as they do to strategy.

Probably the best way to handle the risk management program is through a "two-trader system." The cash bond traders should keep doing what they know how to do. Someone else should become the basis trader. The two should operate independently because their concerns and goals differ. If they pay too much attention to each other, the most likely result will be confusion. At the same time, the cash trader has to keep the basis trader informed concerning the "cash department's" activities. That way, everyone knows the company's position.

Risk managers are usually designing a structure to protect against a short-term danger. Any one strategy is likely to be kept in place for a few months, seldom more than a year. As a result, basis traders seldom even look at yield. After all, as they know, over the short haul, the basis operates in such a way that the investment yields something less than the short-term rate. Yield hardly motivates basis traders.

Basis traders derive their gains from the basis change rather than from the yield rate. Therefore, to choose a cash bond, they have to perform a more involved analysis. First they have to define their business goals, what the risk management program is supposed to accomplish for the company as a whole. Next they have to design a strategy that will enable them to achieve those goals. Then they have to decide what they think the basis situation will be during the period of concern. Finally, they have to choose the right instrument.

If the basis will work in favor of their strategy, the right bond is the one that will produce the greatest basis change. Given the psychological set that many cash bond buyers have in favor of discounts, that creates an obvious conflict. For often the bond that will produce the greatest basis change is a high coupon premium bond. If the basis is going to work against the strategy, then a bond that will produce less basis change is the better choice.

Often the high coupon premium bonds produce the most basis change (the basis of those bonds converges most rapidly toward zero). To a cash trader, bonds like the 13.25% May 2009-14 or the 12.5%

August 2009-14 may seem expensive. That sways a basis trader not at all. Basis change is his guide.

Basis traders also have to be aware of a variety of other circumstances. Changing yield rates alter basis performance. Where one bond might be preferable at one level, another might be if the yield passes a certain benchmark.

The basis trader has a far more complex responsibility. He will act like an in-house dealer in a sense. And he and the cash buyer will be in competition. That follows from the nature of buying and selling. When the basis trader is selling on the cash market, he wants to get a good price. But the basis trader, if price interests him at all, is far less concerned with price than with the basis. Where a low price is almost surely a good buy for the cash buyer, a low price—signalling a narrow basis—could be a good sale for the basis trader (think, yet again, about Georges Andre's comment). Accordingly, these two traders complement each other in a way that may seem counterintuitive to the uninitiated. Competition is inevitable, therefore, and the company will surely benefit from it.

Furthermore, the company can set up a kind of profit and loss statement for the basis trader. By keeping track of his costs of doing business—the trader's time, interest expenses when he has to finance a cash transaction, overhead, and anything else that enters into the cost—the company can determine just how successful the hedging operation has been.

IX

Wrapping Up

26

Summing Up

The idea of risk management is to convert an inherently risky business situation into one where the risk becomes a predictable, manageable factor. Risky risk management is a contradiction. Yet as more and more people enter the field, there is a growing folk lore of hedging horror stories. (One company, the story goes, keeps a potted bush in its trading room and has ruefully labelled it "the perfect hedge.") As a result, companies that could reap substantial benefits from hedging shy away. The tragedy of these stories is not that the companies lost huge amounts of money from hedging but that these people need not have suffered at all. The runaway losses were avoidable.

Careful study of the horror stories suggests that they are not accidental but well motivated. The approach of those "would- be hedgers," who were

- hedging by habit
- shortcutting on their homework
- not keeping basis books

made the horrors a near certainty. Any one of those traits can be dangerous to a hedger. The package is incendiary. Under the circumstances, it is hard to imagine any other results. However, again, properly approached, hedging does not produce that kind of result.

In all the examples of hedging strategies and discussions of how to keep track of risk positions, two themes have sounded over and again:

1. Risk managers must define business goals, analyze the market situation, and choose the strategy that will achieve those goals in that situation.
2. Hedgers must keep careful records of their positions and results because outward appearances can be deceiving.

Habit

People who hedge by habit ask for trouble. It is by now well-known that financial basis converges toward zero. It widens. Also, a strategy which gets the risk manager short the basis is the right one in that kind of market.

Except there are a number of strategies in which the risk manager designs a position where he is long the basis. To be sure, some are losers. Yet others are not.

Recall that even in cases where the basis works against the position, the long basis strategy may allow the risk manager to achieve his business goals.

Sometimes the basis actually narrows. The narrowing period may be a market aberration. It may last only a few days. Yet such events, which are perfectly ordinary, present opportunities to alert risk managers— times when they want to be long the basis in order to enhance their yields.

In short, a risk manager who operates according to rules of thumb like "bond basis always ... therefore ..." or "last year at this time ... therefore ..." may well find hedging dangerous.

Shortcuts

For some reason, though, people try to shortcut the preparation process. Perhaps that comes from the general sense that the commodity markets move rapidly. They do. That makes incomplete thinking even more dangerous.

Some of the new hedgers seem to think of their risk management activities as ends in themselves. Risk management, to them, is an autonomous activity, divorced from the rest of the overarching strategic plan that guides the other branches of their business.

To be effective, risk management must operate in a context. A company wants to limit the cost of building a new plant, protect its cash reserve, improve its borrowing rate, enhance investment yields. Whatever the goal, each kind of objective requires a certain kind of strategic response.

Further, given an articulate goal, the hedger must relate the right strategy to the right market. Sometimes that will be T-bonds, sometimes notes, and sometimes foreign currencies. In addition, to manage risk effectively, the hedger has to respond to the markets as they are. Not as rumor has it. Not as they were last year. As they are now.

Records

An amazing number of people try to hedge without keeping a basis book. Major companies commit vast sums of money to the markets without charting the basis and without keeping effective position records. In point of fact, those people are speculators who just happen to be doing things with both cash and futures more or less at the same time.

The trouble with that is that speculating is risky. Speculators eventually have to face losses, which the big traders in Chicago understand. They risk only "risk" capital, so they are willing to accept losses in exchange for the chance to achieve an occasional major gain. Some of the biggest speculators say their losing trades outnumber their winning ones.

In contrast, a risk manager is hardly trading risk capital. Few companies consider their cash reserve or the bond issue for the new plant risk capital. The very idea is absurd.

The whole idea of risk management, the essence of the basis and the storage problem, is its predictability. Predictability makes for safety. Anything else would be counterproductive—as the horror stories aptly illustrate.

Good risk management is anticipatory, not reactive. Risk managers typically design strategies whose intent is to get ready for events several weeks or months ahead. These markets are fast. If risk managers waited until something happened to respond, they would be certain losers.

Rather, able risk managers anticipate. They imagine situations and think about the response each calls for. That kind of anticipation depends on the risk manager's being able to predict. That, in turn, depends on carefully kept basis books.

In fact, the only way to achieve genuine hedging is to keep records. Every grain trade hedger keeps a basis book. He charts the basis. He painstakingly records positions. He calculates weighted averages. All this allows him to think ahead. The basis book is the foundation of the risk management structure.

Basis trading is hard work. It is no time saver. It requires mental agility. The basis trader has to escape the shackles of common sense. That takes incredible intellectual effort, mental discipline.

The Two Strategies

To outsiders, much of what goes on in the name of risk management must seem forbiddingly complex. While it is true that basis trading is not easy, the strategic side is less complex than some people make it seem. Trade journals and financial newspapers help that impression along with their fascination with "rocket scientists" and their "new technology." Never mind that technology, in any traditional sense, plays a minor role in risk management. All of that makes good copy but obscures the actual risk management situation.

Ultimately, risk managers employ one of two strategic patterns. A basis trader can be long the basis (buy cash, sell futures) or short the basis (sell cash, buy futures). That makes sense in terms of the basis and the storage incentives. The basis can narrow (become more positive) or widen (become more negative). Anticipating a narrowing basis, traders know the market wants them to store, to go long the basis. Anticipating a widening basis, they know the market wants them not to store, to go short the basis.

The legitimate variations in those fundamental positions amount to no more than ways to create beneficial positions relative to an anticipated basis development when a normal business situation creates obstacles of some kind. A forward purchase tactic enables a basis trader to create the effect of a short cash position so he can design a short basis hedge and capitalize on the widening basis of a normal yield environment. Forward loan commitments, PC transactions in the mortgage market, reverse repos, and foreign currency swaps are all ways to use normal basis patterns to attain business goals. Hedge placement variations and trading in and out of the market allow traders to respond to variations in the basis patterns which result from such events as Treasury refundings or interest rate changes. Further, these variations and strategic ploys respond in quite natural ways to predictable basis developments, events that alter the storage picture in foreseeable ways.

Notice, too, that in all cases a risk manager starts out with a definable cash risk. Rising interest rates can make a capital project unfeasible. Floating assets create an unstable situation. A cash reserve needs to yield greater returns. The value of a mortgage portfolio could erode sharply before the banker can sell it off into the secondary market. Thus in all cases, risk managers need to work on the cash and futures sides simultaneously. Further, they often cannot control when a premium stream or pension payments will arrive. Customer funds may not come in at the moment it is convenient to create a permanent investment. As a result of circumstances like those, they need to be in the market consistently, not just when the market seems friendly.

Speculators and Risk Managers Distinguished

To some extent, speculators and risk managers operate by different rules.

If a speculator has a position in T-bond futures that goes against him, he should get out fast. He may have to take a loss, but it will be smaller than it would be if he waffles and the market continues to run against him. Many speculators, to be sure, give in to the temptation to wait a bit in case there is a "correction" ("correction" often seems to mean the market turns back the way the speculator wishes it would). Those people lose big. The speculators who ultimately win get out quickly under those circumstances. If the market turns, they get back in and try again.

Writers on the commodities trade make much of the steel nerves it takes to be a speculator. Certainly, the commodities pits are no place for the faint of heart.

Hedging requires more courage than speculating. Hedgers, by definition, anticipate. They design positions to cope with anticipated events. The market can wander through exquisite contortions on its way to the point they expect it to reach. In the meantime, things can look bleak. Self-doubt comes with the territory. And of course, something there is that doesn't love a margin call.

Faced with a big margin call, nervous would-be hedgers often succumb to the temptation to get out. They rationalize that when the market "improves" (a term much like "correction") they will get back in, saving a lot of margin money. Nonsense.

That's good speculating technique. An often-cited rule for speculators is never to make a margin call. And at that point, that is exactly what those people are—speculators, not hedgers.

Probably one reason margin calls so upset those make-believe hedgers is that, in the absence of a basis book, they have no idea what is happening on the other side of their hedge. They forget that hedging involves both cash and futures.

A true hedger knows in advance that his position may run against him. He hardly welcomes margin calls; but he knows that, like penalties in football, they're just part of the game. More to the point, the true hedger evaluates that kind of situation in terms of what his basis book reveals to him. The futures market may be bleak looking at that point, but that means the cash market is his friend.

Secure in that knowledge, the hedger stands fast in his positions. Not that he is not concerned. Hedgers always check new developments, reevaluate positions, and worry. But they do not get in and out of the markets unnecessarily. Armed with their basis knowledge, they have the courage to maintain the positions they know will produce the results they want and allow them to attain their business goals.

A Word of Caution

Newcomers to the field of risk management cannot, in all probability, go it alone in risk management just from having read this book. But they should be in a position to get good advice and to put that advice to work—to approach risk management confidently and with open minds, well aware of the limitations.

Most risk managers need to remember that the commodities markets provide tools to help them with their primary businesses. An insurance company officer or corporate financial manager needs to resist the temptation to, in effect, change businesses. Even though they may find the markets very useful, they are still primarily in another business.

The discussions of this book should be thought of as guidelines, food for thought. Before people commit real money to risk management strategies, they should get in touch with someone who really understands basis trading. Sad to say, most futures brokers do not. Yet an awareness of the ideas here should enable financial managers to evaluate consultants—to determine their level of basis awareness.

Finally, in this conception risk managers master a few fundamental market characteristics—like the basis and the storage problem—and learn to control a small repertoire of hedging strategies. Based on that, and with proper backup consultation, they evaluate risk situations, consider business goals, and then use those fundamentals to frame a response which will enable them to manage the risk. They can create whatever strategy will fit their situation exactly, helping them to achieve their business goals.

For
Further Reading

O f all the books that have appeared in recent years concerning various aspects of commodities trade and investment strategy, remarkably few relate directly to basis trading and hedging. Most books say the basis is extremely important, then drop the subject.

The one short book which does deal with the basis is Jerome Lacey's *Financial Instrument Markets: an Advanced Study of Cash-Futures Relationships* (Chicago: Board of Trade of the City of Chicago, 1986). Though not a model of clear exposition, Lacey's book includes a good bit of useful analysis.

Valuable background material is available in various forms. Thomas A. Hieronymus's *The Economics of Futures Trading* Second Edition (New York: Commodity Research Bureau, Inc.,1977), though it deals with agricultural commodities, provides helpful background concerning the way the markets operate and their economic foundations. Since bond pricing derives from present value theory, risk managers need to be especially familiar with that material. J. Fred Weston and Eugene F. Brigham's *Essentials of Managerial Finance* Sixth Edition (New York: The Dryden Press, 1982) contains a succinct account of the theory itself and the illustrative examples enable readers to see how these formulas apply in particular situations.

Several recent books contain chapters, many by risk management professionals, which provide interesting insights about particular aspects of financial hedging. Well worth consideration are such collections as the ones edited by Frank J. Fabozzi: *Floating Rate Instruments: Characteristics, Valuation and Portfolio Strategies* (Chicago: Probus Publishing Company, 1986) and *The Handbook of Treasury Securities: Trading and Portfolio Strategies* (Chicago: Probus Publishing Company, 1987).

Two trade magazines, *Intermarket* and *Futures*, provide occassional help to risk managers. *Intermarket*, while it often focuses on peripheral issues, does publish directories which provide useful guides of which firms provide relevant services. Also, it publishes helpful articles on related topics from time to time. *Futures* has published some extremely interesting material by such risk management professionals as Marcelle Arak and Laurie Goodman and John Labuszewski. Of special usefulness are Arak and Goodman's "How to Calculate Better T-bond Hedge Ratios," *Futures* (February 1986, pp. 56-57) and Labuszewski and Kamradt's "Cash Factors that Make Treasury Futures Tick: Tracking the Cheapest," *Futures* (August 1985, pp. 80-84) and "Cash Factors that Make Treasury Futures Tick: Wild Card Delivery Play," *Futures* (September 1985, pp. 78-80). Helpful tips on the interpretation of market signals are contained in McKinzie and Schap's "Reading Markets for More than just Price Information," *Futures* (March 1987, pp. 72-74).

The major exchanges regularly publish useful information. The Chicago Board of Trade's monthly *Interest Rate Futures Review* provides updates on market information such as margin requirements and trading volume, prices, spreads, options, and conversion factors for all deliverable instruments. It also includes a "financial calendar" which lists the first position, first notice, first delivery, last trading, and last delivery days for the next three futures contracts and the last trading and expiration days for options.

In addition, the exchanges publish the proceedings of symposia and other research efforts. These often contain very practical discussions of strategies or risk management topics. For example, *Take it from the Experts: Treasury Note Futures and Options Trading Strategies* (Chicago: Board of Trade of the City of Chicago, n.d.) contains four short articles: "Some Pointers on Mortgage-Backed Security Hedging," "Treasury Note Yield Enhancement," "Hedging with Futures— Navigating the Rapids," and "Determining the 'Tail' in the NOB Spread."

As full of suggestions and intriguing as some of these materials are, readers need to keep in mind that often the formulators of the strategies utterly disregard basis and storage considerations. As a result, hedgers need to *adapt* these ideas rather than merely *adopt* them.

Glossary

This highly selective glossary includes terms which appear often in writings about the commodities trade and which are frequently misconstrued or used in conflicting ways. Italicized terms appear elsewhere in the glossary.

Ask: the price at which a trader can immediately buy. See *bid* and *bid-ask spread.*

(The) basis: the difference between cash and futures. Because T- bonds differ in coupon and maturity, the CBOT developed a system of *conversion factors* to align the futures contract with each cash issue. Accordingly, the bond basis derives from the formula:

$$\text{Cash} - (\text{Futures} \times \text{Conversion Factor}) = \text{Basis}$$

The basis reflects the storage impulse of the market.

Basis play: a strategy in which the trader structures cash and futures positions to benefit from an expected basis change.

Basis trader: a risk manager who designs his strategies in terms of basis factors and expectations rather than in terms of price or other market signals. His primary goal is to benefit from the basis change.

Bid: the price at which a trader can immediately sell. See *ask* and *bid-ask spread.*

Bid-ask spread: the difference between the *bid* and the *ask*. If a T-bond price quote is "135-15 bid and 135-17 asked," there is a two *tick* (or 2/32nd) *spread*.

Call date: a time, in advance of *maturity*, at which a bond issuer has the right to prepay the note.

Commodities month: the delivery months for a commodities contract. Commodities markets offer between four and twelve delivery months or contracts a year. Where petroleum delivers monthly, U.S. Treasury bonds deliver in March, June, September, and December. Those are the *commodities months* for the T-bonds.

Conversion factor: a set of multipliers, developed by the Chicago Board of Trade, which align the generic futures contract with a particular bond.

Deferred: any futures contract other than the *spot*, or *nearby*, month. With regard to T-bonds, on April 20, 1988, any contract after the June '88 (the *nearby*) is a deferred.

Delivery: the exchange of a futures contract for the actual product. A trader long bond futures would thus acquire a T-bond; a short would have to deliver a T-bond. Actually, fewer than one percent of all financial futures contracts reach delivery. Yet the delivery possibility exerts a strong stabilizing influence on the performance of the markets.

Edge: the difference between the last trade and the *bid* or the *ask*. In effect, it is the premium the local takes for making a market.

Financials (or financial commodities): commodities which entail the trading of currencies, financial instruments, or securities. Though the category includes, on the futures side, the stock indexes, there is no practical basis play in that area. Accordingly, in risk management discussion, the financials are the currencies and the U.S. Treasury instruments and related futures.

Floor broker: also known as a *paper trader*, a floor trader who trades customer accounts for a brokerage firm, as opposed to a floor trader who trades his own account and is called a *local*.

Floor trader: any trader, local or floor broker, who owns or leases an exchange seat and so can trade on the floor of the exchange.

Forward: in cash markets, the quoted prices for delivery of a product at some deferred time, in some ways parallel to a futures quote.

Forward purchase: to agree to buy a cash product at a future date.

Futures (futures contract): an exchange traded contract for delivery of a particular physical product or financial instrument at a future time.

Hedge: to balance cash and futures (or cash forward) positions in order to protect against risk and take advantage of a basis change.

Hedge placement: refers to the futures contract selected for trade in a hedging strategy. The usual choice is the *nearby* relative to the *unwinding* date, though other choices are possible.

Hedger: a risk manager who uses futures and forward cash markets to protect against risk and enhance yield by designing strategies which, among other things, involve balancing cash and futures positions and managing the basis change.

Hedge ratio: the multiplier which establishes the number of futures contracts needed to balance a cash position. Often the CBOT *conversion factor* provides the most useful hedge ratio; but other ratios are possible, depending on the objective of the strategy.

Local: a floor trader who trades his own account in a commodities pit.

Long: a position in which a trader buys futures in the absence of an offsetting position, cash or otherwise.

Long the basis: a hedge position in which a hedger buys cash and sells futures.

Margin: a sum of money which must be on deposit with a brokerage firm to protect both parties from a futures trade. Exchanges establish minimum rates, though brokerage firms may set a higher margin rate.

To make a market: when a local takes the opposite side in a trade. Without that action, the trade cannot be effected.

Market: in commodities trade, this can refer to (1) futures exchanges in general, (2) a particular futures exchange, (3) trade—cash and futures—in a particular commodity, and (4) the role of a *local* with another local or a *paper trader* in an individual transaction (see *to make a market*).

Maturity: the date at which a U.S. Treasury issue achieves par value.

Narrow: a relatively positive basis value. In the case of T-bonds, a value of 350 is a narrow basis.

Narrowing: a basis change in which the value moves from a relatively negative to a relatively postive level—e.g., from 5 to 212.

Nearby: the futures contract closest to the present date. With regard to T-bonds, on April 20, 1988, the nearby will be the June '88 contract.

Paper trader: also known as a *floor broker*, a floor trader who trades customer accounts.

Par value (or par): the face value of a financial instrument.

Physicals (or physical commodities): commodities which entail the trading of physical objects such as agricultural products, metals, or petroleum. The agricultural markets gave rise to the original futures exchanges and were the original focus of hedging.

Position: any long or short cash or futures trade. A hedger who buys $10 million of a given T-bond has a $10 million long cash position. At that point, he will also have an appropriate short futures position.

Risk manager: a business person who develops strategies for the purpose of protecting against price risk. The traditional approach is hedging.

Rollover: the replacement of a hedge from one futures month to another. To roll over a short futures position, the trader buys that month and sells the next, or some other deferred month.

Short: a position in which a trader sells futures in the absence of an offsetting position, cash or otherwise.

Short the basis: a hedge position in which a hedger sells cash and buys futures.

Speculate: to trade in either futures or cash markets with the hope of capturing the benefits of favorable market action.

Speculator: a trader who deals in either cash or futures in the expectation of capturing the benefits of favorable market action.

Spot: the current or *nearby* month in either the cash or futures market.

Spread: the difference between two prices or rates, as in *bid-ask* spread, the difference between two futures months, or the difference between a banker's rates paid and earned.

Spreads: the display, or quotation, of a set of futures prices or cash forwards.

Tick: a minimum price increment. T-bonds move in 32nds of a percentage point which have a cash value of $31.25.

Wide: a relatively negative basis value. In financials, which cannot sustain negative basis values, a basis of +2 is wide.

Widening: a basis change in which the value moves from a relatively positive to a relatively negative level—e.g., from 212 to 5.

Index

Carnegie-Mellon Univ.